One Life:
An Afghan
Remembers

by

ABDUL QAYUM SAFI

ONE LIFE: AN AFGHAN REMEMBERS

by

Abdul Qayum Safi

Introduction

L ooking back on my past, a certain image forms in my mind of the trajectory my life has followed. Born in a remote village in Afghanistan, with the first few years of my childhood spent in another, I had never dreamed that I would not only leave its confines and venture out to major cities inside my country, but cross its borders into a wider world to find a better life and help my family members who had stayed back home. I see myself now as I must have been then—a young boy, just graduated from elementary school and traveling alone to unfamiliar destinations, where he knew not a soul. In hindsight, I look upon it as an uncharted journey through alien territory, during which I have, time and again, fallen back on my ability to adapt to

1

new circumstances and succeed without sacrificing my heritage and all that it means to me. I visualize myself now as a person who had been swept away by a storm or a flood and held on to anything that might help him survive. I have faced moments of danger quite a few times in my life, but have emerged from them, relatively unscathed, primarily because of the support from my immediate family and caring relatives. My story is one of many hardships, of ups and downs and twists and turns, but it has turned out well so far. I have not, however, given up the habit of keeping my fingers crossed and hoping that my life will stay on a safe and successful track.

I don't remember anything about Pech, where I was born and spent the first year of my life. My earliest memories are of the wuluswali of Khas Kunar, east of the Kunar River. I remember spending my early years gazing wistfully from a distance at trucks, buses and cars moving back and forth along a road, without being able to approach it for a closer look. I was probably too young to board a local raft on my own and cross the river to the other side or too satisfied with life on my own side of the watercourse to be impelled by the urge to discover its mysteries on the western bank. Apart from the road and the mountain beyond it, there was nothing on the other side anyway. Barring, of course, the White Mosque, which Sarkatib Abdul Wahid from Tanar had built along the road to provide a rest stop for travelers. The ones who did cross the river to the other side were either those who went up the mountain to cut trees for firewood and carry the chopped pieces back home on their backs or those traveling south to Jalalabad or north to Chaghaserai (now renamed Asadabad). I did not know at the time that, one day, I would cross the river too.

Once I had passed the fourth grade at the elementary school in my village, my father came down to Khas Kunar and took me back with him to Chaghaserai, where I would join the rest of the family and continue my elementary education. I remember how, after crossing the river, my father and I had waited by the road for the first vehicle to arrive, halt and pick us up for our trip to Chaghaserai. The vehicle which stopped for us was a large loaded truck and soon, I was riding in the back, clutching the metal bars for support and enjoying every moment of my very first trip. I remember eagerly scanning the areas we passed, never having set eyes on them before. The road was rough and the truck sped along, with the driver in an obvious hurry to reach his destination. Chaghaserai was an hour's drive along a dirt road from Khas Kunar; if you chose to cover the distance on foot, it would take you the entire day. While this was my first foray into the world beyond the river, I would subsequently travel along the same route three times, either taking trucks and buses to my destination or walking all the way.

I remember one of those occasions well. I was traveling with my father and two younger cousins. As we waited by the road, a military truck came along and stopped just long enough to pick up my cousins, leaving my father and me behind. Burdened by the basket of grapes he was carrying on his back, my father had not been quick enough to board the truck. Since it was the last vehicle for the day on that particular road, my father decided to cover the distance on foot, with me trailing behind him. He was worried about my cousins who had already left on the truck, for they were too young to be traveling on their own. He also needed to report to work the next day at the government office where he was employed. After trudging along for sometime, my father got tired of carrying the basket of grapes and sold it for five Afghanis to someone at the very first stop. We continued on our way, walking the whole night and arriving at our destination early in the morning. We managed to catch up with my cousins, because the driver of the truck they had boarded had decided to stop on the way and let the passengers sleep.

My next trip on foot from Chaghaserai to Khas Kunar would be undertaken in the company of my father and my brother, Wadood. Refusing to pay the bus driver the full fare for his young sons, my father had ordered us to start walking. Mere children at the time and weighed down by the two hens we were carrying, Wadood and I were unable to keep up with an adult's rapid pace. As a result, we had to halt overnight en route.

Years later, I would take my third trip, accompanying my cousin, Abdul Wahab, to Chaghaserai to resolve the matter of his military service. However, my first trip to Chaghaserai was the most significant one, as it would offer me exposure to the world at large.

Chaghaserai, I discovered, was a very different place from the village I had been living in earlier. It was here that I would first discover the existence of newspapers, for my father subscribed to the weekly, Itihad-e Mashriqi, the only newspaper published in Jalalabad, the capital of Mashriqi, a province that includes today Nangarhar, Kunar and Laghman. Living in Chaghaserai for two and half years, I would also become acquainted with some examples of technological development that filled my life with marvelous new experiences. There was, for example, a switchboard for telephone communications at the Government Center. The operator would sit in front of the board and keep inserting pegs in different holes and talking to someone invisible on the other end. I wanted to find out what a radio was and was informed by someone that I could see one in the treasurer's house. So one evening, I walked down to the judges' family complex, where I was shown into a room full of people listening to a box sitting on the windowsill that reported news from all over the world. I found it hard to believe that the voice I heard was actually emerging from that box, which was covered with a very fine fabric to protect it from dust. I remember the newsreader reporting on the battles between Egyptian and British forces. Later, I would understand that this had something to do with the war over the Suez Canal. I had read the news in Itihad-e Mashriqi, the newspaper my father would get from Jalalabad twice a month. Although I was in the habit of reading that paper from cover to cover, hearing the news broadcast from a radio was a brand new experience.

The short film about toilet training that was shown in the open space in front of the Government Center was my first encounter with animation movies. I watched the fictional character, Gul Jan, going out to relieve himself in a cornfield and then washing his hands to maintain personal hygiene before going home. During the rest of my years in Afghanistan, I would have access to a more advanced version of the same technology, but nothing that was particularly novel.

My first exposure to television would be in the 1960s in my dormitory in Lebanon, where everyone went down to the basement to watch the news and the programs on the entertainment channels. Although we had to make do with a black and white television set, what I saw on the screen seemed miraculous and unbelievable. Teachers College at Columbia University, New York City, offered me my first experience of computers, when I signed up for a course entitled, Treatment of Mass Data, in the 1970s. To fulfill the course requirements, I had to work on a research project involving the calculation and interpretation of new data collected by distributing a questionnaire. I worked in two different rooms, punching the data cards in one and sorting the punched cards in the second. By the time I graduated and went to Kuwait in the early 1980s, I had bought my first computer for the office. My secretary had to go for a two-week training course to learn how to use it for office work, but I had learned how to use a manual typewriter at my office in the Ministry of Education in Kabul during the early 1970s and had no problem adapting to the computer keyboard.

I even had my first taste of being a rebel of sorts, when I discovered that the king, our spiritual father, could not speak Pashto. His Majesty was due to visit the area and a crowd of locals had gathered in the field in front of the government compound to meet him and listen to his words of wisdom. When the king began his speech, I realized he could not speak Pashto and the provincial governor, Mr. Farouq Osman, had to translate his words for us. The reverence I had harbored in my heart for him dimmed considerably. If he were, indeed, my spiritual father, I had reasoned silently, he should not only have understood my language, Pashto, the national language, but spoken to me in it.

There would be other firsts in my life. Among them was the joy of being the owner of a home, when I built my house in Kabul in 1970 on the plot of land I had purchased earlier. I would buy other homes too, but the first one would always have a special place in my heart.

An autobiography is an ongoing reality show, focusing on an individual's life with its moments of tragedy and comedy, happiness and sorrow, success and failure, laughter and tears, anger and forgiveness, elation and disappointment—all in one package. The Afghans have a saying that a man is both as delicate as a flower and as hard as a rock. Only the human body and soul can endure what happens to them both during an entire lifetime. The real survivors are those fortunate ones who can look back on their lives and write about their experiences so that other people may read about them and compare them with their own. Survival is the ultimate reward for a person who has managed to overcome the difficulties in his life by setting himself a goal and summoning the will to attain it, despite the tribulations that came in his way. Looking back on my own life, I can claim without any hesitation that I needed to work more rigorously, endure greater hardships and surmount more obstacles to succeed than my children ever did. Of course, my father and other members of my immediate family always stood by me, but they had no means of contributing in concrete ways to the achievement of the goal I had set myself: to continue my education and get a good job after graduation. My father's dream was that I should become a teacher, because members of that profession in our country were earning more money than he did as an official at his government office. After moving to northern Afghanistan, where he worked for the Spinzar Company, his dream probably changed: he began wishing I were a doctor or a military officer.

It wasn't, however, the potential income alone that fueled my father's dream. He was the only person in our extended family who understood the value of education. In fact, he was the first member of his family to graduate from elementary school. Unlike his brothers, who stayed home to help the family financially, my father graduated from the government-run school and continued to improve his literacy level through studies at the local and regional mosques, despite stiff opposition from my grandfather. Then he obtained a government job as a volunteer and later as a salaried employee. As the family grew and my father felt the need to earn more to support them, he traveled north to seek better professional opportunities. He returned to Kunar only to take his family with him. To my knowledge, he would go back to Kunar only once more to organize my brother's wedding.

Like most parents in Afghanistan, my father yearned to see me succeed in life, but probably had no idea how to guide and support me academically or financially. First, he could not afford to send me to high school. Kunar had no high school of its own and to enroll in one in faraway Kabul meant having to live there. Neither my father nor I had ever been to the country's capital; nor did we have any relatives living there. Six years of paying for my accommodation and living expenses, in addition to school fees, was not the kind of financial burden my father could have borne under any circumstances. He must have heaved a sigh of relief when, following some stiff competition among participating candidates, I was awarded a government scholarship for pursuing my secondary and high-school education at a boarding school in Kabul. My father must have been glad to pay my travel expenses and get me out of the village which provided neither opportunities for education beyond elementary school nor jobs worth having.

I guess both my father and I felt, early in life, that in order to get ahead, it was necessary for us to break away from the traditional way in which we had been raised. Had my father not served as a pioneer of sorts and paved the way for me, I doubt if it would have been quite so easy for me to leave the family and seek a better life beyond my village. With my academic performance in Kabul and my proficiency in the English language opening doors, I was able to pursue higher education abroad and successfully complete both undergraduate and graduate studies. With Afghanistan's once-stable political situation rocked by violent turmoil, I had no desire to go back home again. Caught between the extremes of communism and religious fundamentalism, my country had become a narrow, stifling space, where I would have found it difficult to breathe, had I returned.

Writing about my life has not been easy, because I have not maintained a diary over the years and must totally depend on my memory. And it retains very little of early childhood events. For those, I must rely mainly on the stories I have heard from my parents and other relatives. As mentioned earlier, Pech, where I was born and lived for the first year of my life, is not even a distant memory. It is a total blank. I am told that my family had to leave the place because the first rumbles of civil war were beginning to affect it. I do remember most of the events in my life in Khas Kunar, where we eventually settled. Graduating from elementary school and leaving Kunar marked the beginning of a journey to the world that lay beyond my doorstep. The window to future opportunities would open and the urge to better myself would sweep me off to new and different places where I had never imagined I would be able to go. New, because I had not been there before and different, because they were all urban centers, quite unlike the simple rural areas I had been used to in Kunar.

A couple of years after I had left Kunar, my father would travel north to find a better life. His target was to get a job, a piece of land and a house and eventually, after an initial period of struggle, he managed all three. He received a plot of farmland as retirement benefits and found a job at the Spinzar Company ("Spin Zar" in Pashto means silver), where he would earn far more than he had as a government employee. Headquartered in the Konduz area, the company had regional offices all over, namely, in the provinces of Konduz, Takhar and Baghlan. The company would help farmers grow cotton by providing them with seeds and fertilizer. In return, the farmers had to give over a quarter of their farmland for cotton cultivation. When the cotton was harvested, they would load it on camels, donkeys, horses or wagons and deliver it to the company's local office. The company would sort the cotton into different categories and buy it from the farmers after fixing the rate for each particular category. The cotton was then processed into fiber and seeds.

I had heard my father say that the fiber was sorted into four categories. The first three were reserved for export, while the fourth was used in local textile factories for manufacturing fabric. The seeds went into the manufacture of cooking oil and soap.

Now that he had a job, my father was able to take the whole family with him and life improved for us. It was a relief for everyone, because we had been scattered in three different places—Khas Kunar, Kabul and further north—with no means of communicating with each other. What sustained us during those difficult times was our abiding faith that everything would work out for the best.

Eventually, my father would move to Imam Sahib, where he had a job, a house and a plot of land. The house in Imam Sahib would become the primary residence for the whole family and it was here that Gul Bebu, my stepmother, gave birth to my three half-sisters, Najiba, Latifa and Ghotai, and my half-brother, Torialai. My brother, Wadood, and I lived in Kabul and would visit the family during our winter vacation. We still had property in Khas Kunar and most of our relatives lived there. This necessitated trips to Khas Kunar, where we visited our relatives and kept an eye on our property.

But no journey would take me further out of my familiar orbit than the one beyond the borders of Afghanistan. My first destination on this voyage of discovery was Lebanon, where I completed my undergraduate studies in psychology at the American University of Beirut. My second was the United States of America, where I pursued higher studies before deciding to settle there with my immediate family. I availed of work opportunities in Kuwait, where I would establish the Center for Evaluation and Measurement at Kuwait University and have a chance to work at the Language Center and at the College of Basic Education, the Public Authority for Applied Education and Training. I experienced many upheavals during my years there. In order to keep my residency in the USA, I had to resign from my job in Kuwait in the middle of the academic year, 1986-87. But I lasted for just over a year in my first job in the USA. During the period following my termination, I was beset by apprehension; I feared I would lose my house and my family would end up on the streets. I went back to Kuwait twice; each time, my contract was terminated and I faced the possibility of unemployment for an indefinite period. But luck favored us. Our ordeals were over by the time our children were ready to go to college and we were able to fulfill our obligations to them and support them financially until they graduated.

I also feel blessed for being able to help my father when he needed it most. I used my savings in Lebanon to buy him his dream house in the town of Imam Sahib. Following President Daoud's ouster and assassination by the communists, anarchy prevailed in Afghanistan. Wadood, who had survived the chaos that ensued, had a hard time, nonetheless, and I felt it was my obligation to help him. I legally handed over my house in Kabul to him, so he could live there, and helped one of his sons to train as an auto-repair mechanic, so he could open an auto-repair workshop. I had his other two sons trained as pharmacists, so they could run a pharmacy in Kabul. Wadood has now retired from his military job and is living with his family in Kabul.

As for my own family, the moment I found a better job in the Washington, DC, area, I began planning for relocating them from Rhode Island. Although I have worked in education, most of the profits I made came from my real-estate investments. Curiously enough, I didn't make much headway as a real-estate agent, but enjoyed surprising success in managing my own properties. In this matter, I was merely following my father's advice; one does not lose money if one invests it in property, he would say. By property, he meant a plot of land or a house.

I bought my first house in Rhode Island in 1980, when our eldest son, Khushal, was only a few months old. I subsequently purchased a five-acre plot of land and a second house that would become the family home. We lived there for eighteen years before selling it. We used the first house mainly as rental property and sold it in 1997. Short of money at one point, we could not retain possession of the land and had to dispose of it, using the proceeds to cover our household expenses. However, by holding on to all three pieces of property for a given period of time and selling them later, we managed to make some profits. I also bought a townhouse in 1999, a year after I had moved to northern Virginia. In April 2005, we would sell the family home in Rhode Island and the townhouse in northern Virginia and move into a new house in South Riding, south of Dulles Airport. It is here that we live now and hope to continue doing so until I retire. Khushal is busy with his job and lives in Washington, DC. Jamal decided to stay on in Rhode Island and is working for the education department in Taunton, Massachusetts. Shireen, who passed the national test and received a license to work as a pharmacy technician, lives with us and is employed in her line of work at a local CVS store. Anna, who worked as a reading specialist in a high school for a couple of years, is now involved in reading as private business. At the same time, she is working on her doctorate at George Mason University.

Given all that I have been through, I feel like an ant carrying a load heavier than the weight of its own body and trying to take it to a particular destination or to the little choo choo train which says it can. We have been pushed to the edge and had the ground beneath our feet removed several times during most of the productive years of our life, but we have managed to keep a roof over our heads and the family united. I was fortunate that when life was really tough, I had youth on my side and was able to work through the obstacles by being patient and determined and buoyed by the hope that things would surely get better. Mine is the life of an ordinary Joe who got caught up in the turbulence of life and managed to hang on and get a foothold, driven by the need for survival. There is no doubt in my mind that without each other's support, none of us would have made it, let alone succeed. It was a joint effort all the way. Yet we were ordinary human beings; none of us would have stood out in a crowd. We have always been a part of that crowd and belonged to it all our life. And I am proud to say that I am speaking for the majority in any society anyone can name. I am glad to be living in a great country, although life here can be difficult at times. But the beauty of this place is that if you have something useful to contribute and can convince others that it will make a difference, nothing can stand between you and success. No wonder I find it ironical that given half an opportunity, those very people from all over the world who spend their time badmouthing America and its citizens, would be the first to land up on its shores, hoping to make it their home.

Among the many setbacks I have faced in life, none was as devastating as the news I received in Kuwait of my father's death. It was he who had been my moral and financial support, encouraging me to continue my education, and his demise left me with a deep sense of loss. After raising Wadood, my sister, Jahantab, and me, my father had brought up four more children—three girls and a boy—the offspring of his second marriage. He had died in November 1995. Surprisingly, I would not get to know about it for a long time. Not even in February 1996, when I visited Peshawar and stayed with my friend, Jalat, and his family.

Wadood, his wife and their four children had joined me there, along with Jahantab and two of her children. We had spent a week together in the same house, but no one mentioned the fact that my father was dead. Perhaps they themselves were unaware of it. Afghanistan was, after all, in the throes of civil war, making it next to impossible to travel within the country and keep communication lines open with relatives living in far-flung places. Or perhaps my siblings knew, but waited until I had left to send me the news, because they felt it would have been too brutal to announce it directly and risked creating an atmosphere of unbearable sadness all through my stay. It was only after I was back in Kuwait that I received a letter from Wadood, informing me about our father's death. It was a terrible blow and I could not stop weeping for a couple of days. I was grief-stricken that despite the modicum of success I had achieved in my own life, I had been unable to take care of my father when he was old and ill and needed me most. It was a particularly heart-wrenching thought; I had simply not been around for the man who had virtually been my backbone through my early years. My stepmother, Gul Bebu, and my half-brother, Torialai, would be the ones taking care of him in his old age. It was some kind of consolation to me that my father had lived and died in the house he had dreamed about every day.

CHAPTER
ONE

Early Memories

Asking an Afghan about his or her exact date of birth may turn out to be an exercise in futility, for most of my compatriots do not record it. Almost all rural Afghans and most urban ones are born at home and no record, official or unofficial, is kept of the day they came into the world. An Afghan will be able to tell you in which year he or she was born and his or her current age. This may be the only information available in most official documents pertaining to the persons carrying them. In most such documents, especially the ones issued in the rural areas, the year of the person's birth is a matter of guesswork. The government official issuing a *tazkira* (national identification card) or a similar document is likely to look at a young man, assess his age and record the year of his birth, based entirely on his own assumptions. I refer deliberately to a "young man," because girls are not even required to apply for a *tazkira*. In fact, no female member of my family has one.

A boy is sent to school when he is approximately between six and seven years old, the decision depending on whether he has lost his lower two front teeth or not. The whole process is initiated by sending a child to the government office, where an official scrutinizes his front teeth and subtracts six or seven years from his present age to determine the year in which he was born. The boy is photographed and a *tazkira* issued in his name. The date marked on it is the one the child is meant to remember as the year in which he was born. The age of a girl is calculated by using the ages of of her brothers or male cousins as a benchmark.

I was born in Pech possibly a year before the Safi War. I mention Khas Kunar as my birthplace, however, because that is where my parents and grandparents were born. Even the *tazkira* I received from the government shows Khas Kunar as my birthplace and I cannot contradict that. If I were to mention Pech as my place of birth, it would cause confusion. However, in my case, the date is important, because it was a precursor to the war that broke out in the mid-1940s, when the Safi tribe in Kunar refused to send its young men to join military service. The story, as I remember it, is that the government sent soldiers armed with heavy and light weapons to subdue the Safis who lived mainly in the mountains west of the Kunar River, from Noorgal in the south to Pech in the north. The people living north of the Safi territory were known as Nooristanis. The soldiers would alight from their vehicles on the main road and start moving up the narrow valleys. The Safis would watch them for a while from their vantage point high above, before rolling rocks down on them. By the end of the day, the soldiers had fled. This progression of events must have been repeated countless times, because it seemed to have become a part of local folklore, with tales abounding about the war between the government and the Safis. The stories were mainly about pride and courage and honor and the tribe's ability to fight the government soldiers with bare hands or, at the very most, with simple, locally made weapons.

The main road between Jalalabad and Chaghaserai—now Asadabad—goes north on the west side of Kunar River. The Safi tribe lived to the west of the main road in the mountains lying parallel to the river. The part of the mountain that lay west of Khas Kunar was called

Teetak. Almost everyone living on the mountain affiliated himself with the Safi tribe, since intermarriage between the Safis and other tribes was extremely rare. Safi men who married women from other tribes usually brought their wives home, where they became members of their husbands' tribe. Similarly, men from other tribes who married Safi women took them home too and the latter automatically became members of the new tribe. Those living on the mountain to the east of the river belonged to the Mohmand tribe. My mother's family, for instance, came from the Mohmand tribe, while my father's family members were Safis. Since the end of the Safi War, the Safis have been law-abiding citizens of Afghanistan, like the other inhabitants of Kunar. The Mohmands, on the other hand, consider themselves residents of the semi-autonomous region of Pashtunistan, carry illegal weapons, flout the laws laid down by the Afghan government, refuse to allow their sons to join military service and cause much inconvenience to the residents of Khas Kunar.

Unlike the people living up on the mountain, those living in the villages along the river in the valley were mixed and belonged to different tribes. For example, my mother's family belonged to the Mohmand tribe, since her father and relatives from his side were direct descendants of the person who built the first house in what is now called Bandai. But by marrying my father, my mother had to move to Tanar to become a member of her husband's family. Her own mother's family belonged to the Shinwari tribe, which lived mainly in the area southeast of Jalalabad near the border with Pakistan. However, by her marriage to my maternal grandfather, Nowrose, my maternal, grandmother would become a member of the Mohmand tribe. Some members of the Shinwari tribe who had come down to Kunar, probably to take part in the Safi War, have settled there. One of my father's elder sisters, Nabo, married Shakar Khan, a Safi who had come from Tagab to Kunar as a mullah appointed by the local mosque and decided to settle there. Their children, our cousins, Rasul and Rabbani, are, therefore, considered Safis. I had once asked my father about our own tribal affiliation, but all he would say was that while he believed we were Safis, he could not be sure.

Like most of the families in Khas Kunar, my father's family too, has taken on identities associated with their occupation, rather than with their tribal affiliation. In the village, they were known as the Julas (weavers). Similarly, some of the other families in Tanar village were carpenters, Qazis (judges), Mullah-Khails, Akhundzadas and so on. The Mullah-Khails and Akhundzadas were the largest clans in the village. As I remember, we always had two Maleks (village chiefs): one from the Mullah-Khail clan and the other from the Akhundzada clan. We also had two summer mosques outside the village along the water canal, each belonging to one of the aforesaid clans. Both places of worship were large enough to accommodate all the village men who would gather to join the special Friday prayers. I say "men," because women did not go to the mosque and prayed at home. The rest of the families had the option to be served by one of the chiefs. Each chief had a Tawachi (assistant), who was responsible for delivering the former's message to his followers. A person who was involved in a dispute either with his neighbor or with another villager would inform the village chief before taking the matter to the government. If the village chief was unable to resolve the issue through negotiation between the feuding parties, the matter would be referred to the government.

The Safis were mainly mountain people living in the range of mountains west of the Kunar River, as far north as the valley of Pech. They also lived in the mountains in the northern part of Laghman province and in most of Kapisa province. Koh-e Safi, where the residents were Safis, lies north-east of Kabul. Traveling north in Kunar province, one has to take the road west from Chaghaserai to go to Pech. The main road goes north to Asmar, Barikot and other areas near the border between Afghanistan and Pakistan. The road to Pech branches off the main road and passes through Du Shah-Khail, north-west of Demkelay, the main village in Chaghaserai. It follows the route west along the Pech River. The river flows east toward Chaghaserai and joins the main river which courses southward from the northern districts of Kunar Province, namely, Asmar, Sheegal, Merawara and so on. A tributary of the Kunar River, the Pech River joins the main river in Mandakul, Chaghaserai, north-east of the provincial government office. The river flows south toward Jalalabad, where it joins the Kabul River which flows east from Kabul through the Tangigharu Gorge and passes through Sarobi, the southern end of Laghman province, and Darunta and merges with the Kunar River north-east of Jalalabad. The Kabul River flows east and passes through the Shinwari territory. The river crosses the border to Pakistan and joins the Indus River in Atek, between Peshawar and Islamabad. The Kabul River is the only watercourse in Afghanistan which flows into the ocean—the Indian Ocean.

The mountains north of Pech are inhabited by the Nooristanis and the area is, understandably, called Nooristan. It used to be a part of Kunar Province, but has recently been separated from Kunar and is a province by itself. The Nooristanis know each other by their local names, which are unfamiliar to other Afghans. However, they use their official names when introducing themselves to Afghans outside their tribe or registering their names at a government office. The Nooristanis were one of the few tribes to resist conversion to Islam, when the Arabs came to the area that is now Afghanistan and went on a conversion campaign. Living as they did in a remote area, they were probably left alone. They did convert to Islam, however, during the reign of Abdul Rahman Khan (1880-1901). It was the Nooristani tribe, in fact, which sided with the government in its fight against the Safis. Realizing, no doubt, that they could not fight on two fronts simultaneously, the Safis accepted defeat and agreed to send their young men to serve in the government's military force.

Some of the stories from the Safi War have become the stuff of legend among the people of Kunar. One of them is about a Safi man who came across a tank which no one was guarding. It seems that he picked up an ax, climbed on top of the tank and tried to smash it into pieces. Being the way they are, the Safis are proud of the man's feat and untroubled by what might have happened to him as a result. Another tale involves two heroes of the war, namely Shahswar and Salemai, who are described as "the two lions." According to folklore, they launched repeated attacks on the government forces in Tsawkai and Robat and destroyed their bases there. I don't remember how long the war lasted, but I have been told that the Safis were defeated and forced to submit to the military service the government insisted their men sign up for. Most of the tribal leaders were relocated to areas far away from Kunar and not allowed to return for a long time. Travel restrictions were eased after 1964, when the country set up a new constitution and members of the royal family were prohibited from taking up an elected government office. Samiullah, the son of Sultan Muhammad, a well-known leader of the Safi tribe in Pech who had been exiled to Sheberghan in the north, returned home and won the local elections, becoming a Member of Parliament in the Kabul-based government. I have known him from the early 1960s, when he was my classmate at the Dar ul-Malimeen (Teacher Training High School) in Kabul.

While the Safi War was on, my father was posted in Pech as the local government's treasurer. During a popular uprising against the government, most of the employees were either killed or forced to flee the area. My father's situation, though, was different. While his Kunar origins had earned him great respect, all who knew him also looked upon the man as a friend and a brother. I recall a certain incident that bears testimony both to his integrity and to the devotion he had inspired among the locals. My father was in charge of collecting money for the sale of lumber and filing the receipts as proof that the merchandise had, indeed, been sold, but payment was pending. Receipts from actual payments were submitted to the government office. My father's office had sold some lumber to a number of locals, but payment to the government was still due. When war broke out, he worried about preserving the unpaid sales receipts intact and eventually found a way. Digging a hole in the floor of the room which served as his storage area, he buried the receipts in it and locked the room. After the war was over, he would travel back to Pech, dig up the receipts and set about collecting the unsettled dues. However, when the battles were still raging in the early years, the locals advised him to go back home to his village and even provided an escort for him and his family. Such was the love and warmth the man inspired in his fellow human beings.

During one of his many reminiscences about Pech, my father would tell me about Fazal Rahman, a schoolteacher and tailor who had lived in the same village. His tailoring job helped him to supplement his income from teaching and among his many clients from the village was one little lad: me. My father recalls bringing Fazal over to the house to measure me for some new clothes and watching, bewildered, as the schoolteacher-cum-tailor shook his head in dismay after he was done. On being asked the reason, Fazal apparently replied in a bemused tone that my width exceeded my height. In other words, I was too fat! It was only later that I would discover that Zahir Torakai, a medical doctor who used to be my classmate in Dar ul-Malimeen, was Fazal's son. While I was working in the Ministry of Education, my father developed a serious hernia problem and had to go to Kabul, where I was based, for surgery. I accompanied him to Jamhuriat Hospital and once the x-rays were done, he was assigned to a room in the evening. The doctor who arrived to perform the surgery turned out to be Zahir. They were happy to be meet each other, particularly as I had told my father that that his doctor was Fazal's son. Needless to say, the operation was successful and my father was soon on the road to recovery.

Having lived in this environment, rendered congenial by the warmth of interpersonal relationships, you can imagine what a wrench it must have been for my family to uproot themselves and leave Pech. My parents, my cousin, Abdul Rawouf, and I would travel to Chaghaserai with an escort of Pech residents. But being quite young at the time, I have no recollection of how we made the journey—in a vehicle or on foot. The Pech River is too narrow and its waters too rough for people to cross over on a *tal* (lumber raft). At Chaghaserai, however, the river widens and the waters are deep and calm so that we were able to make it all the way to Khas Kunar aboard a lumber raft. The lumber used to make such rafts is transported to Jalalabad by river for commercial reaons and trucked across the border to Peshawar. By carrying passengers, the owner of a raft can make some extra money. So we had no difficulty whatsoever in boarding one to go home. It was a long journey and, according to what I have been told, a rather eventful one, but I was too young to remember much about it. It is said that while disembarking at our destination, the person who was carrying me slipped on the river-bank and inadvertently released his hold on me. I promptly fell into the irrigation canal and had to be rescued by someone else who dived into the water to do so. The family, lugging along a thoroughly drenched child, then trooped down to the home of one of my aunts who lived within walking distance, where they spent some time getting me into warm, dry clothes and recovering from the shock of their recent ordeal.

My cousin, Rawouf, was the only offspring of Mehmed Wali, my eldest uncle and my father's brother, who had died before my birth. His widow, Haleema, then married Faqeer Mehmed, my father's older brother, and Rawouf decided to live with my father in Pech. He was one of the few elementary school graduates from Khas Kunar to get a scholarship to the military high school in Kabul and go on to college, graduating from there to become a second lieutenant in the army. A few years later, when I graduated from elementary school and was accepted as a student at Ibn-e Seena Junior High School in Kabul, he was the person I would look for when I arrived for the first time in the Afghan capital.

During the tragically short span of her life, my mother would give birth to five children. I, the firstborn, survived, but the sister and brother who followed did not, leaving this world early in childhood. My siblings, Wadood and Jahantab, were born after their death. The three of us were resilient enough to survive the harsh conditions of life in Tanar village. The water we drank was polluted and the fruits and vegetables we washed in the same water before eating them were, therefore, contaminated and unsafe. This was hardly surprising as the source of our drinking water was two canals, separated from the Kunar River, that flowed south and were used mainly for irrigation purposes. The upper canal that ran along the eastern side of Khas Kunar near the desert and the Shalai Mountains provided water for irrigating the upper half of the farmlands. The lower canal flowed parallel to the upper one and provided water for irrigating the lower half of the farmlands near the river. But the canal water did not serve the purpose of agriculture alone. Residents of villages situated along the canals would swim in them during the hot summer months. We also washed our sheep in their waters and led our cattle to drink from them. Each of the mosques built along the canals had a platform, where men would perform their ablutions before kneeling in prayer. The local mosque I attended, however, stood far from both canals and was equipped with a pool, where we would wash up before our prayers. The small stream of water that separated from the lower canal and flowed west toward the marshy land called the *jaba* was used for irrigation. The women in the houses located along this narrower watercourse would go out early in the morning to fill their *mengai*—ceramic pots—with water, which they used for drinking and cooking. They reasoned that if they could get to the stream before anyone else did, the water they brought home would be as clean as it could possibly be under the circumstances.

It did not help that our village was devoid of sanitation facilities, compelling us to go out into the fields to relieve ourselves. The dung we collected from our cattle was stored in a *dairan*, a place specially made for the purpose and located near our home. In fact, we had three *dairans* close by, each belonging to one of the three families living there.

The animal dung in the *dairan*, along with human waste, mixed with other garbage scattered around in the farmland and created an unhygienic environment that attracted swarms of flies during the summer months. They contaminated our food supplies and were the root cause of a number of recurring stomach-related infections and diseases. *Is-hal* (diarrhea) and *paichesh* (dysentery) were rampant during summer. In winter, on the other hand, we were seized by colds and coughs, because we lacked both adequate woolen clothing and a proper heating system to protect us from the freezing weather.

Autumn did not spare us either. The temperatures in late summer and early autumn were still high enough for villagers to prefer sleeping outdoors on the roofs of their houses or in their gardens, leaving them exposed to swarms of mosquitos. For the standing water in the rice fields, where the seeds were scattered in summer and the crop was harvested in early fall, served as the perfect breeding ground for these disease-spreading insects. Inevitably, malaria struck with a vengeance during the harvest season. Among the more dreaded diseases, tuberculosis and smallpox were common. I was vaccinated twice against smallpox and I remember the experience well. A dab of the vaccine was smeared on my wrist and the area jabbed with a needle so that the vaccine would penetrate the skin. I was then advised to cover the "vaccinated" spot with the leaf of a plant locally called the *shalkhai* (a species of potherb) to keep the wound from healing, the underlying logic being that as long as the wound remained fresh, the vaccine would continue entering the bloodstream and protect me from smallpox germs. I consider myself fortunate that I did not come down with the disease which was considered fatal. I would also be vaccinated with BCG against tuberculosis in high school. I was told that my body was cancer-free, but since my immune system was not strong enough to keep the disease at bay, I was given an injection to boost it.

A common sight in winter was families sunbathing in the shelter of a wall. Women would busy themselves with the task of parting the strands of each other's hair to look for lice, plucking the vermin out when detected and squeezing the life out of them with their nails. Men would take off their shirts or loosen their pants so that they could locate some of the lice hidden in the folds of their garments and pull them out. I remember sprinkling DDT powder on my clothes and even on my hair to kill the lice that had taken up residence in my body. The problem of lice infestation was compounded by the lack of running water in our bathrooms. Most of us heated water and poured it into a bucket to wash ourselves. The more fortunate among us had a private corner in their homes, where they could sit in solitude and run water over their bodies at leisure. The rest had no option but to go outdoors, even in bitterly cold weather, and furtively seek the shelter of a wall or a tree to undress and bathe. Imagine going outdoors on a freezing winter morning and looking desperately for some nook or cranny affording enough privacy to allow you a moment to take off your clothes and have a wash! And by the time one found such a spot, the water often cooled and a bath turned into a torturous experience. Yet one had to bathe at all costs, for even those who had enjoyed sex or had wet dreams the previous night were considered unclean and were expected to bathe and purify themselves before prayers.

As small children, we would go out into the fields to perform all toilet-related functions and the fact that we were not required to wear any clothes in warm weather made the task that much easier. And it was during these sessions that many of us would notice worms in our feces. It was a common enough discovery, but it would scare me all the same. Not that there was much I could do to get rid of those worms, for their eggs were probably in the food we ate and in the water we drank. Once they had made their way into our stomachs, the worms hatched and grew in what was, no doubt, a conducive breeding environment. Evacuating our bowels while in the grip of the disease was no mean task. We often had to push hard, waiting for this strange red object to emerge from what seemed the bottom of the stomach. I assumed it was the other end of the stomach.

A locally available medicine could treat the disease, but its taste was so discouragingly bitter that swallowing it involved a heroic effort on my part. However, it did its job and I would subsequently find a few dead worms in my feces as proof. But the cycle of infection and treatment was a never-ending one, for I could hardly stop eating or drinking, the very source of the recurring disease.

There were other contributing factors as well. Whenever my friends and I took our cows out to graze in the desert near the mountain, we had to quench our thirst at the same source from which our cattle drank—the pond where rainwater accumulated—although we chose to do so further down the bank. We would occasionally spot tiny worms in the water and try to strain them out with a piece of cloth before quenching our thirst, hoping that this precaution would prevent them from invading our insides. If this method succeeded in keeping the worms out, it probably did nothing to stop their eggs from infiltrating into our bodies and hatching into full-fledged worms. In retrospect, I cannot help wondering how I survived my early childhood. Two of my own siblings did not. I suppose many children must have succumbed to the very diseases the more fortunate among us survived and developed some form of immunity to, which eventually prolonged our lives.

Looking back, I realize that every situation has its positive aspects. The hardships we endured and the primitive conditions in which we were raised helped us to become independent at a tender age. Our parents, for example, did not need to potty-train us. We children picked up this essential skill from each other. We would usually follow someone a year or two older out into the field and learn from his or her example. It was not as if we didn't have the odd accident. When we did, our parents or older siblings would wipe the evidence clean both from our bodies and from the site. At that age, we were untroubled by a sense of shame and unembarrassed by our nakedness, which we regarded as our natural state. As we grew older, however, our parents impressed on us the need to be clothed and to keep our private parts concealed.

Although ten children were born into our extended family, my parents are unlikely to remember how we potty-trained ourselves. In hindsight, I feel we must have saved them a lot of trouble and expense. My children, of course, were born in different circumstances. Diapers were available at the supermarket in Kuwait, when Khushal was born, which was just as well, for the use of fields for teamwork and self-training, a necessity in Khas Kunar, was just not an option.

Given the unsanitary conditions in which I grew up, I am certainly lucky to have survived my early childhood. Besides, unlike many children, we had parents to look after us and owned the house we lived in, apart from some farmland. Although my father, a government official, did not know how to work on his land, we did have an income from it, supplemented by the earnings that came in from local landowners with whom my father had invested some money. He had loaned some of his money to Bismillah Khan and Uncle Piro (his real name must have been Peer Mehmed) for profit so that we would receive a part of their grain from the harvest as an interest payment. I don't know what kind documents were exchanged between the lender and the borrower, but my father, the lender, got his money back when he needed it. Besides, he was a responsible parent, meticulous in handling the lumber account that his office had entrusted him with and ensuring that all dues were settled by those who owed the government money so that his children would not be burdened with unfinished business after his death.

TWO

Childhood: The Pre-School Years

My parents were born in Khas Kunar and all our relatives lived there. It was our permanent home, though we would relocate a few times to other places. And it was to Khas Kunar that we returned after leaving war-afflicted Pech. Deciding to settle there, my family bought a parcel of land jointly with my eldest cousin, Rawouf, who had accompanied us back from Pech, and Shakar Khan, husband of my Aunt Nabo, my father's elder sister, and father of my cousins, Rasul and Rabbani. They had lived in Tanar before relocating to the last *qala* down from Pachianu Banda, a small village of the Sayeds. My father and Rawouf bought half of the property, while Shakar Khan bought the other half. It consisted of a piece of farmland, a garden and a residence we called the *qala*. Each section of the property was divided in half. My father and Rawouf split their half, each retaining for himself a quarter of the total property. The *qala*, where all three families lived, was surrounded by a high mud wall, with a common door facing east. Each family had its separate living quarters in the residence and shared the main door, which was locked at night. All three residences opened on to the center of the *qala*, where the entrance to each of our living quarters was located.

Mulberry trees grew in the garden in front of the *qala*, with grapevines climbing up the branches. The garden in the back and along the southern side of the *qala* was abundant with fruit trees bearing apricots and pears, plums and figs. After their father's death, Rasul and Rabbani would plant orange trees on their part of the property. We also used the land under the fruit trees for growing vegetables. A mud wall surrounded the garden, separating it from the rest of the farmland.

The irrigation stream, originating in the lower canal to the east, ran west, north of the *qala*, to the *jaba*, a marshy area at the end of our property on the west and along the eastern side of the river. A public walkway, located between the waterway and the *qala* and used by both people and cattle, ran parallel to the stream. Our property, separated from that of our neighbors to the north by a wall erected along the stream, lay nearest to the river bordering the *jaba* to the west and the watercourse we had to cross in order to reach the main road between Chaghaserai and Jalalabad. Teetak, the high mountain to the west of the road, offered an ample supply of firewood for those young and strong enough to climb it and carry the wood down on their backs.

Our family quarters included a large room on the ground floor, which we shared with the animals we owned: a couple of cows, a donkey, a couple of calves and the sheep and goat that would be added later to our menagerie. The room had a small hole for a window, which looked out on to the center of the common residence. We kept it covered with a piece of old fabric rolled into a ball. The room served as our winter residence and was furnished with cots, one for each family member, lined up against the eastern and southern walls, leaving the area in the center free for us to sit in. The northern part of the room served as a stable for our animals. The door, our only entrance to the room which was also used by our animals, was located in the western wall. The room's centerpiece was an elevated area with a fireplace (actually, a hearth), where my mother cooked our meals, with us sitting around it. We burned wood or dried animal dung as fuel and placed pots over the fire on a *negharai* (metal tripod). Since it was an open fireplace, it emitted a great deal of smoke which we were forced to inhale. When we felt choked, we would open the door to let the excess smoke out. But we couldn't keep it ajar for long, for fear of letting in the cold. After eating our supper and chatting for a while, we would say our last prayers for the day, bid each other goodnight and go to bed.

About one-third of the room was given over to a stable for the animals. A wall that rose only halfway up separated their area from our own and there they ate, rested and relieved themselves. There was a *mena* (shelter) above the stable, on top of which we stored firewood and animal dung for fuel. The space between the *mena* and the room's ceiling was not wide enough for a person to stand upright. We would usually get a small-built person to climb on to the *mena* and squeeze into the space there to bring down the firewood or dried dung needed for daily use.

Our bathroom stood in the right-hand corner of the room. It was a small elevated space with a hole in the wall, where we could only wash our faces and complete our ablutions before prayers. The used water would drain out of the hole through a length of pipe to the center of the common residence, where it joined streams of used water from the bathrooms in the other two residences. This water would then pass under the main door to the garden and on to the farmland that lay beyond. Whenever the stink of the waste water became unbearable, we would scrape the dirty mud over which it flowed and replace it with fresh mud from outside. For security reasons, we could not put in a window in the wall that surrounded the *qala*, though the presence of one would surely have allowed the breeze to waft in and dispel unpleasant odors.

In front of the room that served as our winter residence was a *mandow* (a sort of shelter with three walls and a roof), where we stored our animal feed. It also served as an entrance to our all-purpose winter living room. Dirt steps in front of the *mandow* went up to the second floor. Underneath the steps was a small room where our chickens sheltered at night, although they were allowed to roam free outside the *qala* during the day. They would come in around sunset and after feeding them, we would let them into their room and say goodnight to them. The next morning, we would open the room, feed the chickens and let them out.

This security measure had been taken to protect them, not from human thieves, but from foxes and jackals which lived in the *jaba*'s marshy area and would steal the occasional chicken from our property. This usually happened when the watchdog that guarded our residence was either taking a nap or away playing with canine friends in the neighborhood.

Right above our winter living quarters, was a room where we kept our groceries; mainly, rice, corn and wheat harvested from our land. We also slept there when the weather was warm. The room had a veranda in front of it, with a fireplace (or, rather, a hearth) against the wall and a space where one could sit and eat. While the room downstairs had a hole for a window, the one above it had a real window, which opened out on to the center of the common residence. Compared to our living space downstairs, the room upstairs was airy and had more light, because we did not have to share it with our animals and cooked our meals in the veranda in front.

This room looked out on to the roof of the *mandow*, where cots were lined up for us to sleep in when the weather was warm. Leaning against the wall in front of the veranda was a wooden ladder, which we climbed to reach the roof of the room upstairs where we dried our grains. Every time the grain from Bismillah Khan and Uncle Piro's harvest was due and brought home on the backs of donkeys, my mother would have to fill a basket, balance it on her head and climb the wooden ladder to take it all the way up to that roof, where she would spread it out in the sun to dry. This had to be done several times, until all the grain had been carried up. Once it had dried, it was again her job to bring it down the same way and store it in the room upstairs. Climbing up and down that ladder, weighed down with baskets of grain, must have been quite a challenge, but my mother took it in her stride.

Adjacent to our living quarters downstairs and in the center of the common residence lay a plot of land which we owned and used as an outdoor stable for our animals during warm weather. They seemed to enjoy their time in this little space outdoors.

It was a local custom for every landowner to keep aside a small part of his property for a vegetable garden, where the family could grow tomatoes, eggplants, okra, peppercorns, pumpkins, squash and even exotic plants such as henna. Our own family's vegetable garden lay on the land under the fruit trees behind the *qala*. The wall surrounding the area afforded all the families living in our residence some privacy so that they could work and rest in peace, undisturbed by the curious gazes of passersby. I loved to go into the garden and eat the young eggplants and okra right from their stems. The plants were plentiful, owing, no doubt, to the animal fertilizer we used to boost their growth and our garden produced enough vegetables to feed the whole family all through summer. Some of the surplus would be dried and stored for consumption during the hard winter months. Like almost all livestock owners in the area, we used a part of our land for growing clover or alfalfa. When the clover was tender, we would pick it, cook it and eat it ourselves. Some would be dried and stored for our meals in winter. Later in the season, when the clover had lost its tenderness, we would reap it, a section at a time, and store it as winter feed for our animals.

Harvest time was a special occasion, because everyone in the community helped out their neighbors in reaping and threshing the crop. The event which inspired such communal cooperation was called Ashar. When my family was ready to harvest the crop, we would inform the neighbors and invite them to help us. Had we undertaken to do the work entirely on our own, it would have taken us a long time to finish the job. But when several people volunteered their help, it could be finished in one day. The harvested crop would be tied in bundles and brought to a designated area, which had been cleared and cleaned in advance. The bundles of rice or wheat, depending on the season, would be placed side by side in the face-up position and a big wooden nail inserted in the middle. Animals, mainly bulls and donkeys, would be lined up and tied together. One end of the rope would be tied around the nail. We would take turns to whip the animals, urging them to move around the nail and on the crop, until the hay was separated from the seeds. The mix of hay and seeds would be lifted into the air in small amounts with the help of a *khakhai*, a large wooden fork. The seeds, being heavy, would fall straight to the ground, but hay, being light, floated off and landed further away. The grain was put into sacks and brought home. The hay from rice was tied up in bundles and stored in a mulberry tree. The hay from wheat, on the other hand, was stored in a *bosarla*, a storage space with an open door that was like a haystack with mud walls, covered on top with a layer made from a mixture of hay and mud to protect it from rain. The door was then blocked, only to be opened in winter so that the hay could be taken out in small amounts to feed the cattle.

The harvested corn was processed in a different way. The crop was brought in bundles to the designated area and each bundle opened separately. A person holding a large wooden needle in his hand would prod open each kernel and separate it from its husk. The plants, divested of their kernels were then tied up, taken to the garden and stored in one of the mulberry trees. Storing them in the tree was probably a good idea, because the rainwater would drain through. The kernels were piled up and a group of men would then get together and beat them with long, heavy sticks until the seed separated from the *toqa* (corncob) inside. The seeds were gathered, cleaned of dust and put into sacks. The *toqas* were gathered and used as fuel to cook our meals. So the plants were meant for animal consumption, the seeds for human consumption and the *toqas* for cooking our meals and heating our rooms. The rice plants were also bundled up and stored in the trees and used as animal feed during winter. The wheat plants were usually broken into small pieces and could not be tied up. The wheat hay was placed in sacks and emptied into a *bosarla* or storage space. While wheat and corn seeds were ready to be taken to the mill to be ground into flour, rice seeds were still rough and had to be processed by the Kashmiris, a group of professionals who would separate the seed from the shaft. The Kashmiris would, of course, undertake the job for a fee, which was paid in kind; they kept a part of the rough rice for themselves. When the rice was ready, the owners would be informed and it was loaded on donkeys and brought home.

The best quality of rice and, understandably, the most expensive in Afghanistan is produced in Kunar, a narrow valley, where cultivable land is limited. It is not available in most of the country's bazaars. During my employment at the Ministry of Education in Kabul, a colleague of mine, whose family lived in Balkh province, had asked me if I would sell him some of the rice we grew on our land in Kunar. I had brought some to Kabul and offered it to him. He had doubts, though, about its origin, and only agreed to accept a sample, which he carried home and cooked. The flavor convinced him about its authenticity and he returned the following day and bought a large quantity of the rice from me. Nowadays, rice comes to the markets from all over the country and mainly from the north. The original residents of the north, primarily from the Baghlan, Samangan and Kundoz provinces where rice is now grown, had shown little interest in cultivating the crop. Its cultivation became widespread, however, when rice-eating people from the overpopulated areas of the east and south migrated and settled there. The new settlers drained the marshy lands and created ideal soil conditions for the cultivation of rice. Today, Baghlan, Samangan and Konduz are the country's rice baskets and the main source of supply for markets all over Afghanistan.

To return to the matter of cultivation, after plowing the land, the farmers scattered the seeds of corn and wheat in the field during the appropriate season. Rice seeds, however, were scattered in a small plot of land, a nursery, but not before the soil was thoroughly irrigated, for the farmer had to ensure that from the time seed was sown in the field to the time the crop was ripe, the saplings that sprouted would remain standing in water. The saplings that sprouted from the seeds were allowed to grow a foot high before being pulled together and tied up in small bundles. The bundles were then scattered across the rest of the land and the neighbors invited to participate in the Ashar. Men and women, in addition to children in their early and late teens, would line up and start the planting process. Each person would open the bundles nearby, pick up a couple of seedlings at a time and plant them, a foot apart, in the soil that had been prepared by covering it with a six-inch-high layer of water. The rice plants needed regular watering, until the seedlings were ripe and the crop ready to harvest. The farmer also had to ensure that weeds did not choke the young saplings, be they of rice, wheat or corn. He would do the rounds of his fields, pulling out weeds wherever they grew. Even these weeds were not wasted, but fed to the livestock.

We had two designated places for grazing our animals. One was the *jaba*, which our property bordered. Our animals were allowed to graze until early evening along this strip of grassy land between the river on the west and the residential area on the east. Between the grassy part of the *jaba* and the farmland lay a wetland, where reeds and *lukhay* (cat-tails) grew in standing water. We called it a *zangle* (jungle). Occasionally, our animals would stray to the wetland to graze. The other grazing area was a desert near the mountain to the east of the residential area, where the grass was believed to be more nutritious for the animals. However, the desert was a suitable grazing ground only during spring, when seasonal showers helped the grass to grow. With the onset of summer and its meager rainfall, the grass usually withered And it was just too cold in winter for us to take our animals there. The grass in the *jaba*, though, was available all the year round. In winter, the animals fed on dried clover or alfalfa and hay from wheat, rice and corn that had been dried and stored in the mulberry trees growing in the garden in front of the *qala* or in a *bosarla*. Some of the hay would be brought in and stored in the *mandow* for daily consumption.

We used the reeds from the *zangle*, the marshy side of the *jaba*, for building shades under the trees that grew in the garden in front of the *qala*. It was here that we usually relaxed in summer, protected from the heat of the sun. The soldiers from the base nearby would cut the reeds, carry them off and use them as fuel for their ovens to bake bread. We cut the *lukhay* (cat's tail) and wound them into ropes that would be used for weaving the stringed cots, the only pieces of furniture we owned, on which we relaxed during the day and slept at night. Similarly, the *lukhay* was brought into the mosque and scattered on the floor for us to kneel on during prayers.

The *zangle* and the farmland were ideal places for hunting birds which would take refuge there, away from the populated areas. We used the branches of trees to camouflage our presence among the reeds above the water and waited there at night. Some of the unsuspecting fowl that landed close to our hiding place would be caught and taken home, appearing on our dinner plates the following day. To trap birds on the farmland, we would use nets. We would first clear a section of the farmland and scatter some grain across it. The net would be placed around the area and tied to a long rope which trailed to a spot where the hunter was hiding. The moment birds alighted on that spot and began to peck at the grain, the hunter would give the rope a sharp tug, causing the net to fall over the birds and trapping them beneath it. The hunter would then approach the net, slide his hands under it, catch the birds, one by one, and bring them out. They would then be killed, cleaned, cooked and served up for the whole family to enjoy. No part of the game was ever wasted, barring the bones. And even these provided, no doubt, a feast for our family watchdog that shared the spoils with its friends in the locality. Vegetarians and animal rights activists may condemn the practice, but will, perhaps, be more forgiving when they realize that for most families living in those areas of Afghanistan, this was probably the only available source of meat.

As long as my mother was living, we always raised chickens. We usually kept a rooster to mate with our brood of hens to ensure a steady supply of eggs. Each hen went through a cycle of laying eggs. As soon as it started clucking, we knew the cycle was about to end and the hen would stop laying eggs. Of the clutch of eggs it laid, we would eat some; the others were placed in a basket lined with hay so that the hen could sit on them. These eggs hatched in due course, giving us more chickens. My mother once encouraged me to test my luck by placing sixteen eggs in the basket. It took twenty days for the eggs to hatch. I was considered very fortunate, because fifteen of those eggs hatched and gave us as many chicks. We also had a cow which provided the family with milk. Mother's job was to milk the cows and process the milk so that we could have butter, yogurt and buttermilk.

The only provisions we regularly bought from the local stores were sugar, salt, tea and kerosene, which we needed to light lamps after sun-down, for we had no electricity. We poured kerosene into a cone-shaped tin container with a hole in its cap. One end of a short cotton twist of rope or felt was inserted through this hole with the other end sticking out of the cap. This served as the wick when we wanted to light the "lamp." Once it was lit, we would watch the smoke from the flame rise in the air and blend with the fumes of smoke from the fireplace in our winter room downstairs so that we could barely see each other. Believe it or not, I have studied for years in the dim glow of this lamp and my eyesight today is still keen for a man of my age.

In the rural community in which we lived, those who were well off breakfasted on yogurt and cold rice that had been cooked the previous night, but they were among the fortunate few. Our own morning meal consisted of a piece of corn or wheat bread, along with sugared tea. Almost every meal we ate in the course of the day was followed by tea. Our mother tongue, Pashto, lacked the word denoting the concept of breakfast and we used the equivalent of the phrase, "morning tea," to convey the same message. For example, we would ask a family member if he had had his morning tea when we wanted to know if he had had his breakfast.

The wealthy families in Khas Kunar would kill a sheep or two at the onset of the winter and dry the meat to consume it later during the cold season. The dry meat, called *landai*, was eaten with a serving of rice and/or vegetables. For those less fortunate, meat was a rarity. We usually killed a chicken when a special guest had been invited for a meal. The presence of a special guest was, in fact, the perfect excuse for having a special meal, with poultry served as a special dish. There were a few other occasions on which people ate meat: when invited to a wedding feast or a *khairat*, a charity meal served to most villagers, after someone had died or when a much-loved member of the family had returned home from a long trip or recovered from a serious illness. Meat was also available to everyone once a year to celebrate the Loy Akhtar (Eid Al-Adha). On this occasion, every family would sacrifice a small animal such as a sheep or a goat or participate, along with a couple of other families, in the sacrifice of a larger animal, usually a cow. In keeping with religious ritual, the families performing the sacrifice would consume one-third of the meat and distribute the rest among those families that could not afford to do so. The sacrifice was symbolic of the act Ibrahim (Abraham) had been prepared to carry out when God commanded him to sacrifice his son, Ismail. Having tested his faith and found it true, God had then sent Ibrahim a sheep for slaughter. The meat-based feast was one of the highlights of Eid, apart from the new or clean clothes we received as gifts and were expected to wear for the special prayers at the mosque, followed by a round of visits to relatives, neighbors and friends.

I remember that period in my life as a happy one. With the yield from our own farmland supplemented by the additional crop that came from the lands of Bismillah Khan and Uncle Piro, we lived relatively well. Our livestock and poultry provided us with milk, eggs and, occasionally, meat. The family was together and I enjoyed being the eldest child, with two younger siblings following in my wake: a brother and a sister. Unfortunately, this golden phase came to an end when my mother fell ill as summer was drawing to a close. I do not know what ailment she was suffering from. It could have been malaria. But the backbreaking work involved in carrying those heavy baskets of grain on her head to the roof of the room upstairs could also have taken a toll on her health. The reason no longer seems important. When my mother died that winter in the bed she had shared with my father in the room downstairs, the prosperity we had enjoyed seemed to vanish all of a sudden.

THREE

Childhood and School

The time to start my schooling was approaching and I was all excited and ready to go. Whenever my father and I were out together, he would point to children on their way to school or homeward bound and ask me if I had noticed how happy they looked. It was due to this steady form of encouragement that I believed school was a cool place, where I would study and play with children my age. Going to school was also an exciting prospect for a more mundane reason: it would give me time off from my chores at home. My father knew the value of education from personal experience. It was because of his education that he had become one of a mere handful of *meerzas*—literate persons—in the village of Tanar, held a government position, received the salary of an official and had a steady income other than his earnings from his farmland. The other two literate people, I remember, were Ala Meer and

Mehmed Younes Krazanadar, the treasurer. While my father probably loved my siblings and me a little more than he did our cousins, because we were his own children, he was genuinely fond of his nephews, his brothers' children, and encouraged them all to go to school and get an education. In keeping with the customs of Afghanistan's patriarchal society, however, cousins from the mother's side were not given the same consideration.

Among the ten male members of my generation, brothers and first cousins from my father's side, seven of us would go to school, graduate at different levels and obtain salaried jobs. Our three cousins, the sons of Uncle Faqeer and Aunt Haleema, were advised by their mother not to go to school. Qudus, the eldest of the three, was blind and would later try to memorize the Quran at our local mosque. Three of us graduated from high school and two of us went on to do graduate studies. Unfortunately, I can neither include our sister nor our female first cousins in this list, because at the time, no school for girls existed in Khas Kunar. However, my three half-sisters, Najiba, Latifa and Ghotai, who grew up in Imam Sahib where there was a school, would manage to graduate from high school. Unfortunately, by the time a school for girls came up, my sister, Jahantab, was too old to be admitted. As a result, she would be denied schooling. A great pity, for she was a very bright girl. I remember that it was summer when she traveled to the north with the family. By the time I joined them in winter, just half a year had elapsed and Jahantab was fluent in Dari, a language she had picked up from our neighbor's daughter, a girl her age. In other words, my sister had learned a brand new language in six months flat!

My eligibility for admission to school depended on two factors: first, I had to be the right age; and second, I had to be circumcised. It is generally believed that circumcision is less painful when performed early in life and that recovery is swifter. Besides, the procedure could be embarrassing for an older boy, since he had to expose his private parts to the medical personnel in charge. In my case, the relative impersonality of a hospital was not an option, for there was no hospital in the whole of Kunar valley, which is now a province. My circumcision could not be entrusted to a doctor either, because there were none in Khas Kunar. The only person who performed circumcisions in the area was Munawar, the village barber. My father, however, did not consider him competent enough to to circumcise his eldest son. He therefore invited Ahmad Gul from another village to perform the procedure.

The big day arrived. I was going to be circumcised, whether I was ready or not. It was a family decision and and also a religious obligation by which every male in the community was bound. I had no choice but to endure the pain, while the rest of the family participated in the ceremony associated with the custom. Only men and children attended the ceremony. While the children were just spectators, with the boys among them learning by observation what they would eventually all go through when their turn arrived, the men usually participated in the ceremony by holding down the poor soul who was being circumcised or helping the barber to carry out the procedure by obeying his instructions. The ceremony involving my own circumcision began under the veranda of the room belonging to Aunt Nabo's husband, Shakar Khan. This was also used as a guest room by all the three families in the qala. I must have been sitting, naked from the waist down, on my father's lap and watching Ahmad Gul sharpening his knife and preparing the material he would need to sanitize the wound after the circumcision was over. Someone must have tried to divert my attention by urging me to look at an imaginary bird or an airplane when the barber was ready to snip the skin off the tip of my penis. Having watched others go through the same procedure, I knew the ceremony usually lasted for a few minutes, leaving the circumcised boy crying in pain. I was mentally ready when my turn came. I knew that going through the painful procedure was unavoidable, because social, cultural and religious norms decreed that every male child would have to go through it. What I could not have known at the time was how important it was for a man to be circumcised before he got married. No man in his right mind would have gone ahead with the wedding if he wasn't. For soon, everyone would have come to know about it. Believe me, you wouldn't dare to be an uncircumcised male in that society!

Meanwhile, the deed had been done and my penis was swelling. But the pain eased considerably later, when our relatives, mainly women, arrived, one after another, and gave me cash gifts. My penis looked gross for about a week. Then the swelling subsided and it began returning to its normal size and shape, enabling me to wear pants again and urinate without pain. My circumcision had taken place in summer and the weather was hot, but by the time I started school in the fall, I had fully recovered. By the end of summer, I was physically and mentally ready to go to school, following in the footsteps of my father and my older cousins.

As I had mentioned earlier, the right age for getting enrolled in school was determined in a rather arbitrary fashion by finding out whether the prospective candidate had lost his two lower front teeth or not. Unfortunately, my father was working in Chaghaserai and not around to advise me when I lost my own front teeth and I had to fall back on Aunt Haleema, who prepped me on how I should respond to the government official's queries about my desire to attend school. My aunt advised me as well as two of her sons, Wahab and Qadeer—the first, a couple of years older than me, and the second a year younger—to tell the man that our families were too poor to afford hiring laborers and needed our help at home and on the fields. Therefore, we could not go to school. I cannot remember if my mother offered any advice on the subject, but Aunt Haleema certainly did.

A soldier from the government office, locally known as a *kotwali*, arrived at our *qala* on the appointed day to escort us to the government office located about three miles from our house. All three of us, dressed in clean clothes, followed the soldier, walking barefoot behind him through farmland as we made our way to the government compound that stood north of Tanar Ghundai (Tanar Hill) along the upper irrigation canal. At Tanar village, we turned north and took the road to Bandai. Passing through Bandai, we turned east and walked through the local cemetery to arrive at the upper irrigation canal. We kept walking north along the canal on the western side of Tanar Ghundai, until we had arrived at the government compound. We entered the compound and joined a group of children who had also lost their lower front teeth and were supposed to have reached school-going age. The official in charge sat on the floor of the veranda, facing the children gathered in the courtyard. He had a list of all the children's names and read them out, one by one. The child whose name was called out had to step forward, stand in front of the official and state his case. My two cousins who were ahead of me parroted the lines their mother had taught them. The official saw merit in the argument they presented and sent them to join the group of children who had been exempted from going to school for similar reasons. When my turn came, I faithfully obeyed Aunt Haleema's instructions and explained why I could not go to school. The official looked down at my name on the list and read it again: Abdul Qayum, son of Faiz Mehmed. Then he looked back at me sternly and said that I was lying. He added that he knew my father and was well aware that my family was not poor, as I had claimed. Then without further ado, he sent me off to join the other group of children who had been selected to go to school. I don't remember how I felt at the time, but I suspect I must have been relieved, because it was my father's wish that I get an education and the government official had realized that. Had my father not been away, he would surely have accompanied me to the government compound and ensured that I got enrolled in school. But in his absence, his name seemed to have been enough to achieve the same purpose. It seems that my destiny and that of my cousins were determined at that very moment.

I spent the rest of the summer at home and when it ended, I was ready to go to school. On the first day of the school in September, I had a new life and a new identity—student—whereas my cousins, Wahab and Qadeer, continued with their routine family chores. Even though elementary education—Grades One through Six—was compulsory in Afghanistan, not all children were fortunate enough to avail of it. In remote areas, especially in the thinly populated mountainous region, no schools existed. And as I had mentioned earlier, there was no school for girls in our own village. Nor was there a special education program for the disabled. Children like my blind cousin, Qudus, were forced to remain at home, unlettered. Finally, the government officials were the ultimate authority, deciding who should go to school and who should not. If, as in the case of my cousins, a child was instructed by his family to come up with an excuse that sounded valid, he would be exempted from school without further investigation of the matter.

I do not know what vision of the future drove my two cousins, but I was already thinking ahead, dreaming of going to Kabul and wearing a uniform like the students I had seen returning home from the military high school and the military academy in the Afghan capital, with everyone in Khas Kunar going out to the riverside to greet them as they crossed over on the raft and landed on the eastern side of the river. It was a special occasion and everyone enjoyed greeting them, because they were related to someone or the other they knew. For my part, I enjoyed greeting my cousins, Rawouf and Rabbani, every time they arrived home to spend their winter vacation. I remember receiving a luscious-looking apple from Rabbani one year. The climate in Khas Kunar is not conducive to the cultivation of the fruit and people coming from Kabul always brought apples as gifts. I had held on to Rabbani's apple for a couple of days, admiring its rich color and gleaming skin before I actually ate it. Although my cousins were students and did not have a lot of money to spare, they would bring back small gifts—a pencil or a notebook, for instance—every time for their family and other close relatives. I wanted to be the one bringing gifts for my relatives and friends, instead of receiving them and looked forward to the day I could.

Some of the schools in the province of Kunar were located in the winter-vacation areas, others in the summer-vacation areas. Khas Kunar was a summer-vacation area, where students went back to school at the end of summer. On the first day of school, I remember walking behind my cousin, Rasul, who was a teacher at the local elementary school that stood half a mile west of Kunar village. It was a long walk and would take us an hour to arrive. This was the winter campus, where everything from the last school year had been damaged or destroyed and had to be reconstructed. I remember how I joined in the activity, virtually rebuilding our classroom from scratch. We erected a square-shaped metre-high mud wall in which we left an opening that would serve as the entrance and exit of our classroom. We each had a wrap-around piece of cloth which we spread on the ground and sat on. The school did own a few *kilims* (rugs), but they had been assigned for the use of students in the upper grades. We made a mud seat for the teacher, attaching it to the wall so that when seated, he could face us as we sat on the floor of the classroom.

I remember having to walk through farmland and jump across a few streams on my way to school. I usually took the same route every day, though I was afraid of the dogs that guarded some of the houses I passed on the way, but I don't remember ever being attacked by them. All they did was bark. I guess my fear of dogs wasn't entirely unwarranted. I had twice been attacked by them during my childhood. The first time it happened was when my family sent me to Shalai to visit Uncle Piruz's family and bring some firewood back home. Uncle Piruz was married to my stepmother's aunt. He and his two brothers lived in houses they had built in the same compound both for the sake of convenience and for security reasons. Shalai village lay within walking distance. My stepmother's aunt was my uncle's senior wife and the matriarch of the family. The three brothers and other male members of the family prayed at a mosque nearby. Uncle Piruz's family was involved in disputes with the families of his distant cousins. Once in a while, they would resort to firing on each other from the trenches they had dug for the purpose. This would be followed by convening a local *jerga* (a local court of justice, as it were) and restoring a period of truce. Life in those parts was unpredictable and it only took a minor incident to trigger off serious fighting between families.

After staying overnight at Uncle Piruz's house, he and I had gone to the village and loaded firewood on a donkey which I would have to lead back home, a few hours away on foot. On my way back, I was passing Ahmad Sayed's house, when two or three ferocious dogs bounded out of his *qala* toward me. I almost panicked, but remembered that I had been instructed to sit down and remain calm whenever a situation like this arose. When the dogs were close, I decided to take refuge behind the donkey. The dogs attacked the donkey instead, but as luck would have it, the beast of burden didn't take too kindly to the assault and kicked one of them hard enough to send all of them squealing back in retreat. I was relieved that no one emerged from the *qala* to shoot the donkey dead. Had I been injured, the incident could have set off a feud between Ahmad Sayed and Uncle Piruz's family.

The second attack took place early in the morning, when the bitch we kept as a pet was in heat and the dogs from the neighborhood were fighting over her. One of those dogs attacked me, launching himself at me so hard that I was flung into a ditch. Later, I found teeth marks on my leg, but the wound healed and I survived.

To return to my days at school, I recall that our winter campus was a strip of grassy wetland, unsuitable for farming, that lay between the farmland and the marshy area. There was no building on the grounds and without a roof over our heads, we were always at the mercy of inclement weather. When the weather was fine, we would stay on the campus and study. On a rainy day or when a downpour surprised us during school hours, our classes would be held in one of the mosques in Kunar village and we would run through the rain and attend them. The village had four mosques. The Charakai mosque was located along the irrigation canal at the northern end of the village, while the Khyber mosque stood at its southern end. Within the village were two more mosques. Students from each class would run through the rain to be in time for lessons at their assigned mosque. Although the space inside the mosque was a bit cramped for the number of students it had to accommodate, we were relieved to have our classes there, protected from the rain. However, we had to finish our lessons and leave by early afternoon so that the villagers could use the mosques for their noon prayers.

Temperatures could dip sharply in winter and making the hourlong journey to school every morning, as most of us did, walking barefoot over frost-laden grass, shrouded in mist, with icicles forming along the streams, was as painful an ordeal as spending time there. Imagine a group of between thirty and forty students sitting in an enclosure, surrounded by a wall no more than a metre high, with no protection from the cold. The area had probably been selected for a number of reasons: the proximity of the hot spring, no doubt, the cleanest source of water available in the whole area; and the unsuitability of the land for agricultural purposes, which automatically ensured that no one would claim ownership to it. The summer campus was at another location, a little further down from the winter campus, and it would take me well over an hour to get there. The warm-weather campus was a garden to the southwest of Kunar village. A dry bed formed by silt left from a flood and locally known as a *khwarl*, separated the village from the campus. The garden, where the students attended their classes under mulberry trees, belonged to Ala Meer. The trees, however, did not protect us from showers and when it rained, we had to run again to the assigned mosques, as we would from the other campus. The saving grace was that the village was closer to this campus even though it was over an hour away from my home on foot.

The campuses were probably selected bearing in mind the location of Kunar village which stood midway between the village of Mangual, the last village in the south, and the village of Hakimabad (locally known as Kuleegram), the last village in the north. The origin of the hot-spring water lay at the winter campus, from where it flowed, ending in the marshy area between the grassy section of the *jaba* and the farmland. During my first year at school, the students and the villagers started to clean the stream. I remember that a few snakes were pulled out of the ditch. Fortunately, the following year, when I was promoted to the second grade, the school moved to a new campus, a big fort that stood about half a mile north-east of Kunar village and to the east of the only road in Khas Kunar. The best part of the move was that we did not have to carry anything to the new campus. The school supplies were stored in a couple of trunks which could be loaded on the back of a donkey and carted off to the new campus. There was no furniture. Just a few *kilims*, which could either be carried by the janitors or loaded on the backs of donkeys.

The fort that stood east of our house had a big entrance door. The rooms inside were built adjacent to its four walls. I would follow the watercourse upstream, passing through Pachianu Banda, walk over the wooden log to cross the lower canal and arrive at the new campus located about 150 metres east of the road that did not lead out of the Khas Kunar area and was, therefore used only by pedestrians, although it was wide enough for vehicles. The fort was one of the two big *qalas* owned by Mariam Jana's family, the wealthiest in the area. Their own residence stood on my way to school along the lower canal. The door of the *qala* opened to the west and faced both the road and Mariam Jana's residence. The courtyard was spacious and in front of the campus was an area where we gathered in the morning before going to our class-rooms in an orderly manner, lining up behind our classmates to do so. We also used that area for playing volleyball.

My first classroom was in the corner of the *qala* and we students had to enter it through one of the adjacent rooms. The classroom did not have a window and daylight came in through a round hole in the ceiling. The classrooms of Grades Three and Four, however, had windows which opened out on to the courtyard. While winters are generally not severe in Khas Kunar, on certain days, the temperature would plunge drastically. Naturally, we were happier being indoors here, rather than out in the open in the old campus, although our classroom was the darkest one on the campus. During the cold winter days, each student would be asked by the school administration to bring a log of firewood so that we could build a fire in the middle of the classroom. All the rooms were interconnected and had flat roofs.

When the weather was mild, classes were held on the roof. Like our other campuses, the new campus was not equipped with indoor bathrooms. We had to wait till recess and find a private corner in the farmland around the *qala* before we could relieve ourselves. This didn't take too long before the harvest, as we could easily hide in the wheat or corn crop. But once the harvest was over, it would take a while, because we often had to cover long distances to find a place where we wouldn't accidentally stumble upon another classmate. For this very reason, the recess was invariably extended. And anyone living in the neighborhood or passing through did not take long to find out about our recess time. I would remain on this new school campus for the next three years.

Mariam Jana, the owner of the new campus, was Lalu Jan's widow and the family matriarch. Of the three sons Mariam Jana had borne him, Malang was older than me, Kabeer was my age and Naeem was a couple of years younger. They lived in a big *qala* and all the land surrounding it belonged to the family. They had a garden to the north of the *qala*, with a stream flowing between it and the residence. While Malang and Naeem lived in Khas Kunar, Kabeer would graduate from Rahman Baba High School in Kabul before going to Germany. Malang was later elected as Khas Kunar's representative to the Parliament in Kabul. The last time I remember seeing Naeem, he was the assistant principal of the high school south of the Government Center. I had visited the institution while working at the Ministry of Education in Kabul, because my uncle, Habib Rahman, was its principal.

I would meet Mariam Jana in 1967, when I came home on vacation from the American University of Beirut (AUB) earlier than anticipated because of the six-day Arab-Israeli War that had broken out on 5 June, causing the university to shut down prematurely for the summer. It was while spending a week with my stepmother's family in Khas Kunar that her mother, Hukumai, whom I regarded as my own grandmother, informed me that Mariam Jana wished to see me and inquire about her son, Kabeer, whom I had visited in Germany during a trip to Europe the previous year.

I considered meeting the lady an honor, because everyone in Khas Kunar and most of the people in the valley of Kunar knew who she was and were somewhat awestruck by the clout she wielded.

I found her seated on a cot outside the door leading from her *qala* to the garden, waiting to welcome me to her home. In our part of the world, women usually do not invite men, other than close relatives, to their homes. However, our equation was somewhat different. Since I was her son's age, she was old enough for me to address her as "Aunt." I sat down on the other cot facing her and patiently answered all her queries about how and where I had met her son.

I had, in fact, met Kabeer in Frankfurt. He was on vacation from the radio station, Deutsche Welle, where he worked in their Pashto department, and we would spend an evening together at his place. I would meet Kabeer again in the family's garden back in Khas Kunar, when I graduated from AUB and was working at the Ministry of Education. I remember the moment well. I was on my way to stay with my cousin, Wahab, for a week. The road east of Kabeer's family residence was operational for vehicles at the time and I had boarded a jeep in Jalalabad and gotten off to the east of the house. I was passing through Kabeer's garden, when I saw him and his brother, Naeem, inside a bush cottage under the trees. It was summer and by sprinkling water on the bushes, mainly the thorny ones, one could create a cool and pleasant environment inside the cottage, with the breezes blowing through.

Coming back to my school days, I have never forgotten that winter morning when I tried walking over the wooden log, as usual, to cross the canal on my way to school, lost my balance and fell headlong into the water. Fortunately, the water was never too deep in winter, because the level of the river from where the canal flowed remained low and I managed to get up and scramble out. The story would have been quite different in the spring, when the river was swollen with rainwater. However, since I was soaking wet and it was a cold winter day, I decided to return home and change out of my clothes. It was a winter that would stay in my memory for other reasons too; my mother was gravely ill when I tumbled into that canal, but I remember her getting out of bed to hand me a dry set of clothes and wrap me in a blanket so that I wouldn't catch cold.

Looking back on all that my mother was required to do to raise us and keep the family together, it seems impossible now that one person could be burdened with so much work. Her daily chores included milking the cow or cows—depending on how many we had at a given time—processing the milk so that the family could have other dairy products to vary and supplement their daily diet, cooking meals for us, doing the laundry and cleaning the house. In addition, she would be carrying the grain from the harvest to the roof of the room upstairs. I was in the second grade when my mother fell ill. I recall how she would seek out the sunny patch that lay between the garden and the farmland and rest on the ground there, going back into the house only when the sun was about to go down. Then she would busy herself with preparing the evening meal for the family.

When winter arrived, it was too cold outdoors for my mother to venture out and she spent most of the day in bed in our room downstairs. There were no hospitals or medical clinics in the area and I can't recall if my father took her anywhere else for medical treatment. Once in a while, a mullah would come to the house and prescribe some herbal medicine for her or give her an injection. She was gone before the winter was over, passing away in her bed, wrapped in my father's arms.

When I consult a doctor for the first time, he or she usually asks about my family's medical history. One of the queries is invariably about the reasons behind my mother's premature death. I have no satisfactory answer to offer. Perhaps I was too young to know what had ailed her. Even the mullah who treated her from time to time did not seem to know what was wrong with her, but gave her medicines to ease her suffering. In retrospect, I suspect she was suffering from malaria. The image I have retained of her, lying in the sunlit garden for some warmth, suggests she was in the grip of some kind of fever and sought relief from the chills that seized her periodically. Deep in my heart, I blame my father for not taking her to Jalalabad, where she could have consulted competent doctors, sought treatment and, perhaps, recovered. She was fated to die young, her illness undiagnosed.

According to local tradition, when a married woman dies, her relations with her husband end and her father's family gets in charge of funeral arrangements The same was true in my mother's case; her parental family took on the responsibility of carrying out her burial ceremony. As far as I remember, it was the first time that my mother's younger brother and her elder brother's family would come to our house to make arrangements for her funeral. I recall sitting on the edge of the area in our room that was reserved for meals and conversation and gazing at my dead mother's face. I did not know what I was expected to do under the circumstances. Should I weep or just stare at her face, I wondered. I had noticed a female cousin of mine, three or fours years my senior, sitting next to me and crying her head off. It was likely that her tears were less an outpouring of grief for my departed mother than the performance of a social ritual whose importance had been ingrained in her. She was expected to weep in the presence of a dead relative who had yet to be buried and she was doing so with gusto. I saw her furtively glance at me between bouts of crying and suspected she was outraged at my silence, when it was own mother lying there before me. Unable to bear it any longer, she poked me suddenly and ordered me to cry. I don't remember if I did or just kept staring at my mother's face. I knew with a certain finality that she was dead and it was the last time I would see her. She would soon be buried and all I would see was her grave.

My mother's permanent departure from the family turned our lives upside down. We lost all the animals and the stable remained empty. The money we had invested with Bismillah Khan and Uncle Piro was, in all likelihood, spent on my mother's funeral. I was, at the time, in the second grade, Wadood was between three and four years old and Jahantab was an infant. Father was forced into playing the role of both parents, although he could not really take over from where my mother had left off. The family sank deeper and deeper in debt. We lost all our livestock and the stable remained empty. We could probably have repaid our debts and regained our financial stability if my father had been a farmer. But he had never in his life worked on the land, busy as he was with his duties as a government official. We hired a farmer who would plow the land, sow seeds and harvest the crop. We had to pay him with one-third of the yield at harvest time. As a result, the income from the land was not enough to cover our family expenses. As we fell on hard times, the relatives we had been close to earlier distanced themselves from us.

That very winter, my brother and I were sitting in the room downstairs one night, when we heard a sound from the empty stable, as though someone were moving about. We both screamed and ran out of the room in fright. Mullah Bebu, my cousin Rasul's wife, came into the room to investigate the source of the sound and examined it thoroughly in the light of the kerosene lamp, with my brother and me looking on.

We expected to see some ferocious beast lurking in the darkest corners, but failed to find it. Mullah Bebu left the room and although we were terrified, we two boys survived the night.

Wadood lived with our father most of the time. Out of sheer kindness, Aunt Mulko, who had a daughter the same age, took Jahantab over to her house to care for her. I would go off to school every morning and when it gave over early in the afternoon, I went straight to my aunt's house and took my sister out to play until sunset. I would then take her back to the house and run home, the journey taking me about twenty minutes. This was my daily routine, except on Friday, a holiday, which I usually spent at Aunt Mulko's house, taking care of Jahantab. Shegai, an open space that served as a playground for the village children, lay north of Tanar village and south of the housing complex belonging to the judge's family. Almost all the children from the village would gather there every afternoon to play *khusai*, *dandas* or *taiqai* until sunset.

Khusai was a game in which two teams were pitted against each other. One team would guard a dirt mound that stood behind them. The other would attempt to hit the mound and bring it crashing down. The players of both teams had to hop all the way, holding one leg up with a hand. The team guarding the mound had to force as many players as possible of the opposing team to release the immobile leg before they reached the mound. Any player who succumbed to pressure or lost his balance and let go would be out of the game until the next round. The players of the team guarding the mound would try to reach the *khusai* (one of the boys of the opposing team who had been so designated, though the word literally meant "a female calf") and force him to let go of the raised leg. If they succeeded, the team he represented would have to concede defeat and the other team would receive a point in their favor. If the other team managed to destroy the dirt mound before this happened, it would gain a point. The losing team would then switch sides with the victorious one.

Dandas was a local ball game similar to baseball and, like *khusai*, played between two rival teams. The attacking team would use a stick to hit a small ball toward the players of the other team who were scattered all over the field. Having hit the ball, a member of the attacking team had to sprint a certain distance to a spot where he was considered safe. The opposing team would try to catch the ball and strike the other player before he had reached his "safe" destination in order to gain a point in his team's favor.

Taiqai was a game played with walnuts and a small stone ball. This was not a team sport; everyone played for himself. A player used his middle finger to try and strike a walnut with the stone ball so that the former rolled into a hole. If he succeeded, the walnut became his property. Every player was expected to contribute a certain number of the walnuts when the game started. His aim was to win back the walnuts he had contributed and win some of those belonging to other players involved in the game. It was a sport based on pure marksmanship.

I was in Grade Three and my mother had been dead for a year when my father remarried. My stepmother's name was Gul Bebu. Now that we had a woman in the house again, we brought Jahantab back home. My father explained that he had remarried for two reasons: to give us a mother and to hand over the homemaker's duties that had fallen to him since my mother's death. A year after his marriage, however, he discovered that if he stayed on in Khas Kunar, he would not be able to support his family and make ends meet. As I had mentioned earlier, the money he had invested in the farmland of Bismillah Khan and Uncle Piro had partly been spent on my mother's funeral and partly on his wedding. The new bridegroom found himself in debt and made the mistake of going to the Mohmands living on Shalai Mountain to borrow money. In his desperation, he did not think of the consequences.

Although the Shalai lies within the borders of Afghanistan, the Mohmands called themselves Pashtuns, residents of Pashtunistan, the semi-autonomous tribal region located between our country and Pakistan. Curiously enough, while all the villagers in Khas Kunar spoke Pashto, the Mohmands from the mountains regarded themselves as the real Pashtuns. They were the only people in the area allowed to carry weapons and would come down to Khas Kunar in large groups, every one of them armed, apparently believing themselves immune to local government restrictions that prohibited Khas Kunar residents from carrying weapons. The authorities were partly to blame for this devil-may-care attitude, with the governments of both Afghanistan and Pakistan trying to placate them.

The tribals would travel to Jalalabad, for example, and put up at the guest house of the Department of Tribal Affairs. There they would be given free meals and even cash gifts to take back home. I am not sure how often they had to go to Jalalabad to get their allowance, but I would not be surprised if they took gross advantage of their privileges just to be there at the appointed time. I suspect that the tribals who received an allowance from the authorities in Afghanistan did not hesitate to present themselves in Peshawar to collect a second allowance from the Pakistani authorities. I would not have put it past these people to send one male member of a family to Peshawar and his sibling to Jalalabad to collect "dues" from the respective governments. On their next trip, they would have switched places and continued to dupe both governments.

The residents of Khas Kunar referred to people from Shalai as the *Tanga Seri*; in other words, those who had sold themselves for a *tanga* (the local name for a quarter of the Afghani, our country's currency). They despised the tribals, but could do little against them, because the authorities were powerless to intervene. The mountain people would come down to the farmland of their debtors at harvest time, load their donkeys with as much grain as they wished and return home to Shalai. No one could protest or argue with them, because the tribals were judge, jury and prosecutor, functioning above the law and immune to its diktat.

There was very little farmland up in the mountain and the desert was mostly barren. The tribals grew some wheat and barley in relatively arid land, waiting for the rain to irrigate their meager cultivations so that their crop would grow and yield some grain for consumption. The amount of rainfall determined how much food they could get from the harvest. In a situation of such terrible uncertainty, they had to find other means of sustenance. Usury, the tribals' main line of business, ensured not just survival, but profits. The mountain people would charge as much interest as they themselves deemed fit. Where our family was concerned, the tribals would carry away the entire yield of our summer harvest, returning for more during the next harvest in the fall. The amount of money my father had borrowed from them would remain unchanged as long as the lenders thought they had received enough crop to ensure a profit on their investment. If the crop failed to meet their demands, they would add to my father's debt. Had this situation been allowed to continue, my father would have lost ownership of his farmland and it was to avoid this eventuality that he chose to accept the government job and hand over his whole share of the harvested crop from his land to the mountain people.

Fortunately, my cousin, Rawouf, graduated from the military academy as a second lieutenant, saved some money from his salary and lent it to my father who added some of his own money to the amount and paid his debts to the mountain people to reclaim his land. Henceforth, life for us would improve a little, thanks to the crop from our land and my father's salary from his government job. However, we would discover later that his total income was hardly enough to support a family of five. Being away at work, my father could not keep an eye on the farmer he had hired to cultivate his farmland and was, most likely, cheated on the crop harvested from his own field.

Going back to the moment my father accepted his job with the government, I remember his move to Chaghaserai. Wadood and Jahantab were not yet of school-going age and accompanied him and their stepmother to their new home. Since it was the middle of the school year, I had to stay back in Khas Kunar and went to live with my stepmother's parents, Abdul Rahman and Hukumai.

I was not unhappy about the arrangements, for Hukumai, my stepmother's mother and, therefore, my grandmother, was the kindest person I knew among all my relatives and the nicest woman in the whole village. In fact, everyone considered my father fortunate to have such a woman for a mother-in-law. As time passed, however, I realized how difficult it was for her to treat me like a grandson, because I was the same age as her youngest daughter and, therefore, old enough to be her son. But I could not be a son to her either, for Khalil Rahman, her third child, who was a couple of years older than me and the only male offspring in her brood of four, would always be the apple of her eye. For my grandmother, Khalil was special and she spoiled him rotten. She ensured, for instance, that he was the best-dressed among the boys who walked with him to school; and the coveted breakfast of rice and freshly made yogurt was reserved for him alone. How I longed for such a breakfast as a boy! I still remember the creamy yogurt that you put into a bowl, the rice which was mashed into it and the delicious mixture that you ate using your fingers. But Hukumai never thought of serving it to me. I recall an occasion when she fed Khalil the special breakfast while I was still asleep or, rather, pretending to be asleep. I knew she would not wake me up to serve me the same meal. So I continued lying in bed, my eyes shut, until Khalil had finished. However, I harbored no resentments against him, for he was a couple of grades ahead and like a big brother to me. He accompanied me to school every day and was there with me on my way home too.

My life in my grandmother's home would come to an end when I was promoted to Grade Five and my father came down to Khas Kunar to take me back with him to Chaghaserai, where I joined the rest of the family and was enrolled in a new school.

Gul Bebu, my stepmother, was her parents' second child. Her elder sister, Gula, was married to Muhibullah, who lived in Arazai and was, like his wife's father and uncles, a carpenter. Gul Bebu and Gula's two paternal uncles, Fazal and Muhib, were also carpenters by profession and helped theirolder brother, AbdulRahman , in the family workshop. They primarily served clients, local farmers, who came to them to have their yokes repaired. In their spare time, the three brothers would make wooden spoons and legs for cots. In time, Abdul Rahman's son, Khalil, would learn the trade and take his father's place after the latter's death. Khalil sometimes traveled to other locations and undertook contract jobs for the carpentry work in a building under construction. Sometimes, he worked independently; at others, in partnership with his maternal uncle, Abdul Ghani, who lived next door to his father and was a carpenter involved in building houses, schools and other edifices. Ghani would sign a contract with the property owner and hire Khalil and other carpenters to work for him. He even went out of the Kunar valley to build houses. I remember hearing one year that he was working on a construction site in Sarobi, located on the road between Kabul and Jalalabad.

Gul Bebu, who was hardly ten years older than me, probably found it easier to relate to my younger siblings as her children. In hindsight, I feel it must have been hard for her to adjust to her new life with us. Imagine being married off to a man and saddled with three children, one of them a mere infant, and none she had given birth to. My father was away at work and the stable was empty. So she felt no obligation to be home all the time. Being close to her parents, she would try and spend as much time with them as possible every day, taking my younger siblings along with her to their home and returning late in the evening. With my father away and my stepmother and siblings at her parents' home all day,

I would come back from school to an empty house. I remember going out to the very edge of the garden umpteen times and gazing across a clear space over the farmland to see if Gul Bebu and my siblings were on their way back from her father's house. Looking on the bright side, not having to take care of my baby sister any more or graze and feed the family cows, for our stable lay empty, did ease my burden and school became less of a slog and something to look forward to. Of course, I was still doing some of the family chores, like fetching water from the canal, carrying wheat or corn to the local flour mills, gathering firewood and carrying it home, but on the whole, my life was certainly easier.

While I was overjoyed to see my younger siblings again when I joined them in Chaghaserai, I did regret losing an entire semester at the new school, because the students there went on their annual vacation in winter. The school was located in a *qala* in Yargul, about an hour's walk from my house in Demkelay. The rooms were built against the *qala's* four walls and we studied there when the weather was cold. A short distance away was a garden of mulberry trees—our summer campus. Classes were held under the trees and a knee-high walls segregated the different batches of students attending different classes. It was like the summer campus of elementary school in Khas Kunar, when I had been in the first grade. In fact, I preferred the new place, since it was located along the Kunar River and we enjoyed the cool breeze blowing across the water. Both campuses were located along the river and the entrance to the *qala* opened toward the river. The *qala* stood on top of a hill, while the garden lay below, closer to the riverbank. We had to walk up a rocky incline in order to arrived at the *qala*'s main door. Each class in the garden was surrounding by a short stone wall. So we did not have to build our classroom from scratch at the beginning of each school year.

The road leading to the *qala* would be crowded with young men walking to school every morning and returning home early in the afternoon. A large group of students would follow Ghulam Sakhi, the Flower Teacher. He was thus known, because he always tucked flowers around the edge of his *pakool*, a wool hat he wore every day without fail.

The Flower Teacher was not from the area, but had come from Khaiwa, which is located at the southern end of the Kunar valley near Jalalabad. He probably had a wife and children, but I don't remember him bringing his family along to Chaghaserai. He was always alone and his living quarters were the guest room of a wealthy person in the locality. The Flower Teacher taught history and geography to the students in the upper elementary level, Grades Four to Six. He usually ran out of money before the month was over and I would ask my father to give him part of his salary in advance. On the way to school, most of the students would stop for a while at Chinar Daba, a shaded area along the water canal. The Flower Teacher would arrive at Chinar Daba and the students would line up behind him. The road from Chinar Daba onward was rough and dusty and clouds of dust would rise from under our feet as we headed toward the school.

Unlike the Flower Teacher who taught us history and geography, most of our teachers were locals. Some belonged to well-known families in the area. Abdul Ghafour, for instance, was our teacher for religious studies and belonged to the Qazianu family of judges who lived in a secluded area near the village of Demkelay, next to the compound of the Khazanadar family of treasurers. This compound lay north of the main village and west of the canal which ran between the village and the bazaar. Abdul Ghias, our language teacher, was a wealthy person in his own right. He had an imposing house behind the village mosque and owned a lot of land, in addition to a flour mill and a rice-processing plant. I am not aware of Murad Khan's family background, but he had a nice house along the dry bed of silt left by receding floods on the southern side of the village. Abdul Baseer was from Kerala, the village across the river. We had to cross the bridge that spanned the Pech River near the government compound, turn left toward the west and walk along the river, against the current, to arrive in Kerala. Whenever I went there, I would stay at the house of Shah Mahmud, who was a year senior to me at school. His father, Sultan Mehmed, and mine were good friends. Moreover, Shah Mahmud was also my father's student and took religious instruction from him as well as lessons in reading and writing.

Graduating first in class, I now suspect, was probably the outcome of two factors: my rigorous study schedule and a little bit of luck, that may have had something to do with my father being in charge of disbursing the teachers' salaries. Not that our teachers spared us. As I have mentioned earlier, most of the local ones had their own farmland. After the soil was prepared for planting rice, our class would be deployed to plant saplings and the job would keep us busy the entire day. At the end of the day, the whole class would be fed. This was our reward. I don't remember being absent from any of these occasions, not even on the days we worked for Ghafour Khan. When work on his field was over for the day and we had washed ourselves, he would bid us goodnight and send us home without feeding us a morsel. It was a perfect example of slave labor, where the religious studies teacher exploited his position had forced under-age boys to work for him for free.

Most of the land owned by the teachers was fertile for reasons most people would never have dreamed of suspecting. It was located near the Government Center that drew a large number of visitors every day. Since there were no public toilets at the center, all visitors and most of the officials felt free to use the surrounding farmland. Bulls would be put to work and helped plow, water and rake up the soil, with a *maala* (harrow) to smoothen the surface. When it was ready, we students would be asked to roll up our pants and shirt sleeves and step into the six-inch-high water that covered the soil, the ideal condition for planting rice saplings. We would move slowly through the fresh human manure, planting the saplings with our bare hands as we went. We were afraid that if we refused to join in, our teachers would find a way of flunking us or expelling us from school and we would remain illiterate for the rest of our lives. I wonder now if anyone had fallen ill because of the unsanitary conditions in which we were made to work. Even if they had, there was little they could have done about it. No one would have listened to our protests, for we were just children and our teachers, being adults, were always right. Even our parents wouldn't have entertained complaints on the subject. They would have scolded us for being disrespectful to our teachers, who were our spiritual fathers, and sided with them and the school administration.

Things had not been that much better in elementary school in Khas Kunar, for discipline in Afghan schools was strictly enforced and harsh, even cruel. Since there were no hard and fast rules, the students often did not know if and when they had violated them. I remember being absent from my first-grade class in Khas Kunar one summer's day and being severely punished for it the following day. It must have taken some ingenuity on the teacher's part to decide that I should carry Sher Alam, one of my classmates, on my back and go around the classroom as punishment. It was the hot season and we students had been sitting under a tree in Ala Meer's garden. Sher Alam was the oldest student in our class, because he would fail, year after year, and remain in the first grade. I have now forgotten how many times I had to carry him around the class, while the rest of the school witnessed my humiliation. After this experience, I would remain terrified of the teacher. I remember one occasion, when I was strolling in the garden in front of our *qala* and spotted the man approaching the house. I did not know that he had come to visit my cousin, Rasul, and fled in panic to the edge of the garden, jumping over the wall to the other side on the assumption that I could hide there till he had left. However, the man had seen me. Approaching the wall, he peered over it and ordered me to go and fetch my cousin. I have never been more scared in my life!

There was another teacher in the same grade, a bearded man who announced in class that he needed a chicken to feed his guests. I was so eager to ingratiate myself with him and thereby stave off possible punishment for perceived misdemeanors in the future that I promptly told him we had one at home. He immediately sent me off to get it. Walking home took an hour, as did the journey back. Moreover, I had to spend some time looking around the farmland to find our rooster and catch it. But I was desperate to do anything to stay in the teacher's good books.

Complaining against any teacher in the local community was unthinkable, for he was "the man with the stick"—a branch freshly cut from a mulberry tree—which he had no qualms about using liberally. The stick was a handy weapon for whacking students, usually on their palms or on the soles of their feet. A student being punished for some infraction would be asked to turn his palms up so that the teacher or the headmaster could hit it repeatedly. Or the boy could be asked to lie down on the ground, while the school janitors came and bound his feet with a *pato* (a cloth). A janitor would stand on either side, holding the ends of the *pato* and pulling on it, so the student's feet were raised above the ground. The teacher or the headmaster would then take up position and strike the soles of the boy's feet with the mulberry branch.

Mehmed Noor, our headmaster at the elementary school in Chaghasersai, was hard of hearing and made up for his infirmity by meting out the harshest punishment. The school would start at eight a.m. and the headmaster would make it a point to stand by the main door, stick in hand, after five or ten minutes had passed to intercept latecomers. A janitor would stand next to him, carrying a bunch of surplus sticks, in case the headmaster's stick broke on a student's back and had to be replaced. In fact, it was the janitor's job to go to the garden, our summer campus, and cut a few branches from the mulberry trees, early in the morning, for that very purpose. Every student who walked in late would be hit repeatedly and although he usually aimed for the back, Mehmed Noor did not care which part of the body he struck in his frenzy. Those whose reflexes were sharp would manage to evade blows after the first one; those who were slow to react obviously took the brunt of the beatings. Fortunately, the headmaster did not follow his victims to their classroom; he probably did not want to miss out on his next potential prey, a latecomer he hoped to intercept at the door.

Timore Shah was one of the students at the elementary school in Chaghaserai who used to fail year after year, without ever being asked to leave. He was the oldest in his class and the others would often ridicule him. Usually, he was a very patient person, but sometimes, he would lose his cool and hit a student in retaliation. The boy would promptly complain to the headmaster, whereupon the latter led Timore out to the courtyard to punish him publicly so that it would be a lesson for everyone. However rigorous the punishment, there were two things neither the teachers nor the headmaster could make Timore do: scream in pain or apologize to them. For Timore, it was a matter of honor. Had he given in, he would have ruined his reputation as the school's tough guy.

Weekends meant we had Friday off and half of Thursday. During that respite from school, I would usually take wheat or corn to the flour mill and remain there until the job was done so that I could bring the flour back home. Sometimes, I went off to the desert or to an island to cut branches from trees or bushes, so we could use them at home as cooking fuel or to build a shelter that would protect us from the hot summer sun. I also helped my stepmother by fetching water from the nearby irrigation canal for drinking, cooking our food and washing ourselves. My favorite place for studying after school was under a mulberry tree along the river near a spring. The area was called Mandakul and there was hardly anyone about. So I clearly remember the day some government officials and their guests turned up and dynamited the river. I watched, appalled, as a few minutes after the explosions, dead fish rose to the surface, their white bellies facing up. I thought this act unspeakably cruel, because in addition to the large fish the men caught and took home, their callousness had killed many tiny fish that did not interest them and destroyed their spawn.

Before I started the fifth grade, I thought I needed a companion. Wadood was at the right age to start school, I surmised, and took him to the government office and got him enrolled. When my father found out, he was a little upset, because he felt my brother was too young to go to school. But given his respect for education, he came around soon enough and actually acknowledged that it was a good idea, after all.

The house we lived in in Demkelay consisted of a big room and a wall encircling the courtyard. The south-facing main door led out to an open space. There was a small mulberry tree in the courtyard under which we usually sat to have our meals and chat with each other. One evening, while sitting under the tree, I was stung by a scorpion. In an instant, the pain from the sting had spread all over my body. Our next-door neighbor, one of my father's colleagues at the government compound, did some faith healing by muttering religious incantations over me. Miraculously, the pain went away.

We built a shelter in a corner of the courtyard to protect ourselves from the hot summer sun. We slept in the room during winter and in the courtyard in summer. Our house stood among others of its kind south of the main village that was separated by a dry bed of flood. The area was arid and trees were few and far between, growing in the yards of some of the houses. Only Gul Rahman had several trees in the small garden in front of his house. A cemetery was located to the east of the housing complex and the main road ran along the irrigation canal east of the cemetery. We would take the path south of the cemetery to go to Chinar Daba and fetch water from the canal. The last house built in the area belonged to Abdul Hakeem who belonged to a wealthy family and worked in government. My good friends in the housing complex were Habib Rahman, Lal Shah and Keerai, whose real name was Noor Hameed. We would gather after school and play in the open space. We also visited each other's families.

We lived in that house for one year and then moved into another in the middle of Demkelay, the main village near the local bazaar. Our new house was the last one at the end of the street. It consisted of two rooms, with a *mandow* in front of the larger room and a small courtyard.

Steps climbed up against the surrounding wall and led to the terrace in front of the small room. Everyone spent a good part of their time on their terraces in summer and we did the same, building a shelter there which would afford protection against the blazing sun during the day and some privacy at night. A casual visit to a neighbor's house was rendered easier; all you had to do was step off your own terrace and on to your neighbor's.

Our immediate neighbor, Ghafar, had three daughters and a son, Faqeer. His eldest daughter was a widow. The second one was single and would later get married. The youngest one was also single. I remember her well, because she would fall ill from time to time and lie on a cot, seized by violent spasms and muttering incoherently. Her family members and some of the neighbors would then surround her cot and try to hold her down. The villager rumor went that djinns had entered her body and made her ill whenever they were in a foul mood. Her incomprehensible mumbling was apparently the djinns speaking in their alien tongue.

Privacy was easy to maintain in winter, when everyone stayed indoors. In summer, however, people preferred to spent time outdoors, either on their terraces or out in the compound. And if they raised their voices while talking to each other, they could be easily overheard by their neighbors. I recall how I had once gone up to our terrace and crossed over to that of a family living in the second house from Ghafar's, drawn by the loud quarrel which had broken out among its members. I had stood there, staring at them, until they became aware of my presence. Caught in an embarrassing position, I had fled back to our own terrace. Of course, my parents reprimanded me when they got to know about it and I never dared give in to my curiosity again.

Meanwhile, in his desperation to make ends meet, my father had accepted a government post that would pay him a lower salary than his previous job had earned him. Although we were not required to pay rent for the house we were living in, because the owner had migrated to the northern part of the country, abandoning his former home, my father could not stretch his salary to meet our monthly expenses and we almost always ran out of money before the end of the month. The yield from our farmland in Khas Kunar was average and did not help ease our financial burden. We found ways of skimping and saving to make the most of what we had. We would buy a quarter-pound of meat from the butcher's next to Gurmek Singh's grocery and general provisions store. The butcher knew me well, because I visited his shop regularly, but I was not exactly a prized customer. Forced to limit my purchase on every occasion to a quarter-pound of meat, I could hardly expect to be. Back home, we would boil the meat in water to make soup. There was so little of it that once the broth was prepared, the morsels of meat were barely invisible and we had to grope with our fingers to fish them out. Then we would mash bread in the soup and eat it with our fingers.

In such trying circumstances, my parents' powers of endurance were tested to the limits when Gul Bebu gave birth to their first child, a daughter. The baby died not long after, but my parents could not bury her in Chaghaserai for fear of hurting the sentiments of the villagers they had lived among in Khas Kunar and, particularly, of their extended family based there, who would wish to be present at the funeral. My stepmother must have steeled herself in advance for the journey we would undertake to Khas Kunar for her deceased daughter's burial, for not a sob escaped her lips as she hid her lifeless baby inside the folds of her burqa, a loose, all-enveloping robe covering her from head to toe that all Afghan women wore in public, and boarded the bus with us, conveying the impression that she was carrying a sleeping infant in her arms. An hour later, we had arrived at the White Mosque, our disembarkation point before boarding the raft that would take us across the river to Khas Kunar. Our relatives and friends were waiting on the other side and the moment they saw us alighting from the raft, the funeral service began.

I am unaware of the reasons that prompted my father to accept early retirement and return to Khas Kunar. He must surely have realized what he and the whole family would be up against without the benefit of his salary. Besides, he had chosen to forego retirement benefits in cash, accepting a tract of land instead. I can only admire his restraint in this matter. However, my parents would, in all likelihood, have discussed the difficulties of remaining in Chaghaserai and come to the conclusion that it was time for us to go back to Khas Khunar.

The move to Khas Kunar would be undertaken in two stages. My father would take my stepmother and Jahantab back first, before returning to Chaghaserai for my brother and me. I had just graduated from the elementary school, ranking first in my batch, and was hoping to obtain admission in a high school in Kabul. Having returned to fetch the two of us, however, my father informed Wadood and me that he had some pending work he needed to complete. He would, therefore, stay back for a while in Chaghaserai and send my brother and me ahead. We duly boarded the bus for Khas Kunar and were waiting for it to leave, when my father suddenly asked both of us to get off. He made it clear that he did not wish to pay full fare for the two of us and asked the driver for a concession on our tickets on the pretext that we were mere children. I would realize later that my father's obstinacy had less to do with principle than with necessity; he could not afford the full fare. The driver obviously did not agree with him and we were peremptorily asked to get off the bus and walk to Khas Kunar.

The journey on foot from Chaghaserai to Khas Kunar takes an entire day, that too, when robust adults are undertaking it. For Wadood and me, covering the distance in a day, weighed down by the two hens we were carrying, was next to impossible. It was nearly midday when we started off. I don't remember if I had any money to pay for food or other necessities on the way. We took the road south, passed by the village, the cemetery and Chinar Daba before walking along the road toward the school. It was still light when we passed through Yar Gul, Salar Bagh, Taisha and Nowabad. The sun was going down when we arrived in Upper Narang, but we decided to proceed to Lower Narang, where we could stay overnight at the house of our father's colleague, Mehmed Ehsan. Darkness was descending when we arrived in Lower Narang at the end of the day. We could have gone to the local mosque and stayed there overnight. But we decided to look for Mehmed Ehsan's house in the village and eventually found it. Ehsan's son, Agha Mehmed, was there and received us graciously. We enjoyed his hospitality and woke up early to continue our journey. It was still dark when we picked up our hens, ready to hit the road. But before we left, Agha Mehmed gave us a loaf of bread to eat on the way.

Dawn hadn't broken when we were passed through the village and heard the sound of movement near the irrigation canal. At the edge of the stream crouched a woman, adding water to the yogurt she had prepared for her family, before stirring it repeatedly to form buttermilk. She was waiting to collect the butter that would form on the surface of the mixture. Local custom forbade women from speaking with strangers of the opposite sex, but the circumstances were unusual and the woman by the canal probably reckoned that we were mere boys and no passerby could possibly take offense if she gave us some buttermilk. We were grateful for her generosity and not having a receptacle in which to carry it, we drank it right there.

The hens seemed to be growing heavier by the minute and we made several halts on the way. We passed through Ghundu, Kanadar, Baberai and Tsawkai village, arriving at the White Mosque late in the afternoon, but had to wait for the raft to return from the other side of the river to carry us across. It usually takes a while for the raft to make a one-way journey across the river, because the water level in summer is high and the *jalawan* (a kind of boatman) uses oars to direct the raft cross the river so that it moves with the current. With the water level in winter being low, however, the raft, attached to a rope which, in turn, is anchored to a pile of stones on either side of the river, operates through a kind of pulley system that moves the vessel back and forth across the water. The raft took a while in coming, but it did arrive eventually and we crossed the river while it was still light. Walking home, we ran into a group of men accompanying Azeem Khan, the provincial inspector, who must have been visiting the local school in Khas Kunar. He gave me the good news that I would be sent to Kabul to study at the Ibn-e Seena Junior High School, a boarding school for rural boys with no access to high-school education in their area. We arrived home and our father joined us after a few days. I don't remember asking him how he had traveled from Chaghaserai to Khas Kunar. Had he walked or had he taken a bus?

Life in Khas Kunar turned out to be really difficult, because without my father's salary to help us make ends meet, we were entirely dependent on the crops from our land. As I had explained earlier, never having farmed the land himself, my father had no experience of cultivation and had to hire a person to do the job for him. While the landowner provided the seeds, the tenant farmer usually received one-third of the grain at harvest time. Things came to such a pass that my father feared he would be forced to borrow money from the mountain people again. He knew that could only lead to disaster and he would probably end up forfeiting his entire property. He felt he could not continue living in Khas Kunar and I would often hear him say that he wanted to get out and stay out until the Pashtunistan problem had been solved. He hoped the tribals from Shalai Mountain would eventually have their own independent country and stop bothering us.

While the situation at home was dire, there was still something I had to look forward to, for Azeem Khan, the provincial inspector, had kept his word. I was asked to go to the education office in Chaghaserai in connection with my admission to Ibn-e Seena Junior High. The day before I left home, I recall my stepmother telling my father that she needed groceries and clothes for the children. Since God had created us, he had replied, trying to appease her, He would take care of us.

The next morning, I woke up and got ready for the trip of my life. I said good-bye to my stepmother and younger siblings and left the house with my father. We had walked some distance when my father reached into the back pocket of his vest and took out 200 Afghanis. He handed me the money and wished me good luck and a safe trip. I could tell from his expression that he longed for me to go out and see the world, but being still quite young, it was very hard for me to leave the familiar security of home and family and venture out into the uncertainties of a world I knew nothing about. The increasing problems of staying in Khas Kunar, however, eased the pain of departure a little.

I had to go to Chaghaserai first in order to complete my paperwork at the Office of Education there and decided to stay over at Habib Rahman's house. My friend lived in my old neighborhood south of the main village and we had once walked to school together. Habib's father, Gul Rahman, managed his own farmland. My friend's younger brother, Lakhkar, was the same age as Wadood and had once accompanied us to school. Habib's mother, a very kind woman whom I was not supposed address by name for reasons I will explain shortly, was like an aunt to me and, therefore, imposed no restrictions on me at all. I could come and go as I pleased. In Afghan culture, it is considered a breach of etiquette to address an older person by his or her name. And that, perhaps, is the reason why the Pashto language has a much richer vocabulary than English, when it comes to addressing family members and a vast assortment of relatives. Whether they are related to you or not, all older men are "uncles" and all older women, "aunts." Within the family, an older brother is addressed as "Lala." A paternal uncle is "Kaka" and his spouse, "Tandar." A maternal uncle is "Mama" and his wife, "Mamai." And the list goes on.

It took a week's stay in Chaghaserai for me to complete the paper-work. Then I headed for Jalalabad, the provincial capital. On the way, I passed by the White Mosque and looked toward Khas Kunar from the opposite bank of the river. And for the first time, I did not wait there to take the raft and cross over to the other side.

The area north of the White Mosque, between Khas Kunar and Chaghaserai, was familiar territory, which I had covered on foot, by bus, on trucks and on a lumber raft. However, the area south of the mosque, between Khas Kunar and Jalalabad, was alien terrain. The road passed through Noorgal, Khaiwa, Shega and Darunta. It was my first trip to Jalalabad and the first one ever to a city. The first time I had boarded a vehicle was on my maiden trip to Chaghaserai, when I was promoted from the fourth grade to the fifth. It was in Chaghaserai that I had listened to the radio for the first time in my life.

The trip to Jalalabad was fraught with both excitement and anxiety. Excitement, because I was heading for new, unexplored territory; full of anxiety, because I had no idea what I was up against. I did not know a soul in Jalalabad whom I could stay with or even ask for information. Everyone in Khas Kunar had suggested that I stay at Gul Wali's *serai*. The other two boys who had graduated along with me—Dilawar from Taisha, who had ranked second in class, and Jalal from Kerala, who had ranked third—and were going to Jalalabad for further studies must have known someone in town, for they planned to stay elsewhere. The vehicle I had boarded for my journey finally reached Jalalabad and passed through a large gate. We were now inside Gul Wali's *serai*, a place where people arriving from Kunar could stay overnight. I am not sure if Gul Wali owned the caravanserai or managed it. I remember alighting from the vehicle which had brought me to Jalalabad and going straight to Gul Wali's room and informing him that I wished to stay overnight in his *serai*. Gul Wali led me to a room where cots were lined up in a row and showed me the one I could sleep on, giving me the option of either reserving the cot with a full bed or half bed at half of the cost exclusively for my use.

Gul Wali's *serai* was actually a caravanserai for vehicles operating on the route that connected Chaghaserai and Jalalabad. Its huge gate opened on to one of the main roads in the small town of Jalalabad so that vehicles could enter and leave easily. The drivers were allowed to park overnight and carry out minor repairs, if necessary, to make them roadworthy for the following day's trip. Near the main gate were a few rooms, each equipped with cots and mattresses, pillows and quilts piled up in a corner for the use of travelers who wished to spend the night. I occupied one of the cots and paid two Afghanis for its use ; the bed linen was included in the price. As you can imagine, the bedsheets were soiled and home to a colony of lice that had set up house after being generously donated by different travelers to those who followed. Since I would stay there for at least two weeks, I was deemed a long-term guest and offered a discount. My desperate financial situation ensured that I had no more than one meal in twenty-four hours. I would go out to the bazaar around noon and buy myself a loaf of bread and a chunk of cheese for two Afghanis. Then I would go to a mosque, settle under a tree nearby and eat my meal. I carried on my person what was left of the cash I had received from my father before my departure and it was a miracle that I neither lost the money nor was robbed. The only precaution I took was to maintain a low profile.

I remember waking up after spending my first night at the serai and walking to the east of the city. I passed by a Hindu temple that stood in the middle of an intersection, walked through the old bazaar, a single street, flanked on either side by a few kabob restaurants, and came to a shrine called Dulgi Shah Baba. Then I turned right to arrive at the Directorate of Education. When all the candidates for secondary school had showed up, we were lined up in the corridor and called into the inspector's office, where our destiny was decided. My turn came and I walked in. Azeem Khan was there, smiling at me and informing his colleagues that I was not only the top-ranking candidate among the three from my school, but also the youngest. He declared that he was obliged to keep his promise and send me to high school in Kabul. The officials there told us that we would have to appear for a written test on a certain day.

All three of us, Dilawar, Jalal and I, along with other candidates, reported in time for the test on the appointed day. We were directed to sit down on the ground, maintaining a certain distance from the candidates on either side to discourage cheating. The officials handed us sheets of paper and pencils and asked us to start writing our answers at the same time. The test took almost the whole morning and the written scripts were collected from us after it was over. We were asked to report back for our results. Based on our performance in that written test, I was selected for admission and informed that I was definitely going to Kabul. Jalal, who had evidently not fared well, was asked to go home. Dilawar, whose uncle had accompanied him to the directorate, was asked to hang around; he had been put on the waiting list. But ultimately, he would be dropped from that list. When the finalists left for Kabul, Dilawar was not among them.

We were all put on a truck heading for Kabul. The directorate paid our fare. The road through Darunta and Sarobi was not open to traffic, so we had to take a long detour over the rough road through Surkhrud, Nimla, Gandumak and the Lataband Pass. Just after passing through Surkhrud, the truck broke down in the Ghaziabad desert. We spent the whole day there, hoping the truck would be repaired soon and we could continue on our way. By the time the repairs were complete, it was after sunset and the driver insisted on turning back. On our way back to Jalalabad, the truck broke down again at Du Saraka, leaving us with no option but to walk back to Jalalabad. It was still a long way off and the night was cold. We arrived the next morning and went straight to the Directorate of Education office to report on our aborted trip. This time, the directorate rented a bus for us and we left Jalalabad on the same day, taking the same route. The bus was filled to capacity and quite a few of us had to travel perched on the roof.

It was late afternoon when we arrived at a run-down bazaar, where the only place open was a teashop. We stopped to eat there. The driver had, meanwhile, announced that the vehicle's axle was broken and he would have to send someone to Sarobi to buy one. We realized we were in for the long haul and since it was very cold there after sundown, some of us decided to walk to the mosque in a nearby village for a place to sleep overnight. The mosque was warm and cosy and we slept on the floor. It did strike me that the floor was unusually warm, but I could not see a fireplace of any sort. Things fell into place when I was told that the mosque had been built as a *tawakhana* and the fireplace was located underneath it.

It was noon by the time the driver announced that the axle had been replaced and the bus was ready to leave. The bus stopped at a caravan-serai in Sia Sang (black stone), which would later be renamed Shah

Shaheed (the martyred king), in memory of King Zahir Shah's father, Nader Shah, who is buried on Maranjan Hill, north of the area. He is probably called the "martyred king," because he was shot dead by a high-school student in Kabul in 1933. His son was only nineteen years old at the time. After his father's assassination, Zahir Shah would become the last king of Afghanistan and reign for forty years until he was ousted from power in 1973 by his cousin and brother-in-law, Mehmed Daoud, while the king was vacationing in Italy.

I got off the bus and looked around me before walking the rest of the way to get to my destination.

I noticed the Bala Hisar building on top of the mountain west of Shah Shaheed. I had no time to waste, because it was already mid-afternoon and I had to make it to the military base in Qargha, where my cousin, Rawouf, was posted as a second lieutenant. I had no idea, however, where it was located and how far it was from Kabul City. I knew the military academy, where my cousin had studied after graduating from his military high school, was at Bala Hisar. Following my mental map, I now made for this place. I turned right on the main road before the gate to Bala Hisar and walked north, passing Chaman-e Huzuri on the right and the Eidgah Mosque on the left, and arrived at the river near Pul-e Mahmud Khan. I turned left toward the west and kept walking upstream along the river. I passed by Pul-e Larzanak, Pul-e Khishti and Pul-e Bagh-e Umumi and arrived at Pul-e Shah Dushamshira. Then I saw the Shah Dushamshira ("king of two swords") Mosque, which Rawouf had described to me. I crossed the bridge over the Kabul River behind the mosque and arrived on the northern side of the watercourse. Then I heard the name, Paghman, being mentioned and noticed a bus parked in the space behind the mosque. I was about to leave for Paghman.

I ran across the bridge and boarded it,summoning the courage to request someone in Farsi (the word, "Dari," was unknown then) to alert me when the military base in Qargha was near. The sun was on its way down, when a bearded gentleman sitting next to me asked the driver to stop the bus and informed me that my destination had arrived. He pointed north toward some buildings at the foot of a mountain and indicated that it was the military base. I stepped off the bus and headed for the mountain, arriving there after dark. I stopped at the checkpoint and informed the security personnel that I was Abdul Rawouf's cousin and planned to stay with him overnight.

I was asked to wait there, while a soldier was dispatched to look for my cousin. The man came back to ask me for my name, my father's name and my place of residence. My answers must have satisfied him, because he asked me to follow him. I was taken to a large room, where I met other officers from Tanar in Khas Kunar. It turned out that I was acquainted with all of them and some of them were even distant relatives. They informed me that they had anticipated my arrival, because my cousin had briefed them in advance and I realized that they had also given my details to the soldier at the checkpoint. The officer informed me that Rawouf was in Kabul at the moment for a training course. Although I was exhausted, I was determined to go there and find the Ministry of Education. The officers invited me to stay at the base overnight and gave me directions to Kabul for my trip the following day, as they would be leaving for work early the next morning, before I was awake. When I woke up in the morning, the officers were out on duty. A soldier came and served me breakfast. The moment I had eaten, I was out, walking east along the dirt road. There was no sight of a city anywhere and all I could see was farmland and villages on the right, mountains on the left, and the dirt road heading east to Kabul City.

Just as I was beginning to panic, a truck stopped beside me and the driver asked where I was headed. He was a Pashtun and we had no problems understanding each other. On learning that I was on my way to Kabul City, he warned me that it would take all day to walk the distance and offered me a ride in his truck. I accepted his invitation promptly. When we reached the city and drove in, the driver gave me directions to the Ministry of Education and I bade him good-bye.

I reached the ministry and walked in through the main door. I discovered that it consisted of a few one-story buildings made of mud. The tomb of Amir Abdul Rahman Khan was located inside the compound which, according to the present map of Kabul City, stands in the north-eastern corner of Zarnigar Park. The buildings I saw then would be demolished later and the area turned into a public park. I knew of Abdul Rahman Khan from my elementary-school history lessons. He was Habibullah Khan's father and Amanullah Khan's grandfather. I had learned that during his reign, the people of Nooristan would be converted to Islam.

I also remembered that he had lost the town of Panjdah to some county in the north. I had little respect for Abdul Rahman Khan, because I had heard of his harem, where he kept women for his sexual gratification. I could not reconcile what I knew about him with the image of a spiritual father. For all our monarchs were meant to be revered as such. The name of Zahir Shah, for instance, the king I had seen in my childhood, was included in every sermon at the mosque during Friday prayers. We all had to pray for his long and healthy life. I was sure Abdul Rahman Khan's subjects too, had mentioned his name in their Friday prayers. I could not bring myself to pray for a king who had violated his religious principles by keeping women at his house to whom he was not married. I had read that there was a queen at the palace and wondered how she felt about her husband's numerous concubines.

When I walked into the ministry office, however, the workday was over and I was asked to return the following morning. I walked out of the building and took the road to Pul-e Bagh-e Umumi. I crossed the bridge and turned right to go back to the bus stop, so I could leave for Qargha from the parking place behind Shah Dushamshaira Mosque. It was then that I ran into my cousin. I was both relieved and delighted to see him. I have no idea what I would have done otherwise. The only option would have been to travel between the military base in Qargha and Kabul City every day, for the only accommodation I could have availed of was at the base, far from the city, with no reliable means of transportation to take me back and forth. Even if there were, I would have run out of money by the second or third day. Given the circumstances, meeting my cousin unexpectedly was the best thing that could have happened to me. I felt I had come home at last.

FOUR

Ibn-e Seena Junior High

Rawouf's place, a room at the fruit market which he shared with another officer, became my temporary residence. The Ministry of Education was a conveniently short walk away and I would go there every day, staying until the end of the workday in the hope of obtaining my admission papers for Ibn-e Seena Junior High as soon as possible. When there was nothing else to do, I would walk back to my cousin's room. It took me a week to finish the paperwork and get officially enrolled in Ibn-e Seena Junior High School, where students of Grades Seven to Nine were taught.

Ibn-e Seena was a boarding school for male elementary school graduates who converged from all over the country for their high-school education. The first day I showed up, I was asked to go to the storeroom, where I was given two blankets, a couple of bedsheets, a set of clothes and a pair of shoes. A white mattress stuffed with *maluch* (cotton fiber) was laid out on the bunk bed assigned to me. I was informed that I had been assigned to Section B of Grade Seven and asked to report to Block Three of the dormitory. Later, I found out that the new students were first grouped by age, then assigned to their respective classes. The youngest students went to Section A; the oldest ones to Section K. I think there were, altogether, eleven sections for the seventh grade. I was assigned to Section B, because I was among the youngest students.

I went to my assigned block in the dormitory and arranged my belongings on the lower level of the bunk bed that stood against the wall. There was a flat wood board at one end of the bed, on which I placed my books and notebooks. There was a small box, somewhat like a nightstand, against the wall to accommodate the rest of my belongings. For security reasons, I was expected to keep that locked. The box on top of my own box was meant for the use of the student who slept on the upper bunk. His name was Ismail Shah and he was from Qandahar. Whenever Ismail tossed and turned at night, the bed would squeak, but I don't remember being disturbed or kept awake at night because of it. The nearest light hanging from the ceiling to my bed was dim, but being young and blessed with keen eyesight, I was able to read my books and write my assignments by its glow. We had a curfew time and were supposed to be in bed by a certain hour every evening. As a result, everyone in the room went to bed at the same time and woke up early for morning prayers. The only person who could be seen out of bed after curfew had been declared was the dormitory teacher, who went on his round, checking that everyone was in bed. He would carry a flashlight, since the room was dark and crowed with bunk beds .

The dormitory was divided into five blocks and accommodated about 1,800 students from all over Afghanistan. A teacher was assigned to each block. Block One was the smallest and located in the north-western corner of the school campus, near the main gate. The rooms here were all rather cramped and accommodated twenty students, mainly ninth graders, in ten bunk beds. In fact, it was to this block that I had been assigned when I was a student in Section B of Grade Nine. The assistant principal's office and living quarters stood at the northern end of the block. The dormitory teacher for Block One had his own accommodation there. This was an L-shaped building, with its southern end almost touching the one that stood parallel to the campus's northern wall and contained the classrooms. Block One was the first building you saw as you entered the campus.

The five blocks were not enough to accommodate all the students. Some had, therefore, been assigned to Block Four in Dar ul-Malimeen, the senior high school (Grades Ten to Twelve) across the street to the west. Dar ul-Malimeen was one of the four senior high schools in Kabul, where graduates of Ibn-e Seena were sent to study for their high-school diplomas. The other three were the School of Agriculture on the road to Darulaman near the Kabul River, the Technical High School across the street, north-east of Ibn-e Seena, and the Sharia and Islamic Studies High School in Paghman. We had to go out through the main gate and turn right to visit the principal's office. The building was located in the north-western corner of the campus and accommodated the barbershop and the storage room for school supplies, in addition to the principal's office.

The other four blocks were lined up against the western wall of the campus. Block Two, that stood at the northern end of the building, had two entrances and more rooms than Block One. All the rooms were small, although there were twenty students to a room in ten bunk beds. Some eighth and ninth graders also stayed in this block. Block Three was the largest. In addition to the small rooms it contained, where twenty students were accommodated in each, there was a large one at its southern end, accommodating sixty students in thirty bunk beds. Most of the beds were lined up against the wall and there was an additional row in the middle. In that dormitory, two small cabinets, placed one atop the other and no bigger than a nightstand, were crammed into the narrow space between the beds. The bottom one was for the student assigned the lower bunk; the one on top was for the student on the upper bunk. On the opposite end of the bed was a board, intended for the use of the student occupying the bed for his reading and writing. The two ends of the board were each attached to a leg of the bed.

A spacious dining hall stood between the third and the fourth blocks. In front of it was an elevated open space. A field lay to the east, where we would line up at mealtime. Either the assistant principal or one of the dormitory teachers would come to make an announcement, reminding us about the importance of orderly behavior while entering the dining hall. If an important announcement had to be made, however, the principal himself would be there to deliver it. The dormitory teachers were in charge of supervising our entry into the hall. Tables were lined up from one end of the hall to the other. We would stand lined up on opposite sides of the table, facing each other. You were expected to share your plate with one of the students seated next to you and the two students opposite you. In other words, four students ate their meals off the same plate.

Blocks Four and Five stood to the south of the dining hall, ending in the south-west corner of the campus. I think there was a small door in the surrounding wall between the kitchen and Block Five, but the students were prohibited from using it.

The kitchen was located south-east of Block Five in a separate one-story building that stood against the southern wall of the campus. Meals were prepared there and carried to the dining hall in large pots. There was a small room adjoining the dining hall, where the food was ladled on to large platters that were then placed on our tables. After this detail was taken care of, we would be allowed to enter the hall in an orderly manner, take up our positions on either side of the tables and begin our meal. For lunch and dinner, we were usually served potatoes or turnips, with a small portion of meat. The monotony of our meals ensured that I would stay off potatoes for the rest of my life. Knowing that I have had enough of that vegetable to last me a lifetime, my wife, Anna, now makes it a point to serve another vegetable on the side, prepared especially for me. It would be unfair to give the impression, however, that as students, potatoes were all we were served. We were also treated to a special lunch of rice and meat twice a week. We really looked forward to Tuesdays and Thursdays for that very reason. These two days of the week were called the *chapchapi* (rice pilau) days, a term exclusive to students and teachers of the institution. I suspect they coined the expression, inspired by the slurping sounds we made while eating the mixture. We usually had a cup of tea, sweetened with sugar, and a loaf of bread for breakfast. Only on special holidays were we allowed to have a glass of milk and some *halwa*, a sweet pudding, for breakfast.

Eating in the dining hall was a sort of competition, where the participants felt they had to ensure they'd had their fill before their rivals could. Fast eaters were invariably the victors, the slow ones, the vanquished. All the boys secretly prayed they would not have to share a plate with either Lahore or Mursaleen in the same group. These champion eaters would race through the meal, making sure they gobbled up every morsel on the common platter before the other three members of their group had had a chance to swallow their first mouthful. If you were unlucky enough to be teamed up with either of these two boys, you could be sure the platter would be empty before you knew what had hit you. Having noticed what was happening, Zar Ahmad, one of the dormitory teachers, decided to teach the two champions a lesson. One day, he served them each a plateful of food and laid a wager, challenging them that they would not be able to finish it in three minutes flat. He timed the event and discovered that their plates had been licked clean before those three minutes were up. Having lost the bet, Zar Ahmad never made the mistake of challenging them again.

During the holy month of Ramazan (locally known as Rozha), we fasted from dawn to dusk, abstaining from eating, drinking and smoking. Neither a morsel of food nor a drop of water passed our lips. I do not mention abstention from sex, because I was studying in an all-male school and sex was a forbidden word. Ramazan being part of the lunar year of the Hijri calendar, which is ten days and six hours shorter than a solar calendar of 365 days a year, could be observed during any of the four seasons. The year I began attending high school in Kabul, Ramazan was observed in winter. During that period, we were allowed two meals a day: one before sunrise and the other at the end of the day, after sunset. The pre-dawn meal was prepared at night, brought to the dining hall, arranged on plates and served on the tables. Our respective dormitory teachers would wake us up at the appointed hour and order us to line up in front of the dining hall when it was still dark. By the time we had all gathered in one place, lined up and proceeded to enter the dining hall in an orderly manner, the food would be cold. How cold it became depended on the temperature outdoors. We had to eat it, whether we liked it or not, because once the sun rose, no food would be available until sunset. After we had eaten our meal, we would go back to our rooms and the job of the dormitory teachers was complete. They could then take their morning nap. We, however, had to get ready for morning prayers before heading for our classrooms.

Fasting is the third pillar of Islam and praying five times a day the second one. Once the month of Ramazan was over, we could have our regular three meals a day for the rest of the year. However, praying five times a day was mandatory all year round. The first prayer of the day had to be recited before dawn. The prayer schedule, especially the early morning session, was strictly observed. For our dormitory teachers, it was the most important prayer session, because they had to prove to the administration how diligently they were honoring their religious obligation in conformity with school policy. They ensured that we woke up and left our rooms while it was still dark. Since we were required to perform our *awdus* (ablutions), we filled our pitchers from the aluminum water tanks lined up in front of the dormitory blocks that had already been replenished by the *saqawan* (water carriers), who would fill their *mushks* (skin containers) from the piped public water supply and pour their contents into the tanks.

The *khakandaz* (literally meaning "the place where clay is thrown") or toilets we used did not have water. They were located at the southern end of the campus, parallel to the southern wall. Housed in a small single-story mud building, they were small spaces, each equipped with a hole in the middle and a supply of clay in a corner. After relieving ourselves, we were expected to rub the clay on our butts to clean ourselves. Once the job was done, we would go out to the least frequented area in the campus for privacy and wash ourselves. We were then ready for morning prayers. By the time this was over, the sun had come up and we had to get ready to have our breakfast, for classes began at eight a.m., an hour later.

Even in such primitive conditions, we had our own sanitary system in place. Farmers from the villages near Kabul City would troop in with their donkeys very early in the morning to clean the *khakandazes*, both in our school and in private houses. Loading the donkeys with human waste that had been mixed with soil, they would finish their jobs and head home before dawn to use the product as fertilizer for their farmlands. Still sleeping in our rooms, we would be roused by the jingle of bells that hung around the donkeys' necks and the melody of the farmers' songs, as they trudged south on the road that connected Ibn-e Seena and Dar ul-malimeen. We liked to crack jokes about the farmers, claiming that if one of them fainted from overexertion, another would revive him by bringing his cargo off his donkey's back for the afflicted man to smell. Given the alternative—the dormitory teacher roughly rousing us from slumber to justify his position and his salary—the sound of bells and singing was a pleasant wake-up call in summer. But winter, with its freezing temperatures, was a different story.

The classrooms were in a building that stood parallel to the campus's northern wall. Its western corner began where the southern part of the dormitory's first block ended. Students sat on benches, two to a desk. We spent Saturday through Wednesday in the classroom, between eight a.m. and four p.m. Since Thursday was a half-day, our classes gave over in the afternoon. Friday was our day off. From Saturday to Wednesday, we had an hour-long lunch and prayer recess before our afternoon lessons. The curriculum covered the two official local languages—Pashto and Dari—two foreign languages—Arabic and English—science, social studies, religious studies, math and practical work.

The practical work was mainly carried out outdoors, the task assigned to our class involving the demolition of the Qala-e Kulukhak, a clay fort. I am not familiar with its history, because by the time I came to enroll in Ibn-e Seena, the fort had already been partially demolished. The plan was to level it to the ground so that the school could put the land to use. The number of students was increasing every year and, with the classes overcrowded, the school aimed to build more classrooms and employ additional teachers.

I recall that the bus stop in front of the Technical High School was known as Qala-e Kulukhak and whenever the Kabul-Mirwais Maidan bus stopped in front of the school, the driver's assistant, who was also the bus conductor, would shout, "Qala-e Kulukhak!" It was the signal for passengers bound for this destination to get off. Once the *qala* had been leveled to the ground, the school began building more classrooms on the land and extending the constructions to the whole area adjoining the campus's eastern wall. But it took an entire year for the bus drivers to rename the stop after the Technical School.

When the job was over, we were rewarded with a daylong picnic in Paghman, sponsored by the Ministry of Education. Located at the foot of Paghman Mountains, about fifteen miles west of Kabul, it was popular as a summer picnic spot for residents from Afghanistan's capital. Its cooler weather, unpolluted air, beautiful gardens and abundant water supply merely added to its popularity. Moreover, our principal, Hafeezullah Amin, was from Paghman and his family wielded a lot of clout in the area. I heard from other students that his brother, a high-ranking official with the Spinzar Company, owned the fleet of trucks that had driven us to the picnic spot. The Ministry of Education had paid for the food and entertainment at the picnic and the school authorities went that extra mile and invited Ustaz Sarahang, the son of well-known musician, Ustaz Ghulam Husain, to sing for us. This gentleman was a fixture at school events and always accepted invitations to sing for us, because he knew how much we appreciated his performances. I remember him sitting on the grass under a tree and sending his audience into raptures with his first song in Dari: "The weather is pleasant, the lawn is green and my friends surround me. All to no avail, however, because the place of my beloved is empty."

Ibn-e Seena was located in Kart-e Char district, west of Deh Mazang, north of the Kabul River and south of the main road that connected the city to Mirwais Maidan. The area south of the river, which would later become the Karta-e Se, consisted mainly of farmland dotted with a few villages and the ubiquitous mud house. Since no suitable place was available on campus for individual study, most of the students preferred to take the road west of the campus and walk south across the river. A tranquil corner under a tree somewhere in the middle of the farmland was the ideal place for studying on one's own. I often used the privacy of the place to wash some of my clothes in the river and spread them out to dry while I studied. These were garments tailored from a fine fabric that I reserved for special occasions like holidays or visits to relatives on Friday, our weekly holiday. However, we usually gave our clothes, made of serviceable material and handed to us by the school, to the laundrymen or *doobis*, who would take them down to the Kabul River for washing.

I had hoped that graduating to secondary-school level and coming to Kabul would spare students like me the arbitrary punishment that our rural elementary schools had meted out in the name of enforcing discipline. I discovered to my dismay, however, that the situation was not very different at the junior high school. Since there were no written regulations to go by, we were often unaware of the fact that we had infringed them. Each teacher had his own way of enforcing discipline.

Some were more forgiving than others. Many were harsh disciplinarians. As in the elementary schools I had attended, a favorite form of punishment was beating students with sticks fashioned out of mulberry branches. It was the same scenario all over again, with janitors holding down students as they lay on the ground and giving the teacher free rein. If the teacher was particularly infuriated, his blows would land on the student's back. The severity of the punishment was arbitrarily determined. The boys who screamed the loudest were usually let off lightly on the assumption that they had suffered enough and were atoning for their sins. Those who endured the beating silently or stubbornly refused to beg for forgiveness were harshly treated. In other words, the teachers were accountable to no one and could do pretty much as they pleased.

I wouldn't be spared either, that too, for breaking the rules unwittingly. I remember the occasion clearly. I remember how cold it was as I got out of bed for morning prayers one winter, before the sun had even risen. Shivering, I had picked up my blanket, wrapped it around my body and gone out, unaware that this was a punishable offense. It was my first year at the school and I was in the seventh grade. I was staying in the large room in Block Three and our dormitory teacher, Ghazi Salik, was infamous for his cruelty. He must have spotted me leaving the room wrapped in the blanket, because when I returned from my prayers, he was waiting for me in the adjoining hallway. A more forgiving teacher would have pointed out that I had violated a school regulation and let me off with a warning. But given the person he was, Ghazi Salik could hardly wait to grasp my right hand in his, turn it palm up and whack it repeatedly with a stick. By the time he was through, my hand was badly swollen and, when released from his grip, dropped limply to my side like the appendage of a corpse. I was unable to use it and had to wait for a long time for the swelling to go down.

I remember another occasion when I was singled out for punishment. According to the school's regulations, we not only had to be in bed by a specified hour at night, but also to be asleep by then. One summer night, I found myself awake past our stipulated bedtime. Faqeer, our dormitory teacher, who was passing by the open window of our room on the way to his own must have spotted me. Before I knew what was happening, he had swung around and flung one of his sandals at me through the window. It was clear that he would have been answerable to

79

none, had the sandal struck and hurt me or missed its mark and landed on another poor soul who had done no wrong and was sound asleep, just the way he was meant to be. Fortunately, the sandal landed wide of the mark and I recall picking it up and politely returning it to Faqeer, apologizing for staying up past the stipulated bedtime.

The school authorities also believed in publicly discipling students, assuming it would serve as a lesson to all. An instance of exemplary punishment that remains embedded in my memory involved a student from Maymana who was brought to the area between Block One and the building where the classes were held. The boy was made to lie on the ground, face down. Two janitors, one holding his hands and the other, his feet, lifted him off the ground. The assistant principal then approached with the required sticks and started raining blows on the boy's back, while some of the dormitory teachers and a large number of students stood there, watching. I wonder how the self-appointed disciplinarian had felt at the time. Had he put himself in the student's shoes, would he have allowed the same thing happen to him? I guess the man had certain things to prove: he had to show his boss, the principal, that he was a strict administrator who knew how to exercise his authority; he also had to make it clear to the dormitory teachers that he was their boss and would tolerate no insubordination.

As I had explained earlier, in Afghan society students are bound by a moral obligation to blindly obey their teachers—their spiritual fathers, so to speak—and treat them with unqualified respect. But given all that I had witnessed and experienced, when I graduated from the school, I felt many of my former teachers did not deserve such respect. Among the shining exceptions were the Flower Teacher and Abdul Ghias, who had both taught me at the elementary school in Chaghaserai. I would meet them after my graduation and greet them with due respect. I recall meeting the Flower Teacher in Narang, where I was sent by the Ministry of Education to inspect schools in the Kunar province. I was sitting with a particular school's principal, when I spotted the Flower Teacher taking classes under a tree. I rose to my feet instantly and went to meet him. He had aged a little and seemed quieter. I introduced myself right away, going into minute details about my years at school and telling him how he had been my favorite teacher, but to my great dismay, he failed to recognize me. I spent some time with him, but could not get over my disappointment.

I remember my other favorite teacher, Abdul Ghias, coming to Khas Kunar to visit my cousin, Rasul. Since the latter was not at home, I had greeted him, ushered him into the room where guests were received and asked my stepmother to make some tea for him, which I had then served. It was only when my cousin returned that I felt my duties were over. On another occasion, I would return to Chaghaserai to help my cousin, Wahab, resolve his military draft issue and while there, visited my former teacher's home behind the village mosque. The night was cold and the stove in the guest room had been lit. Ghias had remained with us, giving us the pleasure of his company until we were ready to turn in for the night. We would have breakfast with him the following morning before leaving for our work at the Government Center.

I would, on the contrary, never have dreamed of staying as a guest of Abdul Ghafour, my religious studies teacher, who lived in the same area. Given my less-than-amicable relations with him, I could not imagine socializing with him in the normal way. I was probably in fifth grade and still to sit for the final exam, when I had shared with him my hopes of going to Kabul and continuing my education there. Ghafour had categorically declared that it would be pointless, as I was simply not high-school material. On another occasion, I recall him swearing that he would fail me in his course. I would subsequently share my apprehensions with the Flower Teacher, who promised to discuss the matter with the inspector arriving from the Education Office in the province as a supervisor for our final exams. The man turned out to be Azeem Khan. In fact, Khan was with Ghafour, when the latter called me in for the viva voce of the final examination in his course. After the test was over and I had left the room, I overheard the two men engaged in serious debate. Khan must have convinced Ghafour that I had performed well in the test and did not deserve to fail his course. For not only did I managed to pass the religious studies course, I also graduated from school with the highest rank!

As luck would have it, I would meet Ghafour again when I was at the Senior High School in Kabul. He was visiting one of his relatives on the campus. I decided to let bygones be bygones and greeted him cordially, even sitting beside him on the bench for a while to talk to him. The last time I would meet my teacher was on an official visit from the Ministry of Education to inspect schools in the Kunar province. I was strolling in the bazaar with my uncle, Habib, the principal of the women's school in Chaghaserai, when I spotted Ghafour. He had retired and opened a shop in the bazaar and that is where I found him. He recognized me and we sat down for a while and reminisced about the past. He remembered I was from Khas Kunar, but he did not know that Habib was my Mama, my maternal uncle.

Life in Ibn-e Seena was agreeable enough and offered its share of advantages. For one, students were given a chance to develop a sense of responsibility and make judicious use of the authority with which they were entrusted. Four student supervisors were appointed on a daily basis and given some duties to fulfill. One would go to the silo to buy bread for the school. Another would be sent to the city bazaar to buy fruits and vegetables. The third one would be dispatched to the slaughterhouse to buy meat and the fourth one would spend the day at the kitchen, super-vising the cook and his helpers. Built by the Russians, the silo was the tallest building in Kart-e Mamureen and stood at the intersection of the road from Mirwais Maidan and the one that ran between Kabul and Qargha. Located near the intersection were the Poly Technic Institute, the Police Academy and the Intercontinental Hotel, which was visible on the hill to the east. The area west of the road in front of the silo lay outside the city limits and was dotted with mud houses. Later, it would be declared a part of the city, feature on its map and be named Khushal Mayna. The slaughterhouse, located east of Kabul, was the furthest of the destinations one of those four students had to reach and involved the longest drive. I remember undertaking all of these duties individually at different times during my three years at Ibn-e Seena.

From the academic point of view, studying at Ibn-e Seena was a daunting challenge for me. The medium of instruction there was Farsi (renamed Dari in 1964), which was new to me, since the medium of instruction at the elementary schools in Khas Kunar and Chaghaserai had been Pashto. We had only started studying Farsi as a second lan-guage in the fifth grade and even the teacher who taught it was not very fluent in the language. The day I had first arrived in Kabul and taken the bus to the military base in Qargha, I recall what courage it had taken to ask a fellow passenger in my faltering Farsi where I should get off. All the students at Ibn-e Seena were expected to read the textbooks and follow the teachers' instructions in the classroom. No distinction was made between those who had arrived from Farsi-speaking areas and those who had originally belonged to Pashto-speaking ones. In other words, no concessions were made for students at an obvious linguistic disadvantage. For me, naturally, it was a matter of sink or swim. I was determined to swim, except that on occasion, I barely managed to keep my head above water. To explain how difficult it was for a Pashto speaker to distinguish it from Farsi, let me give you an example. I was reading a passage about a Farsi poet in the classroom and pronounced his last name as "Khawrai," meaning, "clay." But the man's name was actually Khawari, which meant "the person from the east." Since the name was written in Arabic letters, its meaning depended entirely on how it was pronounced. I have never forgotten how everyone in class, including the teacher, made fun of my pronunciation that day.

But despite these setbacks, I was determined to succeed. The alternative would have been to return to Khas Kunar and the hard life that awaited me there. And so I forced myself to learn Farsi. I eventually managed to master it well enough to be among the top scorers when I graduated. Pashto, which we had as a second language, was a bonus for me. I don't remember if we had a textbook for the Pashto course, but do recall our teacher making us memorize *Zayrai* (good news), the weekly newspaper published by the Pashto Academy. I was relieved when the teacher was transferred in the middle of the school year and his successor desisted from adopting the same method of teaching the language. As for the two foreign languages, namely English and Arabic, that we were required to study, we were taught some Arabic terminology in the religious studies class and concentrated on grammar during the language lessons.

Our school had a library, but it was too small to accommodate students who wished to sit there and study. I would, therefore, borrow a book, usually a volume of Pashto poetry, and read it for my pleasure in my spare time. In almost all the courses, rote learning was encouraged and students capable of faithfully memorizing the contents of their textbooks were most likely to get the highest grades, both in the class tests and in the final exams. Originality and inputs based on a student's own interpretation of the text were frowned upon. This kind of rote learning would follow us all the way to college. I remember my first year at the College of Education, Kabul University. We had an older student there who was working with Americans at the Institute of Education. He was, naturally, fluent in spoken English. Yet every time we had an English test, I, who could barely speak the language, always scored higher marks than he did. While I had mastered the rules of grammar pertaining to the use of tense, he had picked up the language spontaneously, without having to delve into the intricacies of those rules. Unfortunately for him, the tests evaluated our knowledge of the rules, rather than our expertise in the language. I could understand that student's frustration only too well.

The school year ended in December and everyone was excited about going home for the winter vacation. However, there were a few unfortunate students from the country's remote areas, such as Ghor and Badakhshan, who could not travel home and had to remain in the school during the entire vacation period. They would stay in the dormitory and the school became their year-round residence. Before the winter vacation began, those of the students who were leaving for home would have to register their names, indicating their residential addresses. The list would be dispatched to the Ministry of Education for approval so that they could either send a truck over or disburse funds for our travel expenses, depending on the distances each of us had to cover. The students who had to travel a long way home did so on trucks provided by the ministry, that would arrive on the date of departure and park in the open area north of the school and south of Sayed Jamaludeen Afghan's mausoleum. These students, however, were required to refund half the expense incurred for the round trip. And it must have been a grueling journey for those of them traveling north through the Shibar Pass, for even in Kabul, it grew pretty cold by the end of the school year. Kunar, on the other hand, was considered a short distance away and the ministry would give students from the area, including me, cash to cover the round trip. For the trip back to school in the spring, every student was on his own.

Secondary education in Afghanistan covered a period of six years. We spent three years in Ibn-e Seena, following which we had to go to a senior high school for a further three years in order to be eligible for a high-school diploma. Graduates from Ibn-e Seena were sent to one of four senior high schools in Kabul: Dar ul-Malimeen (the Teachers Training High School), located across the street and west of Ibn-e Seena; the Technical High School that also stood across the street from our school, but to the north-east; the Agriculture School down the road to Dar ul-Aman and near the Kabul River; and the Sharia and Islamic Studies School in Paghman. Among them, the Technical School, with its rigorous academic standards, was considered the toughest to gain admission to. Usually, graduates with the highest scores were sent there. Next in line was the Agriculture School. As for Dar ul-Malimeen and the Sharia School, it was not very clear as to which ranked higher in terms of strict admission procedures. Graduates of the Technical School would eventually proceed for further studies to the College of Engineering. Those from the Agriculture School would naturally go to the College of Agriculture. Those who completed their studies at the Sharia School would pursue higher studies at the College of Sharia and Islamic Studies. However, while graduates of the other three schools had a chance to study at Kabul University, those of Dar ul-Malimeen were given teaching positions in elementary or secondary schools and had to forego the option of going on to college.

The year I graduated from Ibn-e Seena, our principal, Hafeezullah Amin, who would soon be transferred to a similar position at Dar ul-Malimeen, created a special group of graduating students from different provinces who had obtained the highest scores. Three of the highest scoring graduates from each province were eligible to study at Ghazi High School, a day school, where mainly graduates from Kabul's elementary schools studied. I had heard of Amin's special relations with the Minister of Education and his ability to persuade the dignitary to tweak the rules a little or do something that was unprecedented. I would be among the three graduates from the Mashiriqi (renamed Nangarhar) Province sent to study at Ghazi. We were put up at the dormitory in Dar ul-Malimeen and spent the day studying in Ghazi, which was a long walk away. Every morning, we would walk down to Ghazi and return to Dar ul-Malimeen after the classes were over. After a month, however, the principal, Mr. Amin who had, by now, been transferred from our former school, directed us to stay in Dar ul-Malimeen and study there.

There was, of course, a reason behind his decision. Dar ul-Malimeen's full-time students resented the privilege we enjoyed of using their dormitory while studying at Ghazi and expressed their grievances to Mr. Amin who, unable to handle the situation, gave in to their demands and closed the gate one morning, thereby putting an end to our daily attendance at

Ghazi. We were divided into smaller groups and sent off to whichever tenth-grade class could accommodate us and became full-time resident scholars of Dar ul-Malimeen. In retrospect, I can understand why students from both the schools resented us. As the top elementary-school graduates from all over the country and the highest academic achievers graduating from Ibn-e Seena, our group was an extremely high-profile one in both the institutions. What had perhaps helped us in attaining this privileged position was our rural background, where work was worship and entertainment scarce. Kabul had once been a distant dream and now that we were here, away from our families and friends, study constituted our only source of entertainment. In contrast, the day students at Ghazi had more exciting lives outside school hours and with more options at their disposal, they naturally did not study as much as we did. The difference was noticeable in the classroom during our interactions with the teacher. Our group obviously took a keener interest in the lessons and classroom activities, responding with greater enthusiasm to the teacher's questions. The day students, on the other hand, would try disrupting a class in progress with different pranks, even daring to make fun of some of the teachers, especially the ones who taught Pashto and religious studies. Since some of these students belonged to Kabul's influential families, they were able to get away with their misbehavior, as neither the teacher nor the school principal dared to confront them. As for the full-time students of Dar ul-Malimeen, they regarded us as a privileged breed that they had never encountered before. Neither of these two groups of students could stand us and their life's goal seemed to be focused on depriving us of our privileges, which they ultimately succeeded in achieving.

When we became resident scholars at Dar ul-Malimeen, Principal Amin struck another incredible deal with the Ministry of Education. In contravention of established precedent, the ministry acceded to his request that approximately one-third of the students graduating from Dar ul-Malimeen be allowed admission into colleges affiliated to Kabul University. Thanks to Principal Amin's special relationship with the Minister of Education, some of Dar ul-Malimeen's graduates would, for the first time in its history, go to college. The new policy was implemented when our group was promoted from Grade Eleven to Grade Twelve. The school authorities divided the students into three batches:

namely, A, B and C. Two students with the highest scores from each province were assigned to Section A. Graduates from this section were eligible to go to college. Among them were Abdul Rasheed and me, the two students chosen from Nangarhar province. The graduates from Section B would be employed as teachers in secondary schools and those from Section C would be appointed as teachers in elementary schools.

Looking back on my years at Dar ul-Malimeen, I can now say that life there was easier and more enjoyable than at Ibn-e Seena. The campus at Dar ul-Malimeen was around the same size as that of Ibn-e Seena, but less crowded and more pleasant because of the trees that grew there. The dormitory building at Dar ul-Malimeen stood along the campus's eastern wall and contained four blocks. Block One, meant for students of Grade Twelve, was located at the northern end, near the main gate. Blocks Two and Three were assigned to students in Grades Ten and Eleven respectively.

The classrooms were in two buildings; one was built parallel to the northern wall of the campus; the other stood right next to it and was parallel to the western wall. We had a field where we played hockey and soccer by changing the goals. But it wasn't the only form of entertainment. The school organized cultural programs, many more, in fact, than at my former school, and we celebrated Teacher's Day with speeches and music.

A part of the campus was given over to a vegetable garden, where we grew different kinds of vegetables, and farmland, where corn and wheat were cultivated. I remember our teacher, Raz Muhammad Zari, teaching me the English names of the vegetables in the farm.

The cafeteria stood between Blocks Two and Three. Block Four, at the southern end, accommodated students from Ibn-e Seena. As in our former school, our dormitory here was equipped with bunk beds, but it was less crowded. Unlike at Ibn-e Seena, we did not have to race to the dining table so as to be the first to grab the food and gobble it down, because each of us was given a plate to eat off and could dine at leisure. Our student supervisors bought white bread from the silo, known as *mahipusht* (meaning, "the back of a fish"), that looked like the Italian bread available in American supermarkets. It was a welcome change from the brown bread we had been served at Ibn-e Seena, which looked like a minibus-shaped brick. Made of whole wheat, it was certainly more nutritious than the refined kind, but rock hard, unless consumed fresh. Breakfast at our new school was certainly a more enjoyable experience, because we were served a plate of *halwa* with a glass of milk on a regular basis.

Our dormitory teachers probably regarded us as responsible young adults and treated us with respect. That is why I don't remember anyone ever being punished in public in my three years at Dar ul-Malimeen. I guess we were regarded as the nation's future teachers and treated as. In fact, we did our practicals by teaching students at the reputed International Elementary School on campus, where some high-ranking government officials had enrolled their children.

The library, a more spacious or, possibly, less crowded room than the one at Ibn-e Seena, was where I usually studied. Mr. Amin remained our principal for one year, before leaving to join the Teacher Education Department at the Ministry of Education. A gentleman called Wazeer Nizami was appointed his successor at the school. His main concern was to ensure that we looked clean. He would time his morning round to coincide with the moment we were standing in line, prior to going to our classes, and inspect our shirts and even our fingernails for the telltale speck of dirt. He would remind those who failed to meet his exacting standards that they should be more vigilant about their appearance.

During the first two years, almost all the janitors were from Panjsher. At the end of my second year there, a gentleman from Laghman called Salem Masudi replaced Nizami as our principal. Within a month of his arrival, all the janitors from Panjsher had been replaced by men from Laghman. Despite the frequent change of principals—three in as many years—the general atmosphere in school remained pleasant.

In addition to the janitors employed on the campus, we had a farmer, an old man who was in charge of taking care of a pair of prize-winning bulls he was devoted to and used them to cultivate part of the land inside our boundary wall. On 21 March every year, he would enter his bulls in a contest sponsored by the Ministry of Agriculture. For quite a few years, those bulls, in which we took a proprietory interest, would continue to win the first prize. One day, I met the farmer in front of the dining hall, carrying his bed. I asked him where he was off to, whereupon he replied that he was resigning from his job and going home to live with his family, because his son had graduated from the military academy and would now take care of him.

It was while I was in the eleventh grade that my father, who had been working for the Spinzar Company in Dasht-e Archi, decided to take my stepmother and my sister, Jahantab, up north. My brother, Wadood, was sent to live with Gul Bebu's parents in Khas Kunar. I had to inform the school administration about my change of address, because this time, I would not be going to Kunar for my winter vacation, as usual, but to the north. Winter came, the school year was over and the trucks that would ferry students to their homes, far from school, arrived and parked in the field across the street to the north of the campus. I had never been to the area beyond the Hindu Kush Mountains, where northbound travelers had to cross the two passes, Salang and Shibar. The government was still working on the tunnel in Salang that would not be accessible to the public before 1964.

We boarded the truck and, an hour later, arrived in the city of Charikar. We took the paved road through its bazaar and arrived in Pul-e Matak, where we would turn west along the dirt road after crossing the bridge, instead of following the paved road to the north that went through the Salang Pass. The dirt road, on the other hand, would take us through Chardeh Ghorband to the Shibar Pass. We traveled seated on our luggage in the back of the truck, wrapped tight against the chill. It was getting dark when we arrived in the area just below the pass. The driver decided to halt for the night at the eatery nearby, as it would be too dangerous to continue driving in the dark.

Our beds for the night would be the rows of wooden tables in the eatery, where travelers stopped to have a meal or drink tea. We had to wait until the other customers had left, before stretching out on the tables.

We set out the following day as soon as it was light. The road ahead was rough and the truck virtually had to crawl along. After an entire day's drive, we arrived in Duab wa Maikh Zareen, where the driver announced a night halt. We passed the night there in much the same fashion as we had the previous night, heading north again in the morning. It was early afternoon when we arrived in Doshi and took the paved road north, after stopping for a midday meal in Ayub Lang's restaurant, a more decent place than the ones I had dined at in the last couple of days. It was almost sunset when I arrived in Imam Sahib.

I got off the truck, hauling my luggage behind me, and waited for a vehicle that would take me to Dasht-e Archi. After an hour, a truck belonging to the Spinzar Company came to the stop and took me to Sharawan, the northern end of Dasht-e Archi, where the company had its offices. I was new to the area and asked the security guard at the entrance to the company compound for directions to my father's quarters. He pointed to a house standing on a sort of hillock. It was barely visible from where I stood, but I found it easily enough.

Our house in Dasht-e Archi stood next to a barber's house on the latter's property. My father must have met the barber at the company and told him that he was planning to bring his family from Kunar. Dasht-e Archi was a new area and most of those living there had arrived from other parts of the country to drain the marshy land and convert it into arable land. No house in the area was available for rent. My father, who must have met the barber at the company and shared his plans to bring his family up from Kunar had, therefore, come to an agreement with the other man and the two had built a couple of mud rooms adjacent to the house. The front room had a *tanoor* (oven) dug into the ground. My stepmother prepared meals there, cooking food on the top, while the dough she had pasted on the inside walls of the heated oven to bake ended up as bread. The room beyond was where we relaxed, ate our meals and slept. The house had no indoor bathroom; we had to go outdoors for a wash or to relieve ourselves.

Our family of four—my father, stepmother, sister and I—slept in the back room at night, taking care to cover our faces with our blankets. That was the only way of protecting ourselves from the clods of mud and droppings the mice scurrying around in the straw of the thatched roof above bombarded us with from time to time. On days when Gul Bebu had to clean the house, I would step out and sit in my usual sunny spot between the house and the stream to the south, enjoying the outdoors or reading. On bazaar days, I would walkdown to the main market place of Dasht-e Archi, an hour away, and spend part of the day there. It was a crowded place, where everyone brought something to sell and bought something to take home.

I had planned to spend all three months of my winter vacation in this manner, but a month after my arrival, my father was transferred to

Khwaja Ghar in Takhar, an hour's journey by bus to the north of Dasht-e Archi. And he was glad of my help as we moved the family to our new home.

Unlike Dasht-e Archi, Khwaja Gahr was an established community, where the Spinzar Company had a more organized office. The company's branch in Dasht-e Archi had been new, its role confined to purchasing cotton from farmers, sorting it and dispatching it to the headquarters in Kunduz. The company branch in Khwaja Ghar, on the other hand, had wider responsibilities and more facilities, including a factory which processed the cotton by separating the fiber from the seed and pressing the fiber into bundles. Moreover, the company in Khwaja Ghar offered housing for its employees. My father was allotted a nice house with glass windows that we could open when the weather was pleasant. It had living quarters, a bathroom, a kitchen, a storage room and a *khakandaz*. The house had its own yard, where we would grow flowers and vegetables. But its most remarkable feature was electricity, the first house I had ever lived in to have that facility. We reveled in the light from three bulbs, one in the family room, one in the guest room and the third in the veranda, to illuminate the yard. Electricity was supplied from around six p.m. till the next morning. When we first arrived, the family of the employee to whom the house had originally been allotted was still occupying it, although he himself had been transferred to Kunduz. For the two more weeks they remained, we would confine ourselves to the kitchen and the storage room. Then the man returned from Kunduz to take his family with him. The house was duly vacated and we settled into our new home, with my parents spending the next twelve years of their lives there.

I returned to Kabul as my winter vacation was drawing to a close and started my twelfth grade in Dar ul-Malimeen. Upon graduation, the students from Section A, to which I had been assigned, prepared to go to college. The three students with the highest grades were allowed to name the college of their choice and among their preferred institutions were the colleges of law, medicine and engineering. This privileged group included Abdul Rasheed, the only student from Nangarhar province other than myself, and he would opt for the College of Medicine. The rest of us were allowed three choices among the colleges that offered courses in arts and literature, economics, science, education, agriculture and pharmacy. I, for my part, had set my sights on the College of Education, primarily because it was new and I would be among the second batch of students to graduate from it. My greater dream, of course, was to pursue graduate studies. My hard work would eventually pay off and I would see myself living the dream when, after completing my first year in college, I was awarded an AID scholarship to continue my studies in Lebanon at the American University of Beirut (AUB). But that was still not on my immediate horizon.

CHAPTER
FIVE

College Education, Kabul

So far, my plans had borne fruit and I was on my way to achieving my goal; I was climbing up the ladder of education and moving toward a better life. I had ranked first while graduatinge from elementary education. It had paved the way for my move to the city and I had managed to survive in my strange new situation. I had learned Farsi, the language of instruction both in secondary school and in college. I was on my way to learning English that would give me an edge when I explored job opportunities and wanted access to information that was not available in either Pashto or Farsi. Graduation from Ibn-e Seena Junior High School with high grades had opened doors for me to a prestigious secondary school in Kabul. I would be among the second batch of graduates from Dar ul-Malimeen to go to college. And now I had reached a stage where I was about to choose the college at Kabul

University where I would study, the stepping stone to a successful future career.

In the fall of 1962, students in all three sections of the twelfth grade graduated from Dar ul-Malimeen. Group A graduates like me prepared for higher studies at a college affiliated to Kabul University, the country's only university. Regardless of the group to which they had been assigned, everyone in the teaching profession was striving to stay on in Kabul, so they could pursue the two-year teachers' education courses offered by colleges or simply hang around in a city where opportunities were more plentiful than elsewhere in the country. Most of the graduates from Dar ul-Malimeen, however, were destined to teach in the rural areas, since that was where they had been born and raised, though a few would be able to move to Kabul later, especially if they had relatives in the capital or contacts with senior government officials.

My own target, the College of Education, was a new institution, temporarily housed in a building outside the Kabul University campus. It was located in the same area of Karta-e Char as the Institute of Education and I surmised the two were related. Most of the faculty members at the College of Education also worked at the Institute of Education with American colleagues. Contact with the American staff had several advantages: learning English was one; obtaining a scholarship to study in the United States of America was another. Even some of our teachers at Dar ul-Malimeen used to work at the Institute of Education. If, therefore, I was fixated on the College of Education, it was with good reason.

My determination paid off and I was in. As a graduate of a boarding high school, I was entitled to stay in the college's dormitory, which was located in an old, run-down house across the street from the southern wall of Ibn-e Seena Junior High School. If my memory serves me well, the house had three rooms, of which one was occupied by five of my friends—all graduates of Dar ul-Malimeen—and me. It was a small room and we shared three bunk beds. In the middle of the room was a space we used for relaxing and having our meals. We would sit on our beds to study.

The classes were held in a less dilapidated looking two-story concrete house by the Kabul River that was walking distance from our dormitory. The building housed two classrooms: one for the first-year students; the other for the second-year students. The rest of the rooms were either given over to offices occupied by the dean, Dr. Mehmed Sedeeq, and his staff or used as storage rooms. The house had one garage, where Dr. Sedeeq parked his official car. It seems that someone had reported to him about the overcrowding in our dormitory room, for Dr. Sedeeq turned up unexpectedly one day and expressed concern that we might not be getting enough oxygen, because the room's door and window were both closed at night. We explained our point of view and he decided to let us be. My five roommates in that dormitory were Jalat, Mobeen, Momin, Zahir and Malang. Jalat and I would each obtain a scholarship and go off to the AUB for higher studies. Mobeen would graduate from the College of Education and go back to teach in his hometown, Khanabad. Momin and Zahir would graduate and get teaching jobs at the Teacher Training Junior College in Kabul. Asad, our classmate at the College of Education who had received a scholarship to AUB and graduated from there, would later joined Momin and Zahir to teach at the Teachers Training Junior College. The Ministry of Education, where I would eventually work after my graduation from the AUB, was a walk away from the college and I would catch up with Zahir and Momin over lunch from time to time. Malang would go to Kunar and start teaching in Chaghaserai. By 1977, when I was leaving Afghanistan for good and heading for the US, he had become the Director of Education in Kunar. Apart from Zahir who would come down with kidney disease and die young, all our friends were alive and well when I saw them before my final departure.

The College of Education was a co-educational institution, where men and women were taught in the same classroom. However, a form of segregation did exist. The women students occupied the front rows, while the men sat at the back. All the women students and some of the men were day scholars, because their families lived in Kabul, and went home after class. The rest of us headed for the dormitory, where we ate and slept. In the courtyard of our dormitory was a vegetable garden, where we grew tomatoes, eggplants, pepper, okra and squash. I don't recall having a dormitory teacher to supervise us and keep tabs on our behavior. Perhaps we were considered old enough by now to take care of ourselves. The only other person living in the house was a cook, who prepared our meals and tended our vegetable garden. The house that contained our dormitory and the one where classes were held were both leased by Kabul University and would be vacated, when my classmates and I were promoted to the second year and had to move to the university's recently opened main campus.

The modern dormitory where we took up residence was a four-story building with four wings, whose construction had been both sponsored and supervised by the US government. As a result, it had all the facilities available to students in a developed country. We ate our meals at the cafeteria, which was located at the heart of the building. We were expected to line up in front of the food counter, where we were also handed crockery and cutlery. We would then proceed to the dining table. There was a cleaning crew to ensure that the building was properly maintained. Unlike the wooden bunk beds we had used at Ibn-e Seena and Dar ul-Malimeen, the ones in the new marble-floored dormitory were made of metal, though after sometime, they would squeak when we lay down or turned. For the first time in my life as a student and possibly in the lives of most of my college mates, the hostel came equipped with bathrooms that had both showers and toilets and were kept spanking clean. It was a refreshing change from the primitive ways we had been used to. As I had mentioned earlier, in the village, we had gone outdoors to relieve ourselves. And at both Ibn-e Seena and Dar ul-Malimeen, as well as in the run-down house that had served as our dormitory the previous year, the waterless toilets were tiny rooms, with a hole in the ground over which we had to squat, that stank from a mile off. I naturally enjoyed using the new facilities, but not before I had gone through a veritable orientation course, with detailed guidelines on how to use them. The instructions were outlined, pointwise, and elaborated on everything from how to sit on the toilet seat to how to use toilet paper. Even now, when I need to go to the bathroom, I find myself checking out the line of perforations in the toilet paper to ensure that I tear it off neatly from the roll. It may seem odd to the reader for a college-going guy to be receiving toilet training, but for us, given the backgrounds from which we had come, it was both useful and necessary and would come in handy when we went abroad for higher studies.

Another novel experience for me was the gym that was walking distance from the new dormitory. There, both men and women students played basketball and other sports under the supervision of a gym instructor and although athletics was part of our college curriculum, I have no recollection of how we scored in the subject.

The curriculum and teaching methods followed during our first year in college were not very different from the ones we had been used to during our six years in high school. We would arrive for the first class at eight a.m. and sit in the classroom, while different professors came to teach us subjects they had specialized in. I remember psychology being part of the first session, followed by English, science and so on. The last class was over by the afternoon and after we had been dismissed, we would return to the dormitory.

I have forgotten the names of most of the professors who taught us during that first year of college, but I do remember Professor Ghulam Hasan Mujaddadi who taught us psychology and Dr. Sedeeq, our dean, who took the science class. I also have a clear memory of the contents of their lectures. Professor Mujaddadi enjoyed debating on the issue of nature and nurture. Would a genius born in a backward society be more likely to come up with a unique invention or one who had been born in a progressive environment? It was his favorite question and his preferred topic of discussion. I remember the discussions thrown up by this issue and the inputs each of us offered on the impact of heredity and environment on an individual's physical and mental development. Although both factors were crucial to a person's growth, some always argued in favor of one to the detriment of the other. While Professor Mujaddadi gave us the freedom of choosing our own perspective, he always qualified it by insisting that we defend whichever position we had chosen to stand by.

Dr. Sedeeq, our science professor, would set us assignments quite unrelated to the subject he was teaching. He had once given me a copy of a medical journal in English and asked me to translate an article on the lymphatic system. The topic had not been discussed in class and I had no idea what a lymphatic system was. Moreover, I was not fluent enough in English to read and understand the subject matter. Keen though I was on impressing my professor, I did not know how to go about it. I finally visited a friend of my cousins, Rawouf and Omara Khan, who had graduated from the university's College of Medicine and was working in a hospital. He listened to my problem attentively and agreed to translate the article into Farsi. He must have skipped some bits, however, because when I received the handwritten translation, it barely covered a couple of pages. To solve the problem, I got hold of a locally made reed pen and copied the translation in my own handwriting, taking care to use large letters that would take up much more space and run into a greater number of pages, thereby creating the illusion that the text had been translated in its entirety. The trick worked and I obtained high grades in the final exam.

I would not meet Professor Majaddadi again after the first year of college. I would, however, have the pleasure of meeting Dr. Sedeeq again, when he was hired in the mid-1970s as an advisor for the Curriculum and Textbook Project at the Ministry of Education in Kabul, where I was working. When I left for New York in January 1977, he was still there.

Toward the end of the academic year, the inevitable speculation arose about who would be the highest ranking student this time, based on the aggregate of the grades he had received for his performance in exams on various subjects. I don't remember if my name was mentioned in this context. Nor was I certain of being the privileged one. The big day arrived and we gathered in front of Dr. Sedeeq's office. He called us in and began telling the students, one by one, what their combined total score was. When I entered the office, he announced that I had scored the highest. I recall how taken aback my classmates were by the news, because no one had expected me to be the one. Jalat ranked second and Asad, third. On the basis of our aggregates, all three of us would be awarded scholarships for higher studies at the American University of Beirut (AUB). But I would not be aware of this last bit of news when I left Kabul for my winter vacation after classes had given over for the year.

I had a long way to travel to our home in Khwaja Ghar and it was an arduous journey as usual, with the truck turning west after Pul-e Matak along the dirt road to Shibar Pass. I don't remember if the mandatory overnight halts on the way also included a third night in Imam Sahib or whether I made it home later in the evening. All I remember was how great it was to be back home, where I was always welcome, no matter how long I stayed. And when it was time for me to go back to Kabul, my father would give me enough money to take care of my travel expenses and leave me with spare cash during the school year.

As soon as I was back in Kabul, everyone began congratulating me; I had been awarded a scholarship for higher studies at the AUB. Of the other two successful candidates, Asad, being a Kabul resident, already knew he had been selected and by the time the new academic year began in the spring of 1964, he had sat for the English Language test and completed all the requisite paperwork. That his older brother was Director of Foreign Relations at the Ministry of Planning could not have been a disadvantage either. He was, therefore, all set to go, while we had not even begun. The previous year, the same scholarship had been awarded to only one student. I now suspect that had it not been for my higher scores and Jalat's at the end of our freshman year in college, the administration would have had no compunctions whatsoever about awarding the same scholarship to a single candidate this year too; and that candidate would have been none other than Asad. Unlike our more fortunate Kabul-based classmate, Jalat and I would have to go through the procedures from scratch and make our way through the complex bureaucratic maze, a difficult enough task because of our rural background and the absence of a mentor or friend in Kabul. However, the university turned out to be an amazing support system and neither Jalat's Pashtun origins nor mine seemed to come in the way in a culture which was fiercely clannish. For example, Abdul Wahid Surabi, the Vice President of Kabul University, was a Hazara, but that did not prevent him from calling the AID office and urging the staff there to provide the two of us with all possible assistance. Shams ul-Abedeen, the Vice Dean of the College of Education and a Tajik, had been our Social Studies teacher at Ibn-e Seena and was there to provide moral support. Both were, perhaps, keen on encouraging us, despite our ethnic and linguistic differences, because like us, they too, had started life in a village and knew the kind of discrimination students from rural backgrounds were up against in a city like Kabul.

Despite their help, there were many obstacles lying in wait that I hadn't even anticipated. The first reared its head when I had my chest x-ray taken and presented the plate to the doctor at Aliabad Hospital to look over and sign. The doctor said there was a spot on one of my lungs and directed me to have another one taken. Since I felt physically fit and was untroubled by coughing, chest pain or breathing problems, I sought the advice of some of my doctor friends before having another x-ray done. I asked them about the spot and what could possibly have caused it to appear on my lung. They claimed it could well have been the outcome of taking aspirin when I was suffering from a cold. The only time I remembered taking aspirin was during my cousin Omara Khan's wedding. I had caught a cold and stayed awake all night before the ceremony, despite it, to enjoy the musical soirée he had organized for the guests. Several hours later, I had taken an aspirin and felt much better. I had recovered quickly and never given the matter another thought. And now it had come back to haunt me. The scholarship was too precious for me to leave things to chance. When my brother Wadood and I went to Ibn-e Seena Hospital to have my chest x-ray taken again and my number came up, I sent my brother in my place. I then took his x-ray plate back to the doctor at Aliabad Hospital and he approved and signed it. I assume from the doctor's readiness to sign the plate that Wadood's lungs were unblemished.

The second hurdle came up when I visited the Ministry of Foreign Affairs to submit my application for a passport. I was carrying all the required documents, along with the three mandatory passport-size photos, but the official in charge turned down my application and returned all the documents to me, claiming that my photos were not in order, because I was not wearing a necktie in them. As a result, I found myself in a photo studio in the city, choosing from a selection of neckties that the studio owner had displayed on a rack for this very purpose. Since I was a novice as far as this fashion accessory was concerned, the photographer even helped me fasten it around my neck before taking my picture. The new photographs met the approval of the official at the ministry and he accepted my application, so he could process the papers to issue my passport. Since I had already paid for the other photos, they were put away for a rainy day.

Despite the hitches, Jalat and I progressed steadily and surely, even soliciting the help of our classmate Asad's brother at the Ministry of Planning to make our way. And it was in 1964, as summer came to a close, that we managed to head for Beirut with the other recipients of the same scholarship.

College Education, Lebanon

E xcited though I was by the prospect of boarding the flight to Beirut, my troubles weren't over yet. While going through Immigration at Kabul's Khwaja Rawash Airport, I must have glanced at the customs officer in a manner that was not to his liking, for he singled me out and made me open my suitcase so that he could take out every single item for inspection, piece by piece. I could see the queue was moving fast, but here I was, stuck in one place because of an officer's whims, and seriously started fearing I might miss the flight. Had the customs officer found anything suspicious in my suitcase, I would certainly have had to kiss that flight good-bye. Fortunately, he did not and asked me to close the suitcase. But he did have a query about the money I had received from theAmerican Embassy as travel expenses and directed me to go to the bank and pay a mandatory tax on the US$900 I was carrying. For a second, I imagined I would have to go all the way back to the city for the purpose and miss my flight. But it transpired that the bank had a branch at the airport, where I was made to pay a tax of US$30 before boarding the aircraft.

With the final hurdle crossed before my departure, I was able to relax and look around me. This was the first time I had been inside what was probably the most basic airport terminal for international flights in the world. Passengers who were waiting to board flights entered the customs and security enclosures through a door and proceeded directly to the departure lounge. Similarly, incoming passengers entered the customs enclosure before leaving the terminal through another door. There was no direct access to the airplanes parked on the runway and everyone had to exit the lounge through a door and follow an official who led them to the designated aircraft. It was all rather new to me, for I had never been to the terminal before. I had not needed to, because I neither knew anyone who had come to Kabul from the provinces aboard a flight nor anyone who was leaving the capital on a flight to other destinations. The closest I had been to the airport was the area where I, along with students from my school, would be made to stand, waving the Afghan national flag to welcome a foreign dignitary who would be arriving on an invitiaton from the government. The lucky ones among us would get to wait in the shade of a tree. The rest had to bear the searing heat, with no clue as to when the dignitary would show up at the location where we had been directed to wait. And this, after marching all the way from our school to the city and lining up along the road in front of the Royal Palace, repeating the slogan of welcome we had been taught to greet the honored guest. The job done, we would line up again and start marching back to our school. It was a long way, because our school was located in Karta-e Char, an hour's walk from the Royal Palace.

As my thoughts wandered to my earlier trips to the Royal Palace near the airport, I reflected on all the journeys I had undertaken so far. My first trip had been on a truck, when I finished the fourth grade in Khas Kunar and joined my family in Chaghaserai. It had taken an hour and I remember standing all the way, holding on to the metal bars and enjoying every minute of the bumpy ride. I will never forget the journey I had undertaken on foot from Khas Kunar to Chaghaserai with my father nor the return journey with Wadood, with my father refusing to pay the regular bus fare and compelling us to walk all the way. The trips I had to take after graduation from elementary school and from Khas Kunar to Chaghaserai, followed by the more momentous journeys to Jalalabad and Kabul were arduous, but rife with adventure. My first trip to the north of the country in winter through the Shibar Pass had been an experience to remember. If I had taken it all in my stride, it was probably because the rigors of life in the village had convinced me that I wanted to leave it behind and seek a more promising future for myself. My journey into the wider world aboard an airplane was merely an extension of my aspirations for a better life, fraught with just as much anxiety about the unknown and the possibility of failure.

As the DC-6 we had boarded soared over Afghanistan, I was overcome by homesickness. I was leaving behind my family and my friends without any assurance that I would see them again. While my feelings were tempered by the excitement that overwhelmed me at the prospect of going abroad for the first time, anxiety too, took hold. What if I failed to achieve my academic goal? What would happen to me then? The possibility filled me with dread. My mind wandered to the few individuals I knew who had returned from Lebanon without obtaining their degrees. One of them had been studying with us at the College of Education. I could not bear to be in a similar situation, where I would end up studying once more at a local college affiliated to Kabul University or working at a mundane job in which I would stagnate for the rest of my life. I hoped to follow in the footsteps of my chemistry, physics and math teachers at Dar ul-Malimeen who had come back to Afghanistan after graduating from universities in the West and were the most respected men in their profession. Our chemistry teacher, Abdul Ghafour Zhaznawi, had obtained his doctorate, moved to France and joined the United Nations. Our physics teacher, Mahmud Soma, and our math teacher, Mansour Hashimi, had, however, become involved in politics and I would only hear about them in the news.

When the flight landed at Beirut International Airport, the aircraft taxied to an area far from the terminal. A shuttle bus arrived to take us there. As I entered it, I could only gaze at my surroundings in awe. The size of the terminal and the facilities available put our own little airport in Kabul to shame. Afghanistan, I told myself with some regret, had miles to go before it caught up with the rest of the world. In fact, two years later, on a trip to Europe, I would enter Switzerland by train from Germany and spend a few days in Geneva, before proceeding to Italy, and be reminded of our school geography textbook that had confidently proclaimed how Afghanistan was the Switzerland of Asia. No two countries could be more different, I would decide ruefully, barring their common feature: snowcapped mountains. I could only conclude that the author of our textbook had probably never even seen Switzerland and had based his views on photographs of the country he had seen in books or newspapers. Comparing the beauty of the area I would pass through on my trip from Zurich to Geneva with the barren land of Afghanistan I had traversed so many times would have been pointless. Afghanistan presented an ever-changing scenario, as one traveled from village to town and from one region to the next. Arid land and rocky mountains could suddenly give way to a settled area, distinguished from its stark surroundings by a patch of green, with trees and farmland. Beyond the small oasis lay more barren land. I also felt that Afghans had to work immeasurably harder to eke out a living from their land and to nuture it than the Swiss who had been blessed by nature. Gentler climatic conditions and the easy availability of water made it that much easier to maintain Switzerland's verdant beauty, whereas the Afghans had to fall back on their rivers and the subterranean water supply to dig canals and irrigate their farmland. Unlike the patchwork-quilt effect of Afghanistan's landscape, with its bare mountains punctuated by patches of cultivation, the area I would pass through during my sojourn in Switzerland was a beautiful, uniform green.

To return to my new life in Lebanon, the sophistication of the airport and the contrast it presented with Kabul's international airport was a kind of culture shock, just as my first view of Switzerland had been, but it prepared me for my first sight of the AUB and its beautiful campus. The university, standing on a rocky hill overlooking the Mediterranean Sea, had two dormitories for men: Penrose Hall and the New Men's Dorm, both located south of the main campus. Penrose Hall stood across the street from the university's South Gate; the New Men's Dorm was on Bliss Street (named after Daniel Bliss who founded the AUB in 1866), south-east of Penrose Hall. A football field lay south of Penrose Hall and west of the New Men's Dorm. Two students were required to share a room in Penrose Hall, while in the New Men's Dorm, students were entitled to individual rooms. Bathrooms in Penrose Hall, equipped with a pair of sinks, two toilets and a shower, were located in the middle of the building; their layout was such that two rooms from either side opened into each bathroom. Therefore, eight students from four rooms shared a bathroom. Jalat and I were assigned the same room on the first floor of Penrose Hall on the side facing the university campus.

I was there in 1966, when the AUB celebrated its centenary year. The main ceremony was held at the university chapel inside the main gate and the guest speaker was Daniel Bliss III, grandson of the founder. I remember certain parts of his speech, where he mentioned that it had taken his grandfather three months to make the same journey to Lebanon that he himself had completed in fourteen hours. Over its 100 years, the AUB had evolved from a missionary college to an American university open to students both from the countries in the area and from the rest of the world. While most of the students were from Lebanon and neighboring Arab countries in the Middle East, the student body had representatives from all six continents. Some of Lebanon's well-known professionals and high-ranking government officials were AUB alumni. I remember Walid Jumblatt, a Lebanese politician and current leader of the Progressive Socialist Party, as a fellow student at the AUB.

Bliss Street constituted the dividing line between the AUB to the west and the city of Beirut to the east. A narrow alley from the street ended at the entrance to Penrose Hall and the southern gate to the main campus. Where the alley ended, a flight of steps began, a hundred or more, going down all the way to the road along the Mediterranean Sea. One had to go down those steps, cross the road along the sea and turn right in order to arrive at the salt-water swimming pool, cut off from the sea by the rock which formed its edge. I would go down to the seaside quite often. On my way back to Penrose Hall, I would climb the flight of more than a hundred steps, passing the American Community School on my right, before arriving at the International School on the way to my dorm. I recall attending both schools for a semester to complete my student teaching requirements. I also taught fifth-grade English (as a second language) with a lady colleague at the International School and fifth-grade math and sixth-grade history with a male colleague at the American Community School. The sea was visible from everywhere on the campus and I usually found myself among a like-minded crowd of people when I was out on the campus grounds, later in the afternoon, enjoying the pleasant weather and taking in the sights.

On entering the main campus from the southern gate, one could see West Hall on the right, where the Orientation Program was held. The first building on the left was the Infirmary, while the second was the Humanity Hall, where the College of Arts and Sciences was located. Proceeding north, one could see the president's house on the left and the university cafeteria on the right. Next came the main gate and the university chapel on the right; the Administration building with the clock tower stood on the left. The university library was located to the west of the Administration building. If you turned left and went down, you would arrive at the two women's dormitories located in the north-western corner of the campus.

In my time at the AUB, the student population, covering male and female students from its four colleges—namely Arts and Sciences, Medicine and Allied Health, Engineering and Agriculture—varied between 6,000 and 7,000. The University Hospital, one of the best in Beirut, stood north of the campus across Bliss Street. The former premises of the American Embassy were located north-west of the campus near the Mediterranean Sea.

Life in Penrose Hall was infinitely more comfortable than it had been in the student dormitory at Kabul University. There were two single beds per room and each bed had its own nightstand. Each of the two students sharing the room had his own desk and bookshelf fitted on the wall. The room had two doors; one opened into the hall outside the building and the other to the bathroom which was shared by the students occupying the other three rooms. Each student had a decent-sized closet to himself. A brand new experience in my life at the AUB would be the television set in the basement. We would go downstairs and sit on a couch, marveling at the fact that we were actually watching people reading the news or acting in a movie. The only source of news and entertainment at Ibn-e Seena and Dar ul-Malimeen had been the loudspeakers (hanging from a pole in front of the dining room at the first school and from a pole in front of Block One at the second) connected to a radio in the office of the assistant principal. I remember listening to the radio while sitting on the platform in front of the dining room at Ibn-e Seena and on the benches under the trees at Dar ul-Malimeen. We could not switch over to another program, because there was only one program and one radio station—Kabul Radio. The only time of the year we were actually able to see the singers in person was during the nine days of our country's Independence holiday, when they performed at concerts organized by the clubs near the stadium, east of Chaman-e Huzuri, or on Teachers Day, when the school administration invited a singer to perform at the school. I was unable to enter most of the clubs, because I could not afford the admission ticket. Only the Pashtunistan Club, run by the Ministry of Tribal Affairs, was free and always my first stop. But my tastes were evolving and I found the TV in the basement of my dormitory at the AUB far more interesting, because I could see moving images of some of the areas from where the news was being reported.

Situated within the AUB campus was the university cafeteria, where I was allowed to select my preferred food items and paid for them from the scholarship money I received from US/AID. At the Kabul University cafeteria, while food had been served free of charge to the students, they had to eat whatever was on the daily menu. At the AUB cafeteria, the salt, pepper and sugar served on the table came free of charge. Except that, initially, I did not know how to tell sugar from salt. In Afghanistan, I had been used to rock salt (it was, in fact, available at the local stores there in the form of solid chunks that resembled rocks and had to be ground into powder at home) that was not white like sugar. In fact, even the sugar available for daily use in my country had been a locally processed version consisting of rough brown granules that was quite different from the refined white product we reserved for guests. I still recall my gaffe at the AUB cafeteria when I put salt in my tea by mistake and had to discard the beverage as a result. To avoid similar embarrassment in the future, I learned to distinguish between sugar and salt. It did make me wonder, though, when doctors detected a small, mobile stone in my kidney in 1968, after I had complained of pain and detected a trace of blood in my urine, whether this was effect of the unpurified salt I had consumed during my early years in Afghanistan. Mistaking sugar for salt in Beirut was a minor error I could laugh off, but I was vigilant about the meat I consumed, taking care to ensure that I never ate pork, since my religion forbade me to do so.

Academic requirements at the AUB made an entrance exam mandatory for new arrivals at the undergraduate level. If I passed, I would be admitted as a freshman to the regular study program. If I failed, I would have to go through the Orientation Program again and study English so that I could pass the entrance exam at the end of the semester. I took the test and failed it. As a result, I had to study English from eight a.m. to four p.m. every day, Monday through Friday, all through the semester. We covered all four skills required to master the language: reading, writing, comprehending the language after listening to it being spoken and, ultimately, speaking it ourselves. The emphasis was on practicing the language, as evident from the word, "practice," printed all over the cap Dr. Richard Yorkey, the director of the program, wore every day. For improving our spoken English, we would go to a language lab, where we listened to a recorded voice asking questions and record our own responses to them. We would play back the tape later to determine whether our responses had been appropriate. Our reading material covered, among other things, abbreviated versions of novels and plays like *Pygmalion*, *A Tale of Two Cities*, *The Red Pony* and *The Old Man and the Sea*. Some had a word count of no more than 1,000 words; others went up to 2,000 or even 3,000 words. We were also encouraged to go to the movies in our free time so that we could pick up the language faster. For example, we studied *Pygmalion* by George Bernard Shaw for a week and followed it up by going to watch the movie, *My Fair Lady*, based on the play. The other musical, which I watched several times, was *The Sound of Music*. I failed the entrance exam again after the first semester, but managed to get through after the second. Therefore, it was in the summer of 1965 that I started my freshman year at the AUB.

Taking my place in the long, slow-moving queue of students who had come for the same purpose, I presented my passport to the man at the front desk and discovered that the process of registration was as educational for me as it was mystifying for him. I saw his expression change to one of bewilderment as he went through my passport and discovered that a single name was indicated on it. Unaware that most Afghans used only a single name, both officially and unofficially, he insisted that I give him my family name. It was not as if the concept of a family name was alien to me, but like most Afghans, especially those living in the rural areas, I had not been given one. I remembered my father telling me years ago that his people were probably Safis, though he could not be sure. So I told the person at the desk to add Safi to my first name and that is what he did. I would discover later that Safi was a common last name in Lebanon as well as in the Arab countries of the Middle East. Wadi Safi, for instance, was a well-known Lebanese singer and there was a female student from Yemen and a male student from Iraq at the AUB who both had Safi as their last name. I have always liked the name and now my wife and all three of our children bear it.

With the matter regarding my name amicably resolved, another hurdle had to be crossed. My passport, flouting international norms, showed only the year of birth, in keeping with the Afghan solar calendar, Hijri Shamsi. The solar year consisted of 365 days, beginning with *nowruz*—New Year's Day—which was celebrated annually on 21 March not only in my country, but in parts of Central Asia and Iran and by Kurds everywhere, probably because it marked the advent of spring and, significantly in an agricultural society, the beginning of the planting season. I vaguely recall hearing my father say that I had been born on 21 Dalwa 1322 (according to the Afghan solar calendar) and at the insistence of the man at the desk that I provide the day and month of birth as well, I did some hurried calculations and came up with 10 February 1943. Later on, I would do the calculations all over again and discover that I had made a mistake and added a year to my actual age. I was unprepared for the man's third demand: I needed to provide a recent photo for my student ID. Fortunately, I found the three that had been rejected by the Ministry of Foreign Affairs in Kabul and handed them over with some trepidation, apprehensive that if they weren't suitable for a passport, they might not be for a student ID. But they were accepted and one copy was pasted in the small booklet that would, henceforth, serve as my student ID.

The registration process took nearly an hour to complete and when I emerged from it, I had a brand new family name and a complete date of birth which I was so unused to that I had to memorize them and keep them for life. The date of birth is for my own use, but I have naturally had to share my new family name with my wife and children. I have no intentions, though, of passing on my family name to my other relatives in Afghanistan. Besides, many have chosen family names for themselves, adding them to their first names in keeping with the new trend in my country, especially among those with high school and college degrees. My cousin, Omara Khan, for example, was the first one to use Alizai as his family name. It means, "the descendant of Ali," the reference being to our paternal grandfather, Abdul Ali. My brother, Wadood, used to call himself Faizi, after our father, Faiz Mehmed, but has changed his family name to Alizai. My half-sister, Najiba, however, still uses Faizi as her family name.

The college program at the AUB was very intensive and required a student deficient in English to study around the clock. Those who managed to survive the grueling routine and graduate from college received a BA or BS degree, depending on the study program they had enrolled for. Those who did not make it were admitted to a year-long career-development program and received a diploma upon graduation. The chance of failure for every student was very real. I knew how mortifying it would be for me if I failed my course and had to return to Afghanistan in disgrace and face criticism and ridicule from my immediate family, relatives and friends. I had no idea what I would do if such a fate befell me. The very thought was so depressing that I forced myself to be optimistic and spent every free moment studying. But little things could trigger my insecurity. I remember an occasion when I was going up in the elevator at Penrose Hall and started chatting with a fourth-year student from Iran. It was clear to both of us that I had difficulty expressing myself in English. The Iranian felt that given the lamentable state of my English, I would be incapable of graduating from the university and did not mince his words while saying so. I was disheartened by his lack of confidence in my abilities, but eventually proved him wrong. After a couple of years in college, my English improved and I could gain more from the lectures in the classroom and from reading the assigned textbooks and supplementary material.

From the mid-1960s till the end of that decade, there were about seventy students from Afghanistan studying at the AUB. One of them considered himself an authority on mathematics. His overconfidence did not get him far, however. He could not finish college and had to return to Afghanistan with a diploma from the career-development program. For me, studying was certainly important, but it was equally necessary to find creative ways to academic success. One of those involved being keenly attuned to those areas of the syllabus a professor prioritized over others. From observation and experience, I had come to understand that an essay-type question, based on our knowledge of those areas, was sure to be included in the mid-term and final exams, where such questions were an exclusive or prominent part of the paper set for us. Essay-type questions, unlike the objective ones, always carried weight; how we answered them determined our final scores for a particular course. Knowledge and some guesswork came in useful for correctly answering the objective questions, especially the true-or-false and multiple-choice ones, but a sound strategy was called for to tackle the essay-type questions. Being aware of a professor's degree of interest in the different parts of the syllabus usually helped me to anticipate the essay-type questions that would be set in the course exam. The professors generally allowed us to choose from three such questions. During the exams, I would rely on a combination of luck and knowledge of the course material to successfully answer the objective questions and fall back on the strategy I had devised to tackle the essay-type questions.

We had to take three courses in English, two of them during the freshman year and one during the sophomore year. It was while taking the second course during the second semester of my freshman year that I would be assigned to a very stern professor of English. On the very first day of class, the gentleman came in and looked around at us. Noticing a couple of students who had been in his class before, he offered them the option of switching to another section and, therefore, another professor. Since it was my first course with this professor, I was obviously not among the lucky ones. We were asked to write an essay on a topic of our choice. Realizing that first impressions were important, I thought of writing something original and yet not beyond my sphere of experience. And so I wrote an essay about the rooster I had gifted my elementary school teacher in Khas Kunar who had declared he needed one to feed his guests. I described the long journey home, the time I spent searching for the rooster on our farmland and the equally long journey back to school with the bird in my arms. I also wrote of the beating I would receive from my mother whom I had kept in the dark about the whole affair. The professor found the story authentic and well written and commended me for my effort. Needless to say, I did very well in the course that semester.

Similarly, in the history course, entitled, Civilization of Arab East, I figured out that the professor, George Ziadeh, admired Muhammad Ali Pasha, the Khedive (ruler) of Egypt and Sudan. For even after we had finished going through the course textbook, he would continue to give us examples to illustrate that particular segment. I naturally surmised there would be an essay-type question on the subject in the exam. I remember memorizing that book. When we received our question paper on the day of the exam, I found that we had been given a choice from among three essay-type questions; one of them was, predictably, on Muhammad Ali Pasha. I did not even glance at the other two options, focusing, instead on this one question. I ended up making both the professor and myself happy by getting a high grade for my performance in the test. Let's put it this way: studying hard is the best way, but not the only way to get high grades in a test. A "creative" strategy, based on a professor's preferences in the syllabus, is just as effective.

The AUB regulations stipulated a compulsory two-year stay in the university dorm for all freshmen. Students were allowed to live off campus during the sophomore year and later. The off-campus accommodation was actually cheaper if two students shared a small one-bedroom apartment. Coming as I did from a poor family, my main concern was to save as much as I could of my monthly allowance of US$130 so that I could either send the money back home or or take it back to Afghanistan after graduation.

But I did allow myself one indulgence. I usually took advantage of my summer vacation and traveled. In 1965, I would spend a month in Turkey with a friend, Hidayatullah Tokhi. The following year, I traveled all over Europe for three months with Burhanudeen Hassas, another friend. We would travel by taxi through Syria and by bus in Turkey, visiting Ankara and Izmir before arriving in Istanbul. There, we bought a ticket on the European Express train to Budapest, staying in Sofia and Belgrade before arriving in the Hungarian capital. During the rest of our trip, we would visit Vienna, Salzburg, Munich, Frankfurt, Geneva, Milan, Rome and Athens, before returning to Lebanon via Turkey.

Before leaving Beirut, we had bought International Student IDs which would entitle us to stay at youth hostels all over Europe, barring the East European communist countries, which did not have such hostels at the time. Some hostels in Western Europe charged us fifty cents a night; others, a single US dollar. In the communist countries, we would seek out the universities and usually found a room to rent, because most of the students who occupied them during the term were away on their summer vacation. If we found fellow Afghans to stay with, we did not turn down the opportunity. We found good friends in Sofia, who reserved a room for us in the university dormitory and gave us food coupons for the cafeteria, where we could buy our meals at subsidized prices. In Frankfurt, we came across equally generous and helpful souls who invited us to stay with them free of charge. Turkey had many inexpensive hotels and we did not need to look for alternative accommodation. In Budapest, where all the hotels were full up because of a conference being held in the city, a family took us in and gave us a room to stay in. By paying them a little extra money, we were able to eat with them as well and had a good time watching programs on their television set, which a couple of families shared. The youth hostel in Vienna was full when we arrived there. The manager was nice enough to take care of our luggage while we went out to look for accommodation elsewhere. We were instructed to look out for the "Zummer" sign, but could not see it anywhere and finally spent the night sitting in a public telephone booth, though it was too cramped to permit both of us to sit down at the same time and we had to take turns to rest, with the other person standing vigil to ensure no one was approaching the booth to use the telephone. When someone showed up early in the morning to make a call, one of us emerged from the booth, while the other busied himself dialing nonexistent numbers. When we returned to the hostel in the morning, the manager had a room with a bunk bed ready for us.

In Europe, we traveled comfortably by train from one city to another. On the train we took from Frankfurt, my friend found himself seated next to a beautiful young German woman. By the time she got off at her destination, they had exchanged addresses. They would keep in touch and the young woman would come to Lebanon, one day, to visit my friend. Subsequently, they even married and had a son, moving to Pennsylvania, USA, where he had received a scholarship to study. Unfortunately, the marriage ended in divorce.

But to return to happier times, we would take the ferry from Italy to Greece and then from Greece to Turkey, sitting out on the deck on both occasions. It started raining on one of those journeys and the only place where we could take shelter was on a ladder standing against a wall with a shade over it, because the gates to the area protected from the weather were inaccessible. I remember climbing the ladder and staying perched there until the rain had stopped.

We went to the port in Greece, seeking to get on a ferry to Lebanon. The tickets for the journey would have cost us each US$40 if we traveled on the deck. I had barely over a forty dollars in my pocket and realized right away that I couldn't afford the fare. The Greek shipping company made us another offer: with a good discount, we could travel to Izmir in Turkey for ten dollars each. We grabbed the opportunity and bought tickets for the trip. We arrived in Turkey after nearly twenty-four hours. On the way, the boat dropped anchor at several Greek islands to allow some passengers to disembark and others to come aboard.

Once we arrived in Turkey, making our way to Lebanon was simple. We took a bus and after a day's trip, spent the night in a hotel room with a shower in Iskenderun. The next day, we managed to cross the border to Syria and decided to stay in Aleppo overnight. We both went to a barbershop for a nice haircut. By the time I arrived back in Beirut at the end of my three-month summer adventure in Europe, I think I had about five dollars left over from the more than $300 I had set out with.

The two hot issues in Europe that year were the Beatles and football. Almost everyone my age was singing the Beatles' songs and listening to the band sing. It was the first time in my life that I would see people walking down a street with a tiny radio—a transistor—in their hands. I was interested in football, not obsessed with it. I would go to the Kabul Stadium to watch football, basketball, field hockey and volleyball teams from high schools competing against each other. I wanted the team from my high school to win the game, but once I was out of the stadium, I could forget about them. In Europe, however, people seemed obsessed with football. I remember that most members of the three families who had watched TV together in the Budapest home we stayed in were football freaks and spent every evening watching tournaments. The football championship tournament was on in Europe and it seemed that everyone had a favorite team they were rooting for.

On 5 June 1967, I was waiting with other students in class for the first lesson of the day on experimental psychology. It was nine a.m. and our professor, Dr. Ward, was yet to arrive. One of the students had a portable battery-operated radio which he had turned on. Suddenly, he shouted in Arabic that war had broken out in Egypt. That was how I learned about the Six-Day Arab-Israeli War. That day was declared the last one of the semester and the university was closed for the summer. The final score for each course was calculated on the basis of our performance in class during the semester. I stayed on in Beirut for six days before a message came from the Afghan Embassy that an airplane belonging to Ariana Afghan Airlines would be arriving at Beirut International Airport to take all Afghan students back home.

The day the war started, I spent the whole day listening to the radio stations of all the Arab countries. Judging by the reported casualty figures their news readers cited, it seemed as if Israel would be wiped off the map by the time I woke up the next morning. A blackout was imposed at night and I had no desire whatsoever to leave my apartment. When I woke up in the morning, the first thing I did was turn my radio on. The tone of the broadcasts from the radio stations in the Arab countries had changed. Seeking more objective news reports, I turned to the BBC, radio stations in Europe and those outside the Arab world. The casualty figures and the situation on the battlefield they reported were very different from what I had been led to believe so far. The Egyptian army, it seemed, had surrendered on the very first day of the war and the Israeli forces were now focused on fighting the Jordanian forces, which had gained a little ground while the Israelis were engaged in battle with the Egyptians in the Sinai Peninsula. By the second and third days, the Jordanian army was also on the run. By the fourth and fifth days of the war, Israeli forces had captured and occupied the Golan Heights and were on their way to Damascus. A ceasefire was declared between Syria and Israel on the sixth day; the war was over. Israel now occupied the whole of Sinai, the West Bank and Gaza and the Golan Heights. The entire Arab world was in turmoil. Although Lebanon was not involved in the war, we would see military airplanes flying over us once in a while and I remember how, while strolling on the campus one day, I had run into my academic advisor, Prof. Levon Malikian, who had urged me to go back right back to my dorm and stay put.

As soon as the war ended, the President of Egypt, Gamal Abdel Nasser, resigned from his post, blaming himself for the defeat suffered by his country's military forces. The day before war was declared, I recall seeing a cartoon in one of the Arabic newspapers that featured a classroom where the teacher, President Gamal Abdel Nasser, had written on the board in Arabic: "The first lesson, the Gulf of Aqaba." Living in Lebanon, I was fairly well informed about what had been reported in the Arab media. I had no idea what the Israeli military was planning and had assumed it would be crushed if attacked by the forces of the three neighboring Arab countries, Egypt, Jordan and Syria. I have to admit in hindsight that my knowledge was not only limited, but biased.

In spite of the military defeat, most Arabs came out in support of President Nasser and begged him to withdraw his resignation. The blackout in Beirut had not yet been called off on the first night the war ended and the city lay shrouded in darkness. But people came out of their homes carrying lighted candles and filled the streets. A still larger crowd gathered in Cairo and other Egyptian cities, urging the president to change his mind. Nasser bowed to their will and withdrew his resignation.

I stayed on in Beirut, which was still under a nightly curfew, although the war was over. It was while taking a shower one day that I got the news from Jalat about the Ariana Airlines plane having landed at Beirut International Airport to take us back to Kabul for the summer. We boarded the DC-6 that had been parked at the airport and it took off and flew north over the Mediterranean Sea, turning east to fly over Turkey. A stopover in Tehran followed; and then we were in Kabul.

My family was still living in Khwaja Ghar where I had left them when I went to Lebanon. Since I had had no telephone contact with them, it was a great surprise for them when I simply showed up at the door after a three-year absence and greeted everyone. My father must have been particularly pleased to see me, because he wanted to slaughter a sheep and invite all his colleagues at the Spinzar Company to partake in the feast. I would have loved to spend my own money on the special occasion he was planning, but it was his decision to take and I had to bow to his wishes and stay out of it.

Converting the dollars I had saved in Lebanon into local currency yielded 90,000 Afghanis. My father had often mentioned his lifelong dream of owning a house in Imam Sahib, where he had a plot of land he had been given as retirement benefits in lieu of cash. He planned to settle there after his retirement from the Spinzar Company. Since he already had farmland, owning a house would be the icing on the cake, as it were. Jalander, the person in charge of the storeroom at the company owned two houses in the town of Imam Sahib, and wanted to sell off one. My father was given the choice of buying either one of the two houses. One was made of baked bricks and had a regular-size yard. The other was made of unfired bricks, but the yard was larger and had an adjoining garden with trees that stretched over one *jereeb* (half an acre). My father preferred the latter and bought it for 100,000 Afghanis, supplementing the money I had given him with the 2,500 Afghanis he received after selling off a radio. At the end of my summer vacation, I returned to Lebanon to continue my studies.

Life in Beirut was almost back to normal. The university campus was quiet, but uniformed security guards of the Falangist party, headed by Pierre Jumayyil, guarded all the entrance and exit points to the campus. I took courses during the summer of 1968 and had a one-month vacation coming up before the beginning of the fall semester in September. I decided to spend it in Egypt with my friend, Asad. Syria and Egypt had arrived at a political agreement and created the United Arab Republic. Since a flight from Damascus to Cairo cost far less than a flight from Beirut to the Egyptian capital, Asad and I decided to make our way to Damascus and fly from there. We bought round-trip tickets and had to wait a couple of days before boarding our flight. The streets in Damascus were more crowded than those in Beirut and almost half the people were in military fatigues. The devastation the city had suffered during the Six-Day War was clearly visible and the people had not escaped unscathed either. During my stay there, I would visit a few places like the Old Bazaar and the Ummayyad Mosque, among others. I liked the mosque for its four *mehrabs*, one for each of the four Sunni sects in Islam, namely, Shaf'i, Hambali, Maleki and Hanafi. The shrine in the courtyard was that of the Prophet Yahya, according to the Muslims, and of Saint John, according to the Christians. Our two days in the city were soon up and it was time for our flight. Asad and I took off for Cairo aboard a Soviet-made aircraft.

Our two friends in Cairo had been fellow students at the AUB, but the stream of medicine in which they wished to specialize was not available in Beirut. They had, therefore, been sent to Egypt to study at Cairo University. They were extremely helpful and with their assistance, we managed to rent the lower portion of a split-level house in Maadi, south of Cairo, for a month. We had three bedrooms, a bathroom, a kitchen and a living room to ourselves. We had plenty of room for entertaining some of our Afghan friends who were either studying in Egypt or working in the Pashto Department of Radio Cairo. If I remember right, our rent was ten Egyptian pounds. The landlord's family lived on the upper level and I remember them well. I recall the day I had jokingly expressed my interest in marrying the landlord's daughter. Her mother had promptly replied that the man she would welcome as her son-in-law should have a house, a job and a car. As a student on a scholarship, I could fulfill none of those three requirements.

Cairo had been hit hard by the Six-Day War and the signs of devastation were still visible. The streets were unbelievably crowded and the buses so crammed with passengers that they could be seen hanging from the doors and windows. The train that carried workers from Cairo to Halwan, the city's industrial area, and passed through Maadi was extremely crowded during rush hour and we made sure we avoided that hour whenever we needed to board it.

During my stay in Cairo, I could not possibly miss out on the pyramids and the Sphinx and visited them in due course. Fortunately, I was young and nimble enough to be able to climb the stairwell inside the large pyramid that led to the tomb of a pharaoh buried there. I remember our guide pointing out the casket in which the ancient monarch was entombed. He indicated a hole in the floor near the casket from where, he explained, jewelry adorning the pharaoh's person had been dug out and taken away for display at the Cairo Museum. Apparently, there was another room just below the one in which we stood. It was where the pharaoh's consort was entombed. The Sphinx, I was disappointed to discover, looked far less impressive than in the photographs I had seen of it. I heard later that it has been restored and looks more presentable now. At the end of our vacation, we returned to Beirut by the same route via Damascas that we had taken for the onward journey.

The university opened for the academic year 1968-'69. After completing the course requirement, I had to pass a swimming test by swimming across the university pool. On the day of the test, the pool was not available for our use and the sea was rough. We were asked to swim across a narrow waterway to the cliff on the other side and back. I was overcome by doubt and wondered if I would be able to make it. But once I plunged into the water and started swimming, I managed to reach the cliff and swim back to the point where the instructor stood waiting. He thought I had performed well and my name was added to the list of students graduating that year.

The graduation ceremony was held on the university playground in the lower campus, where the colleges of engineering and agriculture were also located. Each of the graduating students was allowed to invite five people—family and friends—to the ceremony and was handed as many cards for the purpose. My family was far away in Afghanistan and my only friends were fellow students who could attend the ceremony without special invitation. I don't remember what I did with my invitation cards, but I was there to walk up to the podium and shake hands with the dean and the university president, Dr. Kirkwood, before receiving my degree—a Bachelor of Arts in Psychology and Education.

I had achieved the goal for which I had come all the way to the AUB. But on returning to Afghanistan, I would have another struggle ahead: I would need to find a job. The Ambassador of Afghanistan in Cairo at the time, Mr. Musa Shafeeq, had visited the AUB to meet students from his country, reserving a private session for each of them. When my turn came, Mr. Shafeeq and I realized that we were from the same province and he advised me to get in touch with him when I returned to Afghanistan after my graduation. He asked me where I would like to work and promised to help me find a job at the place of my choice: Kabul University, from where I had obtained my scholarship. Back in Afghanistan, I spent six months waiting for a job at Kabul University, but forgot to ask Mr. Shafeeq for his help. By the time I would meet him again at the Kabul Hotel and have a drink of Coca-Cola at his suite, I was gainfully employed at the Ministry of Education and did not have to seek his help.

SEVEN

Work and Study Program

W hile Jalat and I were still looking for jobs in our own country, both of us would regularly visit Kabul University in the hope that some vacancy for a post would come up. The university president, Fazal Rabi Pazhwak, was considerate enough to start paying us salaries from the very day of our arrival in Afghanistan. We were actually being paid for doing nothing and keen on obtaining a regular job to justify our salaries.

With nothing to do and nowhere to go, I began observing that student gatherings at the university and in Kabul's public places had become common. Youngsters would congregate and openly express their grievances against the government. Their ideology was often extreme and they held open discussions in local restaurants, debating over the country's plight and the measures they felt should be taken to improve it. Some of the young intellectuals in these groups were socialists, faithful followers of the Soviet Union's version of communism. A few swore by the ideology promoted by the Peoples' Republic of China. The Soviet-inspired socialists belonged to two different factions: the Khalqis, under the leadership of Noor Mehmed Taraki; and the Parchamis, led by Babrak Karmal. The socialists who believed in the Chinese version of communism were called the Shu'la-e Jawaid (Eternal Flame) and regarded Mahmudi and Ghubar as their leaders. Those at the other end of the spectrum were guided by their religion , determined to defend Islam against the infidel socialists. It was not as if I hadn't heard the names of all these parties before leaving for Lebanon in 1964, but I had never imagined them being allowed to hold meetings in public places to air their anti-government sentiments.

The ground for such freedom of expression had probably been laid by the setting up of the Constitution of 1964 that had declared Afghanistan to be a constitutional monarchy and barred members of the royal family, excluding the king, from seeking political office. The commission that would draft the Constitution had been formed right after Daoud's resignation from his post as Prime Minister. The Loya Jerga (tribal grand assembly) was convened in the spring of 1964 (afghanland.com) and met in September 1964 to sign the new draft. The king signed the draft and it became the Constitution. One hundred and seventy-six members of the Loya Jerga were elected by the people from all the provinces, while the king appointed thirty-four more persons to add to the group. These men represented all the provinces in the country and, therefore, all its religious, linguistic and ethnic groups.

Appointed by the king to succeed Daoud as Prime Minister, Dr. Mehmed Yousef was the first commoner to rise to that post. The orthodox sections of the population, which looked upon the socialists as infidels and wished to see Afghanistan become an Islamic nation ruled by Sharia, had no choice but to accept the existence of parties whose members were inspired by a liberal ideology. While respecting the Islamic aspect of Afghan society, the nationalists of the Afghan Millat Party and the democrats of the Musawat (Equality) Party were opposed to the imposition of Sharia. Supporters of these parties were quite vocal about defending their respective ideologies.

Supporters of most of the existing parties would congregate for a public meeting in Park-e Zernigar on 1ˢᵗ May, International Labor Day, attracting crowds of spectators. Their spokespersons would take their turn on stage, trying to rally public opinion in their favor. Soldiers from the national army and police personnel were present in sizeable numbers to maintain law and order. Sometime after I began working at the Ministry of Education across the street from the park, I would, on one occasion, emerge from my office and join the crowd in the park on the first day of May to observe the gatherings and listen to the party leaders holding forth. But while I was unemployed, I had all the time in the world to observe the developments around me.

The party that chose a spot in the park closest to the Ministry of Education was the Musawat (Equality) Party. Its leader, Hashem Maiwandwal, a well-known scholar, would stand on a table, addressing a small group of supporters and others who had stopped by to hear him speak. Since I had read *Musawat*, the party's publication which outlined its ideology, I had no desire to while away the hours listening to Maiwandwal's monotonous speeches. It was apparent that other people in the crowd shared my feelings, for few paused to listen to his words of wisdom.

Not far away was the spot where the Khalqis congregated around their leader, Deputy Chief Hafeezullah Amin, my former teacher and principal and second in the line to the party leader, Noor Mehmed Taraki. His supporters were mainly students who had come to Kabul from the rural areas and were studying in the city's boarding schools. The spectators were primarily male, but a few young women were also visible in the crowd. Amin was invariably in full cry, expounding on the ideology of his group, as the crowd looked on and listened. With his years of experience in teaching and administration at the boarding schools in Kabul, he knew exactly how to motivate or, rather, indoctrinate its students. Whenever he paused for breath, a woman would spring to her feet and spout an emotion-charged slogan, swearing by her honor and chastity and everything that was precious to her to stand by the cause she had espoused. Everyone would be very moved and acknowledge her words with a round of applause. It was just the impact Amin sought to create. I hoped to get a glimpse of Taraki, Amin's boss, but he was not present at the gatherings I attended.

The gathering place for the Parcham party was along the road which divided the park into its southern and northern sections. Its supporters, mainly students and officials living in Kabul, would stand around their leader, Babrak Karmal, who wound take up position on top of a mound on the northern side of the road. Karmal was fond of narrating the story of Abdul Rahman, one of his followers, who had been killed by villagers near Mehterlam, the provincial capital of Laghman. The story went that the Imam of a local mosque, where the villagers were gathered for Friday prayers, had branded Abdul Rahman a communist and exhorted his congregation to kill him. After their prayers were over, the villagers, led by the Imam, had emerged from the mosque and headed for Abdul Rahman's village to look for him. They had hunted him down and beaten him to death.

South of the mound which Babrak was using as a platform, a large number of people walking down the road would stop to listen to his declamations. While the supporters of the Khalq faction seemed composed and less prone to excited outpourings, those of the Parcham faction appeared more volatile. Inevitably, the crowd in the northern half of the park was easier to handle, while that in the southern part needed greater surveillance. The security forces deployed by the administration had their hands full trying to keep the two rival groups, the Shula-e Jawaid and the religious faction, apart.

The Shula-e Jawaid and its adherents congregated on the southern side of the dividing line behind the Spinzar Hotel, where a heavy security detail ensured a safe distance was maintained between this faction and members of the Islamic parties and other communists. The Islamic party members gathered at the southern end of the park near the Spinzar Hotel and the Pushtani Tejarati Bank. The other communists, namely the Khalqis and the Parchamese, were to be found across the street to the north. One religious party had set up a platform at the bus stop in front of the Spinzar Hotel. A table would be placed on the sidewalk for a member of the group to stand on and hold forth, the target audience mainly being party supporters and those waiting for the bus to go home from work. Because of the heavy security arrangements, I thought it prudent not to linger too long in the area. I cannot be sure if the Afghan Millat Party was there or not or if I had simply failed to notice its presence. It was, in fact, the only nationalistic party which claimed Afghanistan for all Afghans, but sought a dominant position for the Pashtuns who constituted the majority of the population.

While these political developments were taking place, I had to focus on my own future. One month swiftly followed another, while Jalat and I were still waiting for a vacancy at Kabul University. We had, in the meantime, been reflecting on the career options available to us. We decided that in case we failed to procure a job at the university, our second option would be the Curriculum and Textbook Project at the Ministry of Education. The project was funded by US/AID and managed by Teachers College, Columbia University, New York. Our third choice was to teach at the Teachers Training Junior College in Kabul. Our six-month waiting period, hoping for a job at the university, finally came to an end without bearing fruit. Ayub Lang, the dean of the Junior College, invited us both for lunch one day, because he was eager to hire us. However, we preferred to wait and see if anything would come of our second option. When Jalat was accepted for a post at the Social Studies section and I was employed at the Testing and Evaluation section of the Curriculum and Textbook Project in January 1970, we were both set to embark on our individual paths to a promising professional future.

The Curriculum and Textbook Project had been set up in 1966 and we were required to work on it with advisors from abroad. Our affiliation with a foreign agency increased our chances of getting a scholarship to study at Teachers College, Columbia University (TCCU). Under the circumstances, our second option had turned out to be the best one. There was also the matter of the military draft. It was mandatory for college graduates to sign up for military service for a period of one year; others had to serve an additional year. Teachers were exempted from the service, provided they taught for a minimum period of six years. President Daoud had issued a directive that those Afghans who successfully completed their study programs overseas and returned to the country with a degree were to be exempted from military service for that period of time. And since I was working at the Ministry of Education and, thereby, enjoying the status of a teacher, I too, was eligible for exemption. My period of employment since January 1970 was taken into consideration and at the end of 1975, I received my military certificate without having spent a single day at the military base.

The Curriculum and Textbook Project was aimed at developing and publishing new instructional material, textbooks and teacher guides for elementary schools all over Afghanistan. When the project was first established and even after I had come on board, the elementary schools in the country taught Grades One through Six. However, in 1976, while Daoud was still president, the government decided to add two more years to complete the elementary-school level. The first two years of what used to be junior high school were absorbed into elementary schools across the country, while the third year, the ninth grade, became part of high school. It created more work for those toiling on the project, because it now covered eight grades instead of the original six.

When I first joined the project, the experts had decided that they had enough material from the basic research and were ready to start writing the instructional material. It was almost toward the end of the basic-research period that I would have to make two trips as a member of an evaluation team: one to Herat and the other to Kunar. But before I broach the subject of those trips, I need to explain how they came about.

Increasing the elementary school years from six to eight and, thereby, doing away with middle school were a part of the educational reform the Ministry of Education had tried to introduce in the summer of 1976. Although I was involved in its implementation and not in its planning, I had heard my colleagues talking about it at the cafeteria on the fifth floor, where almost all staff members of the Ministry of Education ate lunch every day. Those employees selected to visit the provinces to implement the reform had been directed by the Deputy Minister of Education to gather at the cafeteria. I had imagined he would explain the reform's main purpose and offer us some material and guidance on how to implement it. But that was not to be. The deputy minister arrived at the cafeteria and advised us to rely on our judgment while evaluating sixth-grade students and deciding which of them should be promoted to the seventh grade. It was clear to me that he was absolving himself of all responsibility and putting the ball in our court, so to speak. I could not help but reflect on a system where high-ranking officials could enjoy all the privileges of their position without being accountable to those they had been chosen to serve; in the case of the deputy minister, students, teachers and school and provincial administrators. Had they been selected on the basis of their competence or given the post because of their connection to people in power? The deputy minister presumed, no doubt, that his position was safe. However, owing to his lack of concern about his responsibilities, my colleagues and I would leave for the provinces with empty hands and emptier heads, clueless as to how we would achieve our objectives.

As far as I was concerned, the trip was outside the purview of the Curriculum and Textbook Project and I was not accompanying foreign experts with whom I was expected to work in collaboration. The ministry's rules stipulated that we would be paid an extra day's salary for each day we worked in the provinces. That additional sum barely covered the cost of three daily meals. Paying for hotel accommodation out of that allowance was out of the question. Moreover, our travel expenses had to be paid for out of our own pockets. When traveling with foreign experts, I had not only received 150 Afghanis to cover daily expenses, but been provided free hotel accommodation and transportation. Unable to afford hotel charges, I hoped I could select a geographical region for my work where I had a relative with whom I could put up. Among my preferred provinces were Qandahar, where Rawouf was posted as an army officer; Kunar, where I had a number of friends and relatives; and Konduz, where my other cousin, Omara Khan, was head of the Customs Office.

I was asked to go to Konduz. Omara Khan's house was within walking distance from the office of the Director of Education in the city of Konduz. We evaluated the students in three centers located in the city, in AqTaipa and in the town of Imam Sahib. My father was still living at the time and while we were in Imam Sahib for our work, I invited my colleagues to breakfast at his house. Earlier, they had found it hard to believe that my family lived in Imam Sahib, because I was a Pashtun and spoke Dari with an accent not native to the area. But having met my father, their doubts were laid to rest.

I was traveling with two other employees of the ministry that I hadn't been acquainted with before the trip, because they belonged to departments other than my own. They would be putting up at the accommodation provided for them by Mr. Orya-Khail, the Director of Education. On the first day of our arrival, this gentleman invited us to his office to discuss our plan. I soon discovered that, like the deputy minister, the director had no plan to speak of. We asked the storekeeper to hand us a copy of the textbook for each subject area for Grades Four, Five and

Six. We left the responsibility of providing the supplies to the Director of Education. The three of us sat together in a room at the Director's office for two weeks, during which we devised three different versions of a test in both Pashto and Dari. Setting the test in three versions—A, B and C—was my idea, since we resorted to the same system to evaluate the students of the project's experimental schools which used the new instructional material prepared by it. For our current purpose, we simply changed the order of the multiple-choice questions in the test to devise the three versions. Our aim was to prevent cheating by students seated next to each other that would have defeated the purpose of the test. We carried out the test in three centers and reported the results to the office of the Director of Education. It was his responsibility to get in touch with the concerned officials at the Ministry of Education and take the final decision on student promotions.

I can only give an account of how things transpired in Konduz and speculate about the methods adopted by my colleagues to fulfill their objectives without having guidelines to fall back on. Konduz is a large city, with Sher Khan Bandar, the main transit point between Afghanistan and the countries to the north being located in the region. Its residents are relatively affluent. It has a lot of farmland and the Spinzar Company was, at the time, operating all over the province, trying to help cotton farmers make a profit by serving as a ready client for their crop. Even in such a large city, we had initially run into supply problems. The Director of Education had sent someone off to buy paper at the city's main stationery store, only to discover that the city police headquarters had purchased the entire stock. Negotiations between the office of the director and the police had ensued, with the latter deciding that the director's need was greater. The director obtained the paper and we managed to finish our work by using the Gestetner machine at his office to print the question papers for the test.

Given the difficulties we encountered in a city as large as Konduz, I wondered how my other colleagues had fared in provinces where material and supplies would have been hard to find. Furthermore, without instructions on how to implement the reform, their task couldn't have been made any easier. I was not only concerned about the low daily allowance granted to officials on the job that did not even cover their travel expenses, but also about their lack of knowledge and experience in devising tests and evaluating the performance of students that would decide the latter's fate. Given the financial constraints under which these officials had to labor and the fear of failure that overwhelmed the students being tested (since it marked the end of all educational opportunity), the temptation for the latter's parents to offer bribes and for the officials in charge of the youngsters' destinies to accept them were very real. While I have no reason to cast aspersions on either group, the situation was certainly fraught with risk.

Coming back to my experience with the experimental schools, as a member of the evaluation team, I was involved in conducting basic research until the instructional material for the first grade was ready to be tried out in the experimental schools. Once the material was delivered to the schools, my responsibiliteis at the project changed. We would test the students twice—once in the middle of the school year and again, at the end. We also conducted one-on-one interviews with the classroom teachers, the school principals and the provincial supervisor who was in charge of visiting the schools. We used the information we gleaned as guidelines for revising the material at the end of the school year in order to make it compatible with the comprehension level of the students. A review committee was set up at the Ministry of Education, in which subject-area specialists and schoolteachers would participate for the purpose of revising the material by using the evaluation results as their guidelines. Following the review, the material would be published and distributed to schools all over the country.

When the material was ready for distribution, the project set up a teacher-training section, undertaking the responsibility of planning and organizing seminars for teachers and for school and provincial administrators to acquaint them with the methods of teaching the new material. As a member of the evaluation section, I was always present at such seminars to explain to the audience that the material had been tried out and inputs from schoolteachers and administrators incorporated in the revised material. We used teachers who had taught the tryout material in the experimental schools as resource personnel at the teacher-training seminars. The project was able to develop new material for all six grades of elementary school, before the communist takeover of the country and the assassination of President Daoud.

The fallout of these developments—the US government's decision to terminate its contract with the previous regime and dissolve the project in 1978—was unfortunate, because it was the first attempt in the history of Afghanistan to have local and foreign experts collaborating on a project to develop new instructional material and establish a policy for regularly revising that material before reprinting it for subsequent use. Before the project was set up, the instructional material used at elementary schools had consisted of a single textbook in each subject, written by one author whose name was mentioned on the front jacket. No information was available about the suitability of the material in relation to the students it was aimed at. I do remember Mr. Asif Mayel, author of the currently used first-grade Dari textbook, joining our project as a member of the Review Committee, when we were revising the first-grade Dari textbook for Dari speakers.

Long before I actively became engaged in the project, a ceremony, presided over by Abdullah Malikyar, Minister of Foreign Affairs, had been held at Kabul University to felicitate us individually for successfully completing our study programs abroad and earning our degrees. When my turn came, Mr. Malikyar had sternly reminded me that I would have to change my last name, as President Daoud had apparently decreed that no Afghan would be allowed to retain a last name that clearly indicated his affiliation to a particular tribe. I promised Mr. Malikyar I would change my last name, but did not keep my word.

The good news was that I would be awarded two scholarships to study at TCCU, one in January 1972 and the other in January 1977. While the first came through easily, I was unprepared for the problems I would encounter before obtaining the second.

All I had to do to avail of the first scholarship was to appear for the TOEFL exam. I remember my feelings of exhilaration when my supervisor, Phil Lange, brought the results down to the office and congratulated me for my performance. I had cleared the first and only obstacle and would face no further problems in going abroad to study in a Western country. I had a valid passport which now met the standard requirements of a first name, a family name and a complete date of birth, indicating the day, the month and the year.

I landed in Washington, DC, where I was expected to stay to familiarize myself with the American way of life, and recall spending a week in a dilapidated building at Dupont Circle, that may have been torn down by now to make way for new constructions. And, indeed, I made many discoveries I had not been aware of earlier. One day, for instance, I joined a tour group and visited the White House. As we were entering the building, I overheard a black gentleman in the group boldly declaring that the furniture on the first floor had been brought over from France and what we were now looking at was stolen merchandise. He carried on in this vein right through, making derogatory statements about the US president's official residence until the tour was over and he had walked out. I was amazed that this man could speak so uninhibitedly without being arrested. Had I or my fellow Afghans ever made a single statement against the king or president of Afghanistan, I would have been in big trouble and so, perhaps, would some of my family.

On another occasion, I was invited to dinner by an American family and forewarned that I should be careful to treat any pets they might have as I would a family member. I recall my own family having a pet dog in our village in Afghanistan, but it would come to the house only when it was hungry. It would visit the three families living in the compound and get a piece of dry bread from each household. The dog would then spend the rest of the night in the garden. His barking at night gave us a sense of security. On the rare occasions the family had meat or chicken for supper, the dog would be allowed to munch on the bones. There were cats too, prowling around the *qala*, coming and going as they pleased. No one owned them or fed them. They usually took care of themselves. My cousin, Rasul, even brought in a few rabbits to keep at his house, but had to turn them out when they proved to be destructive, digging holes all over the area between their house and the garden. The way we Afghans saw it, dogs and cats could only belong to families of their own species. We were prepared to take care of their young, while they were helpless, but that was it. A dog or a cat could not be a member of a human family. I no longer remember if the family I visited in Washington had a pet, but if they had, I was ready to accept it as a family member and treat it as such.

After acclimatizing myself to American life and culture, I arrived in New York City, with instructions to go to Room 210 on the main campus of Columbia University, the following morning, where I would have to sit for an entrance exam. The required minimum score was 600, but I managed 572 and was accepted on probation. My performance must have been consistently good henceforth, because TCCU accepted me as a regular graduate student when the probationary period was over. But it wasn't smooth running all the way. I had to undergo a hernia operation at St. Luke's Hospital in May 1974. The problem began one evening at a WCCI (World Council on Curriculum and Instruction) dinner in a Japanese restaurant in Lower Manhattan to which the conference organizer, Prof. Alice Miel, had invited me, promising to give me a ride back to my room near the TCCU campus. I had enjoyed interacting with the other guests and we were just winding up when I felt a piercing pain slice through my lower abdomen. I excused myself and went to the men's room, assuming the pain would subside. But it persisted and became more acute. On the ride home, I politely asked Prof. Miel if she could drop me off at the emergency room of St. Luke's Hospital, as she was driving north along Amsterdam Avenue. She did so and I was admitted as a patient. The operation was performed early the next morning and Prof. Miel came over to visit a couple of days later. She confessed that she had known I was in pain, but hadn't imagined it could be so serious.

Jalat and I completed our study program together in 1974 and decided to return to Afghanistan together. On our way back home, we would be stopping over in England to attend to the WCCI conference to which we had been invited. We were delighted at the opportunity and could not wait to get there. It did not occur to us, however, that we should apply for our visas at the British Consulate-General in New York, assuming that our letters of invitation to the conference would pass muster at the Immigration Desk at London's Heathrow Airport. It did not quite work out that way. We were stopped at Heathrow and British Immigration busied itself trying to arrange to put us on the first flight to Kabul. They booked us on an Iran Air flight and made sure we boarded it. I found myself sitting next to an Iranian who kept drinking through the flight. During the conversation I had with him, we talked about the end of the monarchy in Afghanistan. I told him that our king had gone and wondered which other royal ruler would be the next to go. The gentleman flushed a deep red and stopped talking to me altogether.

We landed in Abadan for a stopover and had to go through Customs. The official who checked my passport decided to retain it. When another official who was going through the contents of my suitcase asked for my passport, I explained the reason why I did not have it with me. I cannot remember if we boarded the same Iran Air flight for Tehran or another one, but I did so without my passport.

Some Iran Air inflight staff member must have been entrusted with my passport, because I do not recall having it with me when we landed in Tehran and no one bothered to ask me about it. At the Iranian capital, Jalat and I had to wait in the transit lounge for our Ariana Afghan Airlines flight to Kabul. I asked the Iran Air staff if we would be allowed to stay in Tehran for a few days before leaving for Kabul, but they ignored me. As soon as the Ariana flight was ready for departure, we were directed to go through the formalities and board the flight. My passport was handed back to me on my way out to the aircraft. In retrospect, I suspect the coup d'état in Afghanistan and its possible impact on the Shah's regime in Iran had shaken the composure of the Iranian monarch. Daoud, King Zahir Shah's own cousin, had abolished the monarchy in Afghanistan and was now the head of a socialist-dominated government, though he would subsequently be ousted by his own allies who would declare Afghanistan a democracy based on Soviet ideology. Perhaps, the Shah's fears were not unfounded. Five years later, the Iranian mullahs would take over the country, abolishing the monarchy, forcing its ruler into exile and declaring Ayatollah Ruhollah Khomeini as their Supreme Leader.

Back in Afghanistan, after returning to the ministry, I was informed that I had received a second scholarship to go back to New York and study at TCCU for twelve months. But this time, things didn't work out so smoothly. When news arrived that the name of one of my colleagues, whose American wife was working on the same project, had been confirmed as a candidate for the scholarship, I suspected I had been sidelined, because the lady's influence with the administration had worked in her husband's favor. I was not going to give up without a fight, however. I approached the project chief, Ralph Fields, and explained that I deserved priority, because I had been awarded the previous scholarship as well and had returned home to join the project and that, like him, I was head of my section. I also appealed for a fair decision to Mr. Sailani, the Head of the Department of Translation and Publication, under whose aegis the project was in operation. The two senior officials must have conferred before deciding that I was, indeed, the more deserving candidate and entitled, therefore, to the scholarship. I would spend the whole of 1976 in Kabul and leave for New York the following year. I heard later that the other contender, having failed to obtain the scholarship, had left for Herat, from where he would travel through Iran to reach the USA.

Back at the TCCU, New York

While my scholarship would only cover a twelve-month period, I planned to work toward my doctorate in education during that time. To obtain the Ed.D degree, I was required to complete the course work, have the topic of my dissertation approved, write an abstract of it and defend my thesis during the oral exam and then write my dissertation and defend it. I had enough material from my work at the project to write my proposal. By the end of the academic year, 1977-78, I had even completed the course work. I was unsure, though, about being able to fulfill all the requirements within the year and hoped that my request for an extension would be granted.

That hope, however, was dashed, when two factions—Khalq and Parcham—of the Communist Party in Afghanistan joined forces and engineered a coup in April 1978, killing Daoud, bringing down his regime and ending the power monopoly of the royal family of which he had been a member. The remaining royals went into exile, joining deposed king, Zahir Shah, in Italy. While the communists who had come to power were concerned about the enormity of the task ahead of them in a predominantly Muslim country, whose citizens regarded the new Soviet-backed government as an infidel regime bent on wiping their religion, Islam, off the face of the earth, I was anxious about the repercussions of the coup on my own future. My apprehensions, it turned out, were hardly misplaced. In the aftermath of the communist takeover of Afghanistan, US/AID terminated its contract pertaining to the project and my scholarship was discontinued.

I was in New York when I first received news of the coup, a development that threatened to destroy all that I had achieved so far. I remember making my way to the office of Mrs. Susan Nanka-Bruce, the Foreign Students Advisor, and the first question she asked me: did I know who the people behind the coup were? I replied that they were either the mullahs who respected the king, but despised his cousin, Daoud, or the communists who might have exploited their influence within Daoud's administration to get rid of him. Everyone knew Daoud to be a communist sympathizer, with a special affinity for the Parcham group, I went on, but even they did not trust him because of his royal antecedents. It turned out that I was partly right, when photographs of Noor Mehmed Taraki, who had established the communist party in my country in 1965, officially known as the Peoples Democratic Party of Afghanistan (PDPA), appeared in the *New York Times* and elsewhere.

Taraki, leader of the Khalq, and Babrak Karmal, leader of the Parcham, were diehard Marxists. Four members of their party had won seats in the Wulusi Jerga, the Lower House of Parliament, in 1965. Their first newspaper, *Khalq* ("people"), had been around for barely a month, before Zahir Shah, who was then in power, banned its publication. It was clear that the monarchy's flirtation with democracy was tentative, for while the king allowed the parties to carry on with their activities, he refused to pass legislation that would have lent them legitimacy. Acquiring a foothold in the Wulusi Jerga, however, gave these parties an official identity and a voice. The united PDPA lasted until 1967, splitting thereafter into the Khalq, under Taraki, and the Parcham, headed by Karmal. Being a much-hated minority in a conservative religious environment could hardly have ensured the survival of the communists, even in their united avatar.

Following the split, the animosity between the two factions would merely intensify, resulting in a veritable killing spree. The media reported that Amin had masterminded their leader Taraki's assassination on the latter's return via Moscow from a conference in Havana, Cuba. The Soviets, it was alleged, had brought Babrak Karmal back to Afghanistan after having the American-educated Amin, whom they distrusted, murdered.

Ostensibly restored to power with the blessings of the Kremlin, Babrak went out of his way to ingratiate himself with his people by trying to play the Muslim born and bred. He made it a point to preface his public speeches with an invocation to Allah, but his Arabic accent was atrocious and he instinctively knew that his Soviet ties would always make his attempts at a makeover suspect. I myself had reason to doubt his sincerity on one occasion, when I heard him deliver a speech in Zarnigar Park during the holy month of Ramazan, when all Muslims are required to fast and even abstain from drinking water between the hours of sunrise and sunset. True to his nature, Babrak would keep drinking water while he spoke, that too, in public. A colloquial expression that is popular with Afghans about a man trying to sit cross-legged to cover up a fart sort of sums up Karmal's situation. To put it baldly, he had never stopped farting and the air was foul with the stink. In Babrak's case, it was a matter of hastily adopting a Muslim persona to camouflage all his misdeeds as the leader of the Parcham Party. It did not take the Soviets long to realize that their protégé's future was doomed and as they withdrew from Afghanistan in 1989, Babrak fled to Moscow, leaving Najeebullah, the country's last communist ruler, to take over the reins of power.

With the departure of the Russians, however, Najeebullah's future as President of Afghanistan was doomed. His attempt to use his Ahmadzai tribal base in Logar and Paktia to his advantage in the hope that other tribes in the area would come to his support was in vain. The *muja-hideen*, who had, until then, been engaged in guerilla warfare, were gaining in strength and after defeating the Ahmad Shah Massoud-led Northern Alliance forces, they captured Kabul, placing Najeebullah under house arrest in the United Nations building in Kabul, where he had sought refuge after failing to flee to India where his family was waiting for him. In 1996, the Taliban came to power, celebrating their victory by arranging for Najeebullah's public execution in the United Nations compound. An era had ended and a far more turbulent one was about to begin, marked by events no one had dreamed of, including the disintegration of the Soviet Union.

But back in 1978, with those momentous events yet to unfold, my main concern was survival. With my scholarship discontinued, I was anxious to convince the TCCU administration that with the money I had saved, I would be able to support myself in New York for a while. I was also able to persuade them to pay my tuition for one semester. I was on my way to earning my Ed.D in Curriculum and Teaching, with specialization in testing and evaluation of elementary school instructional material, but my sense of satisfaction was clouded by a serious dilemma. On the one hand, I had no intention of going back to Afghanistan for several reasons: firstly, with my US education, I had no chance of getting a suitable job without joining the Communist Party in my country; secondly, I could not bring myself to accept the party's ideology; thirdly, although Hafeezullah Amin had been my school principal at both Ibn-e Seena and Dar ul-Malimeen and the head of the Teacher Education Department at the Ministry of Education when I joined the Curriculum and Textbook Project and was likely to give me a position for old times' sake, I knew I could just as easily fall out of favor. And that would be dangerous, for he was a vindictive man who did not hesitate to imprison close friends and relatives who had incurred his wrath by failing to toe his line; fourthly, I had grave doubts about the communist regime's survival in an Islamic nation like Afghanistan, the majority of whose citizens regarded it with deep distrust.

Being in the US on a student visa, however, I could not stay and work there indefinitely. Anna Scott, whom I was seeing at the time and would, subsequently, marry, had been working, while pursuing her undergraduate studies, at the International Students' Office of her college and knew how to help me out of my predicament. We subscribed to the *Chronicle of Higher Education* and concentrated on the "international job vacancy" section. After sending out multiple job applications, I received a few offers. One was an offer for a teaching job at the Pahlavi University in Shiraz, Iran, but I it was clear that I would be on my own where accommodation was concerned and would have to look for a house upon arrival. Looking for living quarters in a strange country was no mean task and I preferred the university to make such arrangements on my behalf. The second offer of teaching came from the College of Education in Abha, Saudi Arabia, but the dean of the college who interviewed me in Houston, Texas, told me categorically that Saudi law forbade women to hold professional positions or even drive and my wife would have to abide by those restrictions in Abha, if I took up the offer. The third job offer was from Berzeit University on the West Bank of Occupied Palestine. An Afghan-American professor who was married to a Palestinian and teaching at the university sent me a personal letter discouraging me from accepting the post and advising me to look for employment elsewhere. She explained that if I decided to go to Palestine, I would have to travel through Israel. And the Israeli visa stamped on my passport might jeopardize my chances of ever getting a job in other Middle Eastern and Islamic countries. The fourth job offer I received was from Kuwait University to work at their newly established Center for Evaluation and Measurement. The contract was itemized and clearly stated the salary I would be earning, along with the benefits. My period of indecision was over. I would be going to Kuwait.

While negotiating for the job in Kuwait, I also had to focus on how I would defend my dissertation for the doctorate. My viva voce was scheduled for 8 May and Anna had booked the chapel at the United Nations for our wedding on the 20th. I had my priorities in order: the viva voce took precedence over my wedding, with our departure for Kuwait coming last. For my failure to obtain my doctorate degree would jeopardize both our wedding and our departure for Kuwait.

NINE

An Exam, a Wedding and a Job

A nna picked a white tunic and a smart two-piece suit for me to wear for my oral exam which would be held in a small room, possibly an office. I had to sit across the table from four professors from the Curriculum and Teaching Department at TCCU and answer their questions. They gave me twenty minutes to present a synopsis of the subject on which my dissertation would be based and elaborate on the steps I would take to implement the testing plan I had developed in my proposal. Once that was over, the questions began and went on for a couple of hours. I was then asked to go out and sit on the chair that had been placed next to the door. Twenty minutes went by as they debated on the merits of my performance in the viva voce. I felt myself tensing as the door opened and Bill Sayres came out. He smiled at me, shook my hand and congratulated me. Elated, I went back in and invited all of them to my wedding. I told myself later that by passing the oral exam, I had, in fact, earned two titles: that of "doctor" and of "husband."

I could now turn my attention to my wedding. Anna and I were both completing graduate school and had no money to speak of. We planned on having a nice wedding, all the same. Instead of splurging on a tuxedo for me, Anna helped me pick out a spiffy suit at Harry's that I would be able to wear to work after I got a job. She had bought a simple white dress for herself. I was no judge of women's fashions to be able to comment on its quality, but I thought she looked beautiful in it. Anna threw herself into the work involved in planning the wedding, while I worked on my dissertation. We called the Islamic Center, asking if we could book it for the wedding ceremony, but the person on the other end informed us it would cost us seventy-five dollars. We began looking for other options. We called the Unitarian place and the answer was the same. Then we found out about the building across the street from the United Nations. Owned by the latter, it had a chapel on the first floor and reception halls on each of the eight floors above. The person who answered the phone informed us that while they did accept donations, no fee would be charged. This was the best possible deal for us and we booked a reception hall for 20 May, going to Staten Island a day earlier to get our marriage license.

Looking back on our wedding, I am glad we did not get married in a place where one religion was considered superior to others. I have always been in favor of faiths that encourage belief in one God and focus on the ultimate objective rather than on the different ways of achieving it. The three Unitarian religions apparently promote belief in the existence of heaven and hell in the afterlife. Their advocates may have sound knowledge of who goes where after they die, but as far as I know, no one has come back from heaven or hell to give living beings on earth an account of life there or information on who is entitled to go and stay there. Adherents of Unitarian faiths can choose between highlighting their differences with the devotees of other religions and focusing on shared concerns to bridge the divide. The first option would lead, inevitably, to friction and disharmony; the second, to unity and peace. It seems, however, that the divide has deepened, since 11 September 2001, between the respective followers of Islam and Christianity and the gap shows no signs of closing, with Jews joining forces with Christians against Muslims and waiting, perhaps, for the same Messiah to save them.

If the situation is allowed to continue, it may become increasingly difficult to reverse the trend, as followers of the Unitarian religions sink deeper into the abyss they have created for themselves, and a return to the era of the Crusades may become a terrifying reality. The pressure to carry out as many conversions as possible that drives rival sects of the Unitarian religions is likely to create animosity and chaos, especially when its members are citizens of the same country. The Afghans have a saying about a person fleeing a shower only to stand under a downspout which is as close as one can get to the English equivalent: "From the frying pan to the fire." The invasion by the Indian Army of the Golden Temple, the most sacred place of worship for Sikhs the world over, in 1984 and the destruction of the Babri Mosque at Ayodhya by Hindus in 1992 are two sobering examples of the mayhem that single incidents can trigger off, with serious and irreversible repercussions. Over 2,000 people would be killed in the communal riots that followed the Ayodhya incident and the Indian prime minister, Indira Gandhi, was shot dead by a trusted Sikh member of her security team. The civil wars between Christians and Muslims in Lebanon, Serbia and Nigeria are other examples of the increasing hostility between the followers of these religions.

I have never lived in Serbia and Nigeria, but I did live in Lebanon from 1964 to 1969 and never imagined civil war was a possibility in a country whose citizens were smart business people, capable of resolving their differences through negotiations. What happened in Lebanon in 1975 was unimaginable, but it did happen and continued for a long time. And while I was not present to witness the tragedy, I did follow developments there from overseas. I found it hard to believe that someone would actually go inside the AUB campus to destroy its tower building, arrest three of the professors and kill three senior members of the university administration. Dean Ghusn had been the dean of the Engineering College and Dean Nujaimi, the dean of students, when I was studying at the AUB.

Determination, however, can take you far and the Lebanese have proved it. They did manage to bring the civil war to an end, although it took them seventeen long years to do so, and devoted all their efforts to rebuilding their stricken country. The damaged clock tower was rebuilt and the university stayed open. Having enjoyed my first experience of a country beyond the borders of Afghanistan, I have cherished every moment of my stay in Lebanon. It gives me a great deal of pleasure to learn that the AUB is not only open, but expanding and opening branches in other countries in the Middle East.

My country has not been spared either from the pitfalls of discrimination and separatism that have created a chasm between different sections of the population. I have lived through the disappearance of Hindus and Sikhs from the villages in Afghanistan. I remember my father telling me that there had been Hindus living in Khas Kunar when he was growing up there. They apparently owned property and lived normal lifes like everyone else in the area. I don't recall any Hindu or Sikh living in Khas Kunar when I was growing up there. I later heard that during communist rule in Afghanistan, some Kabul-based Hindus had laid claim to their ancestral property in Khas Kunar, but since I was living overseas at the time, I am not aware if they managed to reclaim it.

When my family moved to Chaghaserai, there were four or five Hindu and Sikh families living in Demkelay. Although I had never been invited by a family from either community to their home nor seen my own family asking them over to our house, it is a fact they were allowed to live peacefully in the village without anyone bothering them. I do remember the solitary Sikh and Hindu who each owned a shop in the local bazaar. The Sikh, Gurmak Singh, owned a general grocery store that stood next to the shop owned by Mullah Ghulam, a Muslim. Both had white beards and wore turbans. While Mullah Ghulam's beard was long and he wore his turban wrapped around a cap which he removed from time to time, Gurmak Singh's beard was folded and pinned under his chin and his turban sat snugly on his head. The Hindu, Lachmy Chand, ran a government owned fabric shop, selling his made in Afghanistan merchandize to his customers and probably receiving a commission on every sale.

Chaghaserai, renamed Asadabad, is now the capital of Kunar province. When my family lived there, it was the main center of Hukumrani, the regional government in Kunar. Khas Kunar, where we had lived earlier was a rural area, where each village had a cluster of local shops from which its residents bought provisions for their daily needs. In Chaghaserai, there was a small bazaar, where people from the area would shop. I am unaware of the reason that prompted local Hindus to move out of Khas Kunar, but I remember them living in Chaghaserai and going about their lives without hindrance. On Fridays, when Mullah Ghulam and other Muslim shopowners closed their shops at noon to make their way to the village mosque for their prayers, Gurmuk Singh and Lachmy Chand must have also closed their shops at noon to go home and have lunch with their families. I am sure they all came back to the bazaar later in the afternoon to reopen their shops and carry on with their business. Later, I would hear that the Hindus and Sikhs in Chaghaserai had had to leave for Jalalabad, the main city in the region, where there is a sizeable community of Hindus and Sikhs who have the freedom to worship at their own temples and pagodas.

It remains a mystery to me as to why, when the kind of harmony I have described is possible between different religions in less developed areas of the world, certain ultra conservative Muslims persist in regarding Christians and Jews as infidels, while some Christian scholars tend to look upon Muslims and even their prophet, Muhammad, as terrorists. Driven as much by belief as by emotion, religious affiliation is, to my mind, a very sensitive issue that needs to be handled with care, with due respect accorded to the right of each group to practice its faith. In my view, the initiative to bridge the existing divide between different religions should be taken at an international level to promote harmony across the world. I envision an international religious center, a kind of mini United Nations council, involving representatives from every faith, fostering a climate of mutual understanding so that all are able to live peacefully in villages, towns, cities and countries across the world. These representatives could be regularly rotated, as is the case at the Security Council. This council should be located in a neutral area, where representatives of all religions, instead of countries, could open offices and attempt to set up a dialogue with followers of other faiths during which they could explain the philosophy underlying their own religions. Since ignorance engenders fear, distrust and hatred of others, acquiring insights into other faiths would broaden the perspective of all and pave the way for a deeper understanding of and respect for religions other than one's own.

It was in the same spirit of religious harmony that Anna and I had chosen to get married at the United Nations chapel in 1978, for it was open to the adherents of all faiths. We had invited a small group of about sixty—family members and friends—to the wedding, but I am sure everyone enjoyed being a part of the ceremony and hope that the bachelors and single women among them, who had been unaware that such a place existed, chose it as the venue for their own weddings when they married later. Our wedding was scheduled for noon and, interestingly, the couple who got married before us was Jewish. We had planned our own ceremony. I myself had no family in the USA. So we invited friends who had taken an active part in planning our wedding and would attend the party that followed. My friend, Hashim Sahraee, read the standard United Nations text for the wedding ceremony. Anwar Husain came with his wife, Diana, and read a couple of verses from the Quran. The verses he chose from the Surah Hujurat, translated by Abdullah Yousef Ali, were as follows: "O mankind! We created you from a single (pair) of a male and a female, and made you into nations and tribes, that ye may know each other (not that ye may despise each other). Verily, the most honored of you in the sight of God is (he who is) the most righteous of you." Ashraf Ghani was my best man. Hashim's eldest son, Qaseem, was our chauffeur, and Anna's cousin, Jean Morrow, was our musician.

Following the wedding ceremony at the chapel, we all went up to the second floor, where a potluck party had been organized with recorded music to liven up the proceedings. Among the guests were Evelyn, Anna's mother, her aunt and her cousins. They were family. The rest were friends who had arrived from different countries. Bill Sayres came with his family and gave us a United Nations coin as a wedding gift. We still have the coin which we will always cherish. Phil Lange, my rotating Ed.D advisor and supervisor at the Curriculum and Textbook Project, had volunteered his services as the official photographer for our wedding. Thanks to his efforts, we have an album full of wedding pictures that become more precious as the years go by. And we have kept in touch with Phil, who had reached the grand old age of ninety-six when Anna and I visited him at his house in Sun City Center during our trip to Tampa Bay in November 2010.

To return to the period following our wedding, Anna and I spent the rest of summer editing my dissertation and arranging for it to be typed. Computers were not around at the time and the person who would type the dissertation had to be registered at the college. Fortunately, Anna found a friend working there and we entrusted her with the job. As she typed the dissertation, we would check it for content and suggest any changes that needed to be made. The job was finally done and the final copy approved. Now that all pending work was over and we were married, Anna and I piled our belongings into a rental car and left for Rhode Island to stay with her mother at the latter's place. As August drew to a close, we would prepare for our trip to Kuwait to begin our new life.

CHAPTER
TEN

Kuwait University

A nna and I had been given complimentary one-way flight tickets to Kuwait by the Embassy of the State of Kuwait in Washington, DC. And having just completed our graduation, we were rather hard up and had just enough money to cover the extra expense we might incur en route. We splurged that "extra" on a week's stay in Rome, where we stopped over to make up for our short, inexpensive honeymoon in New England earlier. Given her half-Italian and half-English ancestry, with the scales tilting heavily in favor of her Italian forebears, it was Anna who had chosen the Italian capital for our second honeymoon. I would be visiting Rome for the second time, having stopped there in 1966 during my tour of Europe while I was still studying at the AUB. Although I would revisit some of the sights, Anna's company made everything seem that much more enjoyable.

For both of us, it was an opportunity to unwind before starting life in a strange new country.

I was excited about taking up a job in an oil-rich country that was less famous than its Middle Eastern counterparts and I would be working as a staff member in Kuwait's one and only university. I had traveled abroad before and adapting to the ways of a new country and culture were part and parcel of my academic and professional life. It would, however, be Anna's first experience traveling to Europe. Besides, while I had a job to go to there, she had been issued a spouse visa and her immediate future was less clearly chalked out. While we were both optimistic that she too, would eventually find a job, Anna was more concerned than I was about how life in Kuwait would turn out. We hoped to rely on each other's support to get over the initial culture shock before we settled down, for our knowledge of Kuwait was scanty. It seemd ironic that while the USA's oil supplies came from this country, few Americans knew about it in 1978. Rhode Island, particularly, was almost provincial in its insularity and people living there neither knew much about what lay beyond their shores nor cared to explore it. In fact, Anna's mother, Evelyn, assumed we would be living in a tent in Kuwait!

It was in the last week of August 1978 that we arrived at our destination. As we emerged from the aircraft at the city's old airport, the summer heat was like an assault on our senses. Neither Anna nor I had ever been anywhere where the temperatures were this high. The airport terminal seemed very basic, considering the wealth at the disposal of the country in which it was located. The ground staff seemed unprofessional. We were asked to leave our luggage in a large room which looked like a warehouse. We were given some papers to take out to another office where they were processed and signed. The entire procedure took us about an hour.

When we came back to reclaim our luggage, we found it intact and handed it to the university driver who was waiting for us outside the terminal. The man explained that this being the month of Ramazan, the staff at the university guest house where we were supposed to put up were asleep, having risen before dawn for their first meal, because they would be fasting all day. He had, therefore, been directed to take us to a hotel for the night.

The car pulled up in the driveway of the Sheraton Hotel in Kuwait City and Anna and I went in, only to learn that a night's stay would cost us US$137. I surreptitiously counted the money in my pocket and was relieved to discover that I just had enough to tide us over for one night.

The next morning, we went to the bookstore-cum-gift shop in the hotel lobby and bought a small yellow phone directory. We looked for and found the phone number of the administration office at the university and dialed it. The person who answered was very helpful. He assured us that the university driver would come to the hotel and take us to the university guest house. He requested me to pay the hotel for our night's stay and promised to reimburse me later.

We spent the weekend and part of the following week at the Kuwait University guest house, where we did not have to pay for the meals we were served. Yousef, a Palestinian and our host at the guest house, was a competent chef and took our orders to prepare our meals. When our apartment was ready for us to move into, a university driver turned up at the guest house, loaded our luggage into the car and took us to Khaitan, a district east of the Airport Road between the Fifth and Sixth Ring Roads.

We were taken to an apartment on the first floor of a building. I noticed that apartments in Kuwait were located on levels above the ground floor. The ground floor was given over to storage rooms, parking spaces for the residents and a room for the security guard/manager. Our apartment had two bedrooms, a bathroom, a toilet, a kitchen and a spacious living room. We had enough space for ourselves and even for entertaining guests.

In the process of settling in, we opened the trunk in which Anna had packed her precious stuff, such as jewelry, perfumes and so on. We were horrified to discover that a great many of the boxes and cases inside the trunk were empty. It was obvious that the trunk had been ransacked and we knew exactly where that had happened. I now realized what the employees at the airport had been up to, when they sent us out to another office to have our papers processed and signed. They must have used special tools to pry open the padlocks on the trunk, stolen Anna's jewelry, perfumes and other precious possessions, and then padlocked the trunks again so skillfully that we could not tell it had been opened. Although we were shocked and furious, we swallowed our anger and let it go. I would like to mention, however, that it was the only such experience we ever had. A couple of years later, the new airport terminal was opened and departure and arrival procedures for passengers became more streamlined.

The university campus in Khaldiah, where I worked, was a fifteen-minute drive from our apartment. Since we did not have a car for the first month of our stay, we usually hitched a ride with other university faculty or employees who lived in the same apartment building. Sometimes, we took a taxi or a pickup truck to work. Anna and I bought our own car after a month and life got a little easier.

On our second day at the apartment, Anna had bought the local English newspaper, the *Arab Times*, and started reading the Jobs section for vacancies. She found one and called the Universal American School mentioned in it. The principal claimed it was an American school, because they followed the American curriculum, and offered her a teaching post right away. The school was run by two cousins from Lebanon, Waleed and Raja Abu Shaqra, who were quite unlike school administrators. As a new teacher, Anna had a lot of innovative ideas on how to improve the curriculum and the methods of instruction at the school, but met with stiff resistance and even had to put up with a form of intimidation when she offered suggestions. Waleed, the principal, even claimed, one day, that he could ruin her husband's life in Kuwait, in general, and at the university, in particular. Anna barely managed to survive the first semester at the school and while still working there, applied for a teaching job at Kuwait University. Selected as a candidate, she was appointed to teach English as a Foreign Language at the College of Allied Health and Nursing in the university's Shuwaikh campus. Anna started teaching at the university as soon as the second semester began.

Since I had an official letter from TCCU certifying that I had completed all the requirements for my Ed.D and that the degree would be sent to me in January 1979, I had assumed that I would receive the salary of a staff member holding a doctorate. Since, however, I did not have the degree in hand when I arrived in Kuwait, the university administration refused to honor the letter from TCCU and insisted on paying me the salary a master's degree holder was entitled to. I dispatched a letter to TCCU, explaining the issue, and requested John Vincent, a staff member I had known, to treat the matter as urgent and send me my degree as soon as possible. I received my degree in the mail either in October or in November and the university administration changed my name from "Mr. Safi" to "Dr. Safi" and adjusted my salary and benefits accordingly.

The next issue I had to resolve concerned my immigration status. Anna was a US citizen, but I had traveled to Kuwait on an Afghan passport, the same service passport I had entered the USA with and used while studying at TCCU. In order to be entitled to a flight ticket to the USA in summer, I had to be either an American citizen or a permanent US resident. I applied for a Green Card at the American Embassy in Kuwait and by the time the university began processing our papers for the summer vacation, my application had been approved and I had received my airplane ticket to the USA.

Kuwait University had campuses all over the city. The president's office and other administrative offices, as well as the Colleges of Science and Engineering, were located in Khaldiah; the College of Commerce, Economics and Political Science was in Adeliah; the Colleges of Education and Sharia were in Keifan; the Colleges of Arts and Education, Law and Sharia and Allied Health and Nursing were located in Shuwaikh; and the College of Medicine was in Jaberia. Later, the Department of Sharia would be separated from Law and the Department of Education separated from Arts and both Sharia and Education moved to their campuses in Keifan as colleges. There were rumors that the university had purchased a plot of land near the airport and was planning to move all the colleges and offices to the new campus that would apparently be built on that plot toward the end of the twentieth century. The university administration reportedly intended to move the whole university to the new campus by the year 2000, but years passed by and all the university did was upgrade the existing facilities for its administration and its colleges.

A shuttle bus was available for students to go from one campus to another. Faculty and staff members who did not own a vehicle or did not want to drive could take the bus too. I would take it several times from the faculty residence in Shuwaikh to my office at the Center for Evaluation and Measurement (CEM) in Khaldiah. Anna usually drove the one car we had, stopping on her way home to pick me up from my workplace.

The environment at Kuwait University was unique. While the Kuwaitis were very conservative and men and women were generally segregated in public places, the university was co-educational and students of both sexes could attend the same classes, eat at the same cafeteria, read in the same library and walk together on the campus, pretty much as students in a Western university would have done.

In this connection, I will never forget the parade organized on Gulf Road, between the Kuwaiti Towers and the Amir's palace, on National Day. It was 25 February 1979 and Anna and I would go and watch the parade together. I got so caught up in the general excitement that I recall climbing on the fence along the road to watch the parade and take pictures. It was as if I were watching Macy's parade on Thanksgivings Day in the USA. Men, women and children sat in moving decorated vehicles that represented various companies and government organizations. I don't remember how long I managed to perch on the fence, but I did take a lot of pictures. I now regret having lost all those snapshots, for it would be the last parade of its kind in Kuwait. I would not get to see another like it, for changes were afoot which would have a significant impact on the Kuwaiti social scene.

That very year, there was an attempt on the life of the Crown Prince, Sheikh Saad Abdullah Al- Sabah, when he was being driven in his car along the Gulf Road between the Amir's palace and the Kuwaiti Towers. That incident changed the security situation in Kuwait and the celebration of National Day became a private matter for the country's citizens and residents. After the Iranian Revolution in 1979, which would send the Shah into exile and bring the mullahs to power under the leadership of Ayatulloh Ruhollah Khomeini, the situation in Kuwait changed. There was a marked movement toward conservatism. As the years passed, an increasing number of women students began appearing in public in black robes that covered them from head to toe. To mark the distinction between Sunnis and Shias, Sunni women would wear a white veil across their faces while Shia women wore black ones.

During the academic year 1995-1996, I was teaching at the Girls' College of PAAET in Shamia. I usually had between thirty and thirty-five students in my class. Barring five or six, all had started using the veil. I remember one occasion on which I was taking the roll call and could not find a particular student whom I had never seen wearing the veil. Yet when I called out her name, she had answered. I finally detected her, because she had raised her hand to let me know she was present. I had not seen her, because she was fully covered and veiled. Henceforth, that is how she would appear in class. I did not, naturally, ask her why she had chosen to dress conservatively, but surmised that she had recently got engaged and her fiancé had obliged her to change her dress code. In keeping with local custom, Anna too, dressed conservatively while teaching at the College of Allied Health and Nursing affiliated to Kuwait University.

The CEM was a year old when I joined the acting director and his secretary as a specialist in September 1978. The acting director, Fathy Abu-Sayf, had been born in Egypt and was, like me, a permanent resident of the United States. As a non-Kuwaiti, this was the highest position he could hold in the country. It was an inference I would arrive at when I discovered that according to Kuwait's Constitution, the position of director was reserved for Kuwaiti nationals. Although abu-Sayf was in charge of the CEM, even his position as an acting director was a temporary one in the eventuality that the administration found a Kuwaiti citizen qualified enough to fill it. Where I was concerned, neither the employees at the center nor those in the administration could decide if I was a measurement specialist or an evaluation specialist. I suspect hardly anyone there knew or cared to know the difference. Even the acting director would introduce me as a measurement specialist to some people and as an evaluation specialist to others. Later, Ike (Ishaq) Ansari from Tennessee and Bob Norton from Utah would join us at the center. Ike was responsible for the planning and implementation of standardized tests at our newly renovated testing hall at the College of Law. The team of an acting director and three specialists would work together to develop the center.

We decided that the CEM would have two sections: one responsible for administering standardized tests such as the TOEFL, the GRE, the GMAT and so on to those applicants who were seeking to obtain an academic scholarship for higher studies in the USA; the other, for evaluating faculty performance during each semester. We developed a local questionnaire for this purpose and later bought the Cafeteria System for US$ 500.00 from Purdue University. Some relevant items were selected from the Cafeteria System, with or without modification. A schedule was set up with each faculty member; an employee or a student trainee would take the questionnaire to a classroom and distribute it to the students for them to fill up during the first fifteen minutes of the class period in the absence of the concerned professor. The administrator would collect the questionnaire from the students and the professor would return to class and take over. The results would be calculated by members of the CEM and a computerized report prepared for each faculty member. This confidential report would be sent to each of the concerned faculty members. The CEM would also prepare a summary report, without identifying the faculty members participating in the evaluation by name, and distribute copies of it among deans, heads of departments and other university administrators.

The CEM would administer the standardized tests in different halls of the university buildings for a couple of years, until it took over a spacious hall at the College of Law in Shuwaikh and converted it into a test-administration center. Kuwait University students and other educated young men would repeatedly send in applications to appear for the TOEFL and other tests, because they were eager to study abroad and especially in the US. In fact, we usually had more non-Kuwaiti applicants, because the opportunity for them to study in the local colleges was almost nil. I will explain the reasons shortly. The Kuwaiti graduates sat for the tests, because they hoped to obtain a government scholarship, but the non-Kuwaiti ones did so simply to get out of the country. The Kuwaiti government was, and probably still is, very generous in awarding academic scholarships to its citizens. During my time there, all a Kuwaiti high-school graduate needed to be entitled to such a scholarship was a letter from a college or university in the USA certifying that the candidate had been granted admission to a course there. And certain colleges in the US were willing to accept them as students if they managed a score of at least 500 in the TOEFL exams. The non-Kuwaitis, on the other hand, had to depend on the generosity of their parents to pay for their studies in the USA.

If non-Kuwaitis were eager to leave the country for pursuing higher education, it was not without reason. The criteria for admission to colleges in Kuwait were far more stringent for non-Kuwaitis. Only the offspring of non-Kuwaiti faculty members and ten percent of non-Kuwaiti high-school graduates with the highest scores were allowed to study at

Kuwait University or in other local colleges. Naturally, the exam hall, which had seating for 300 candidates and a sound system to play the aural-comprehension section of various tests, was filled to the brim when the TOEFL test was scheduled to be held, whereas the number of candidates who appeared for other tests was significantly lower.

I would like to elaborate on the respective cases of a Kuwaiti candidate and a non-Kuwaiti one who tried to obtain a scholarship to study in the USA. Abdullah was a Kuwaiti and a graduate of Kuwait University who had started working with me when I was Assistant Director for Curriculum at the Language Center. He was assigned to work at the center, because he was a candidate for a scholarship and had earned a score of 502 in the TOEFL exam. He had applied to various colleges and universities in the USA, but every time, his application was politely turned down. Frustrated by all the rejections, Abdullah ultimately turned to me for help. I asked Anna to intervene, because she knew someone at Rhode Island College (RIC), who could push Abdullah's case there. It was the right thing to do, because thanks to her efforts, Abdullah was accepted as a student at RIC to work on his Master's degree in English as a Foreign Language.

Abdullah arrived in Rhode Island in the summer of 1992, when I was there. We made a reservation for him and his family at the Marriott Courtyard and went to meet him at the airport. Abdullah landed with his wife, six children, a maid and fifteen pieces of luggage. He rented a house with a swimming pool in North Providence and sent his children to school. Abdullah was a full-time student, while his wife took some courses in English. A check would arrive from the Embassy of the State of Kuwait in Washington, DC, to cover all his expenses. Abdullah eventually received his Master's degree from RIC and went back to Kuwait to teach at the College of Education.

Consider, on the other hand, the case of Ashuq, who was originally from Afghanistan and had graduated from a high school in Kuwait. His father was a government employee, but that did not entitle Ashuq to a government scholarship. He sat for the TOEFL several times, but it would take him quite a while to gain admission to a college in the USA. He and his brother, Ehsan, finally managed to go to the US and, presumably, studied and worked there. Although I would never meet these young men again, I did get an opportunity to speak to Ehsan over the phone in 1999 and learned that he was living in Northern Virginia. I asked about his brother, to which he replied that Ashuq was working for a company as an engineer and traveling overseas most of the time. Ehsan added that his parents had also migrated to the US and were living in Maryland.

The evaluation program at the CEM was more difficult to implement. It was new and marked a departure from the traditional values of faculty-student relations in the Middle East and, particularly, in Kuwait. Until then, a teacher was considered the infallible authority on his subject and students were supposed to follow him unquestioningly. Most faculty members claimed that their students were not qualified to pass judgment on the merits or demerits of their teaching. On one occasion, I even received a phone call from the only female college dean at the university, asking me to go down to her office and explain the concept of faculty-performance evaluation to the heads of four departments at her college. I jumped at the opportunity and promptly presented myself at the dean's office, where I met her, along with the heads of department, and explained that the main purpose of our evaluation program was to offer the faculty an idea of how they were faring as teachers and to help them improve on the selection of course materials and update teaching methods used in the classroom. I was at pains to point out that the evaluation was not a one-shot study, but an ongoing process from which they could benefit, semester after semester, for years. I further explained that since the evaluation project was in a nascent stage, administrators should focus on using the results to help faculty members improve their performance in class. Relying on them to justify decisions relating to their promotion or demotion would be unfair. In this context, I would like to add that once again, it was the Kuwaiti faculty members who were at an advantage. Since they were the privileged ones with tenure, no action could be taken against them. Non-Kuwaiti faculty members, on the other hand, were hired on contract and their positions were, therefore, vulnerable.

The questionnaire for evaluation had two parts. Part One pertained to statements on the course material that could be positive or negative, with a choice of options for students to pick from that followed a five-point Likert scale ranging from "Strongly agree" to "Strongly disagree." Part Two contained positive or negative statements on the methods used by the professor to teach the course material and the same choice of options was available for participating students. A score against each statement would appear on the evaluation report, along with the total score for each of the two parts and a grand total for the whole questionnaire. We would include an open-ended question at the end of each part, enabling the students to not only express their opinions about the course material and the methods used to teach it, but also to suggest new items which could be added to the questionnaire in the future to make it more relevant to the evaluation. The reports of the results were sent to individual faculty members in sealed envelopes. Whether they chose to share them with the concerned department heads and the college dean was up to them.

Looking back on the seven years I devoted to managing and conducting the program, I can firmly conclude that student contribution was negligible. The professors did add a few items to the questionnaire, but most of the suggestions they made were redundant and did not add anything to what was already on the list.

During my eight years of employment at Kuwait University, I published research studies in reputed professional journals and made a presentation at an international conference almost every year. I was entitled to a two-month annual summer vacation, which Anna and I spent in the USA to escape the heat of Kuwait. If I had a paper to present at an international conference, the university usually paid my travel expenses or, at least, paid my round-trip airfare. I took advantage of their generosity to attend my first WCCI conference in Manila, the Philippines, in 1981. The main themes I followed in reporting at other conferences dealt with student admissions policy at Kuwait University, the course and instructor evaluation project and the career aspirations of Kuwait University graduates. I presented the reports at the American Psychological Association (APA) Annual Convention in Los Angeles and at the same convention in Washington, DC, in 1981 and 1982 respectively; at the WCCI Triennial Conference in Manila in 1981 and at the same conference in Edmonton, Canada, in 1983. I also presented them at the International Association for Educational Assessment (IAEA) International Conference in Oxford, England, in 1985.

When I returned to Kuwait after its liberation to work at the university's Language Center and later at the Public Authority for Applied

Education and Training, I realized that the privilege of attending international conferences had been restricted to Kuwaiti faculty members. Even when I tried to get funding from some offices outside the university, I found that such privileges for non-Kuwaitis had been discontinued.

Anna continued to teach at the Allied Health College. In the meantime, we had been blessed with three children: Khushal, born on 5 February 1980; Jamal, who arrived on 12 November 1981; and Shireen who appeared in our lives on 21 February 1984.

In 1985, Anna's mother fell ill. Being her parents' sole offspring, my wife made a decision to leave for the USA, taking Shireen along with her, and stay with Evelyn in Rhode Island. Fortunately, in Anna's absence, we had a live-in maid to take care of us: Paulina Machado, a pleasant woman from India, whom our children addressed as Auntie. Between the two of us, Paulina and I managed to take care of Khushal and Jamal until Anna returned from the US. However, having left her full-time job in Kuwait before her departure for Rhode Island, Anna now had to teach at the College of Arts on a part-time basis. Soon after she returned to Kuwait, however, Evelyn's condition took a turn for the worse and in June 1985, my wife received the news that she had passed. Anna had to make an emergency booking and leave for the USA to make arrangements for her mother's funeral.

This was the beginning of a number of developments that would serve as a warning that our days in Kuwait were numbered. The following year, when I landed at Boston's Logan Airport, an Immigration Officer took me aside, led me to a private room and informed me that I had been out of the country on my Green Card for eight years. He advised me to establish my residency in the USA or elsewhere. During my summer vacation, I submitted the immigration papers to the court, hoping for an extension. Extension was denied in October 1986, when I was back in Kuwait. Meanwhile, Anna had fallen ill and had to be hospitalized. She stayed there for a few days, but the doctors could not find anything serious enough to justify extending her stay and she was discharged. But it did not stop her from continuing to feel unwell and complain constantly about her poor health.

Anna's indifferent health and the lack of proper facilities at the local hospitals was, in fact, one of the primary reasons for me to contemplate leaving Kuwait and settling in the US. The second was the risk of losing my residency in the United States if I kept traveling overseas on my Green Card. And the third one was the job offer of an evaluation specialist that I had received from the Department of Education in Rhode Island.

As our summer vacation in the United States of America drew to a close in 1986, we left for Kuwait, hoping that the US immigration court would grant me an extension so that I could stay in Kuwait for at least another year. Anna's cousin, Jean, called us in September and informed us about the rejection notice from the court, saying that I had to be back in the US by 26 October. Given the circumstances, I was forced to type out my resignation letter and deliver it to our director, Jasem Al-Kandari, at his office the day after I had received the notice. Much as I disliked the awkward position of having to leave my job in the middle of the academic year 1986-87, I was left with no option but to head for the US. The only silver lining that edged the dark cloud of despondency was the job I had waiting for me.

Departure from Kuwait and Life in the USA

A s a non-Kuwaiti staff member working at Kuwait University on a private contract, in which the university was named the first party and I, the second, I could tender my resignation any time without stating a reason. Similarly, the university could end my contract any time during the academic year without assigning a reason for it. However, by submitting my resignation a month into the academic year, even though I had a legitimate reason for it, angered the Kuwait University administration and the director of the CEM, in particular. I felt I was justified in taking the decision, for as a non-Kuwaiti, my position was vulnerable and if a Kuwaiti replacement had been found for my post, none of my expertise would have helped me to save my job. As a non-Kuwaiti, I could neither own property nor live on government handouts.

And as a family man with young children, I was aware of the urgency of securing my future.

Besides, the USA was my country of residence. By fulfilling the requirements for residency, I could become a citizen. And American law was impartial, entitling every citizen to the same rights. I had a job waiting for me and we had a house. In addition, we had saved some money that we could invest in the US to cover emergencies and secure our future. I thought returning to the USA and starting life again was the best decision I could have made under the circumstances.

We arrived in the USA on 21 October 1986, just in time for the court order to keep my residency from expiring. Our two-bedroom ranch house in Narragansett, Rhode Island, had been rented out, but we negotiated with the tenants and persuaded them to move out, so we could live there. Our firstborn, Khushal, began attending second grade. Jamal was a kindergartener in the Narragansett Elementary School. At two, Shireen had not yet reached school-going age. I traveled to Providence to report for work at the Department of Education. We planned to buy a house somewhere near Providence to shorten the time of my commute. Anna was optimistic that she could find a job there too. Life was looking up again.

It was in Narragansett that our children witnessed their first snowfall. They found it hard to believe that what they had seen in cartoon movies—the stuff falling from the sky and making the whole world look white—was real. Our next-door neighbor had two sons almost the same age as our own and the four boys spent hours in the front yard, making a snowman and a snow house.

In December 1986, we bought a house in the Gaspee Plateau section of Warwick and moved in. Our home in Narragansett was rented out again. Driving to work from our new home took a mere twenty minutes, cutting my usual commute to half the distance. Moreover, the house was walking distance from the Wyman Elementary School which Khushal and Jamal now attended, having taken a transfer from their old school in Narragansett. In fact, the school was so close by that one day, our pet cat followed Jamal there and actually peeped in through the window while he was in class!

Anna was equally pleased with the location. Born in Cranston, a five-minute drive from our new home, she had always wanted to return to her familiar surroundings. When she was a child living in these parts, there were apparently few houses in Gaspee and people from neighboring areas were still exploring the possibility of building their homes here. It was, in those days, an affluent locality and few people could afford to buy a house in Gaspee or in Governor Francis Farms across the street from it. By the time we started looking for a house, Gaspee had become a stable, middle-class neighborhood of resident-owners, with no tenants in our immediate vicinity. Our house had a private backyard, where we installed a playground for the children. We made friends with some families who had children of the same age and we were content. Our first Christmas was a joyful one, with a large group of neighbors standing on our front lawn and singing Christmas carols. Compared to our life in an apartment in Kuwait, our neighborhood in Gaspee seemed the ideal place to raise our family.

Optimistic about our future, I went out to South Kingstown and bought a five-acre parcel of land for our future home. I expected the scenic area overlooking vast expanses of farmland at the foot of the hill around Route 2 to develop and even envisioned a time in the future when our children would graduate from high school and attend the University of Rhode Island from our new home nearby.

I was on a high and felt the same confidence about my career. I was sure I had the basic knowledge required to handle the demands of my job at the testing and evaluation section of the Department of Education. As its representative, I attended a meeting on evaluation in New Hampshire. However, being a newcomer to the department, I was unable to participate fully in the discussions, though I did feel I had answered most of the questions to the best of my knowledge. I subsequently had a chance to visit a few schools and even presented the evaluation results to a group of public-school teachers. Certain that I was on the right track, I hoped to keep working at the Department of Education to support my family.

I did not know that my first six months at the department were the lull before the storm. The storm broke when my supervisor declared that she was dissatisfied with my performance on the job and warned me that she expected significant progress before my year-long probation period was over. I got the distinct feeling that she was not optimistic about my prospects there and was contemplating termination of my contract long before I had been given a chance to prove myself. Despite being under tremendous pressure, I managed to visit a few schools and even discussed the results of a pilot testing with the administrator of a school district. The main purpose was to go over the responses to each multiple-choice question on the list and take a call on retaining, deleting or revising it. I did not think I had done a bad job, falling back on the knowledge I had gained from my measurement courses at the graduate school and on the experience I had acquired at the Center for Evaluation and Measurement at Kuwait University. However, my supervisor had also attended the meeting and it seemed that she did not share my confidence in my abilities. Although I was allowed to stay on for a few months after the first year ended, the termination of my contract was inevitable and I was asked to resign.

The department gave me the option of working for a further six months, while I looked for another job, but I was hurt and angry, stubbornly believing that my dismissal was illegal. I turned down their offer. Unperturbed, the department went ahead with my termination. I received the letter in the mail and thought it was the end of the world. The termination letter would ruin my chances of getting a job in education anywhere.

The problem was compounded by the fact that I was new to Rhode Island and did not know how to look for a job in the area or even in the US. Although I did get a chance to attend a few job interviews, my humiliating experience at the Department of Education cast a shadow over the sessions and I was traumatized by interviewers asking me if I had ever been dismissed from a job. Wherever I went and whatever I did, I felt the termination of my contract hanging like a dark cloud over my head. Going back to Kuwait was no longer an option. I had to stay in the US to fulfill my residency requirements. Moreover, Kuwait University was not likely to rehire me, because the administration disapproved of foreign contractors resigning from their jobs in the middle of an academic year. So here I was, blacklisted both in Kuwait and in the USA. I found myself caught between the devil and the deep blue sea, with nowhere to escape to.

Now jobless, I had to dip into my savings to pay the premiums relating to my family's health and life insurance policies. I was going through the worst days of my life and feared that we would exhaust our savings and the whole family would end up on the streets as a result. To stem the tide, I took up temporary jobs. I was working at the cash register of Cumberland Farms, a grocery chain in Rhode Island, when an employee of the Department of Education came in to buy something. The moment he recognized me, his eyes welled up and he left the store immediately.

While the department was still working on my termination, Anna fell ill and had to be hospitalized for almost a month. The doctors could not arrive at a diagnosis, suspecting she was suffering from some tropical disease she might have picked up in Kuwait, and put her through a battery of medical tests. The day she was diagnosed with lupus I went to the hospital, Pawtucket Memorial, and tried to comfort her. Those were my last days on the job. Soon I would be unemployed and without health insurance for either my family or myself. I had three young children to bring up and a house with a mortgage. We still had some money, but it would soon run out. While I held Anna in my arms, my mind kept wandering to the future that seemed dark and devoid of hope.

Desperate to earn a living and unsure of obtaining employment in Rhode Island, I started looking for a job in education in other states. Traveling beyond Rhode Island for an interview meant covering long distances and paying steep fares. I became a regular visitor to the state's Employment Security office, where I had listed my résumé, going there to do a computer search of job vacancies. I even went to a private employment agency in Providence and wrote them a check for $1,000, so they could scout around for suitable positions for me. Wondering, however, if I had been too hasty, I post-dated the check to give myself a chance to discuss things with Anna. Sure enough, my wife vetoed the idea of the private agency right away and asked me to stop payment on the check, which I did the following day. After being repeatedly disappointed, I decided to find a job in a field other than the one in which I had specialized.

I had always been lucky dealing in real estate and tried moving into this area in an effort to forge a second career for myself. I thought I could work at a full-time job in this field, until I found a job commensurate with my qualifications. I could even earn additional income from it after getting a full-time job in education. I had bought my first house in 1980 from a full-time teacher who was a part-time real-estate agent and working for Executive Realty. He had confided in me that he had taken up this second career, because the salary from his teaching job was not enough to support his large family. I felt he would serve as an appropriate role model for me. I applied for a real-estate license and passed both the local and national requirements to become a licensed real-estate agent. I started working for Century 21, but realized I wasn't making much headway. Passing the tests and getting a real-estate license was much easier than succeeding at the job. Although I worked hard, at no office meeting did my name come up as the agent who had sold any property. I even tried to sell my own house in Narragansett, but naively priced it above the going market rate. As a result, it stayed on the market for a long time. When I finally conceded defeat and realized I would not be able to sell it, I took it off the market. Since my job at Century 21 was on a commission-only basis, I ended up earning very little money. Once again, I was at a dead end and decided that real estate was not for me.

Now I had to look for a job which would bring me a regular income. It was while I was at an all-time low that I responded to an ad for a job in inventory taking, because it did not require any experience. The company representative was waiting at the local employment security office. By the time I walked in, he was quite fed up of waiting, because no other candidate had showed up. I was the first. He asked me to report to work on Monday the following week. The person who had hired me was a crew chief who would take his workers to a drugstore, mainly CVS or Brooks, to take inventory of the merchandise on display, the medicines in the pharmacy and the additional stock in the storeroom. One person was assigned to take stock of the medicines in the pharmacy. We were paid by the day and the duration of that day depended on the number of employees reporting to work and the size of the store we were supposed to inventory.

We had to meet in a parking lot early in the morning and take the company van to work. While riding in the van, half the employees usually smoked and no one ever thought of objecting. When I did bring up the issue with the crew chief, he replied that while he was not a smoker, it did not bother him to sit in the van with men who were. It was obvious that I had to adapt. Almost everyone in the crew was younger than me, including the crew chief. The drop-out rate was so high that after a month, I felt as if I were a senior employee of the company.

The fifty-seven dollars a day I was earning were certainly not enough to support a family of five. Desperate to make ends meet, I applied for a second job in the local grocery chain, Cumberland Farms (where the employee from the Department of Education would see me later and be moved to tears by my plight), and my application went to a store manager, originally from India, who was managing a store in South Providence. I told him that I was free to work in the evenings. Soon, I found myself waking up early in the morning to meet the crew chief in the parking lot and going to work with him. On the way back from work, I would drive to the store after the van had dropped me off. Then I would go home and sleep for a few hours before waking up to the next working day. Sometimes, I would go home early in the afternoon, because the store we were inventorying was a small one and every member of the crew had shown up for duty. On those days, I could rest for a few extra minutes before leaving for my second job at Cumberland Farms. However, it was the exception rather than the rule. Sometimes, we had to spend almost the whole day in a store to finish our inventory. On such occasions, I would call the store manager and inform him that I would be going directly to the store. The store closed at ten p.m. and I was allowed to leave right after. I would usually arrive home half an hour later and go to sleep right away so as to be ready for my day job the next morning.

In 1990, I resigned from my job at the grocery store and went to work part-time for the national census. This was a temporary job which lasted till the end of spring and required me work till ten p.m., checking the accuracy of information provided by the individuals who had answered the questions on the form. As soon as I was through with this job, I bought a kiosk of dried fruit and nuts at Rhode Island Mall. The mall was open twelve hours a day from ten a.m. to ten p.m. six days a week. On Sundays, it was open from noon to six p.m. I had two employees and each would open the kiosk in the morning on alternative days. I would take over at four p.m., when I returned from my inventory job. I would close the store and would arrive home at around eleven p.m.

Given my tight schedule, I could not afford to even think about my level of exhaustion. Christmas Day and Easter Sunday were probably the only two days of the year during which the mall was closed, offering me some reprieve from my punishing routine. We went to Connecticut to spend one Easter Sunday at a friend's house. Our hosts were Kathy, Anna's childhood friend, and her mother, Susan and we were meeting at Kathy's parents's house in Newington, Connecticut. With Anna and the other two ladies busy cooking and the children watching television, I sat down beside Kathy's father who had Alzheimer's disease and could neither speak nor move. I must have dozed off the moment I sat down, because when I opened my eyes next, the food was ready and the table all set. I felt embarrassed for not being there to help the ladies, but I must have subconsciously enjoyed the quiet environment after a long hectic period, because I felt very relaxed when I woke up. However, the thought of being in a kind of professional limbo was never far from my mind. I knew I was wasting my time and not making a conscious effort to think about the future. But I could not get over my disappointment at not being able to find a job in education.

In 1989, I received my US citizenship and was free to travel again on my American passport. I wasted no time in getting in touch with my friends in Kuwait and received news in 1990 of an opportunity to work in the Language Center at Kuwait University as Assistant Director for Curriculum. I sent in my application for the post, but before I could progress further, disaster struck. On 2 August 1990, I had no idea what was waiting for me when I went to the parking lot as usual and boarded the van to join the inventory crew. On the way to work, I listened to the news on the radio and saw my future collapse in seconds. Iraqi President Saddam Husain's forces had invaded Kuwait and occupied the country. No one else in the van was affected by the news, but I was devastated. I could only hope the occupation would be a temporary one.

Back in Kuwait after its Liberation

Kuwait's liberation on 26 February 1991 (later declared a holiday, right after the country's National Day that is celebrated as a holiday on 25 February) opened the doors, once more, for employment opportunities in the country. As soon as the Iraqi forces had been forced to withdraw, I contacted the Kuwaiti Embassy in Washington, DC, and reminded Richard Stevens, the man in charge of Kuwait University affairs, about the status of my application. The embassy had apparently been working on my case. For I received a phone call from them, asking me to report for an interview with Dr. Elham Al-Bassam, Director of the Language Center, who had expressed an interest in hiring me.

I remember taking the train from Providence and arriving in Washington after seven or eight hours. I had an overnight reservation at a hotel for which the Kuwaiti Embassy was paying. The next morning,

I went to the embassy to see Dr. Al-Bassam and took the evening train back to Providence, arriving early in the morning.

I had called ahead to inform the crew chief that I would be waiting for the company van in Providence, rather than in our usual parking lot. I boarded the van when it arrived and it was soon moving along Interstate 95 South and heading for a CVS store or pharmacy in Connecticut that was near the state border with New York. I found it ironical that I had just returned from Washington, DC, by the 95 North route and was heading right back again in the opposite direction. Fortunately, the store where we were to take inventory turned out to be a small one, ensuring we could return home by the afternoon. I continued working for the company and waited to hear from the embassy. The good news arrived toward the end of summer and I was on my way to Kuwait by the end of August 1991. However, this time, I would be traveling alone, because given Kuwait's precarious situation in the early days following the withdrawal of Iraqi troops, its government had advised against spouses and children accompanying non-Kuwaiti employees. I did not intend doing so anyway, because I did not want to disrupt the lives of Anna and our children.

If we had survived in the US so far, it was because of her teaching job at Johnson and Wales University and the health insurance we had taken out for the family. However, her salary alone was not enough to make ends meet. I considered the job in Kuwait a blessing, because not only would I be earning a respectable salary once again, I would also be working in my area of specialization. The downside was that I would have to live in Kuwait during the academic year, far away from my family, while Anna single-handledly juggled three jobs: taking care of the children, teaching at Johnson and Wales and supervising the manager of the kiosk we owned at the Rhode Island Mall. Buying the store had been a big mistake, because it had turned out to be like the oil-producing factory I had read about some years earlier. The story went that the factory was producing oil to lubricate its machines, while the machines were being lubricated to produce more oil. But no one knew what greater purpose that oil served. In my own case, that store brought us no income and was even running at a loss. I would have sold it off, but did not have enough time to put it on the market before leaving for Kuwait. Besides, Anna had assured me she would be able to help the manager run it. I hated burdening her with so many responsibilities, but didn't seem to have much of a choice.

I knew I would miss my children badly. The day before I was to board the flight to Kuwait, I took them to an ice-cream parlor in the neighborhood called Dear Heart. We strolled down to the shop, bought our ice creams and started walking back home. On the way home, my daughter, Shireen, asked me why I had to leave home and go overseas. I don't remember how I answered that innocent question, but however clever my answer might have been, it could not assuage my guilt over leaving Anna and the kids to fend for themselves. All three of my children seemed dejected at the prospect of my departure and expressed their sadness in unique ways. When I finally left for Kuwait, my heart stayed back in Rhode Island.

I had corresponded directly with Kuwait University before my departure and its administration was already aware of the date and time of my arrival. As I landed at the airport and passed through Immigration, I found the university driver waiting for me. The heat was unbearable and the signs of war-related damage clearly visible along the road to Kuwait City. Most of the buildings had been destroyed and the air was heavy with smoke from nearly 350 oil wells—of more than 700—that were still burning. But the Kuwaiti government and the people were determined to rebuild their country as soon as possible and restore normalcy.

The driver explained that the university accommodation allotted to me was not yet ready and he had been instructed to take me to the Meridian Hotel in Kuwait City, where I would be put up temporarily. When I entered the hotel, I found signs put up by the management apologizing for the establishment's less-than-pristine appearance and warning guests that they might have to bear with a water shortage, the consequences, no doubt, of the ravages of war. I would stay in that hotel for a month until the apartment at the university housing complex in Shuwaikh was ready for me to move into.

During my stay at the hotel, I would take a walk every evening, exploring different parts of the city and trying to recall how they had appeared during the years I spent there earlier with Anna and my growing family. In 1978, I recall the city and its suburbs being on a development spree, as it were, with new roads, buildings, parks and other facilities coming up in the short time we spent away from it during our summer vacations. After the Iraqi invasion, those constructions and facilities had been partially or totally destroyed. In fact, every edifice that had been damaged or ground to dust reminded me of the old days. The beached ship along the Arabian Gulf, which had been remodeled and opened as the Marriot Hotel, then renamed the Al-Salam Hotel, was an utter wreck. The surrounding area looked like an abandoned lot, with no human movement around it at all. The Kuwaiti Towers stood intact, but the area around them had been dug up. One day I visited the Gold Souq (market) behind the Sheraton Hotel. The *souq* was piled with rubble, although cleaning operations were under way. The plate-glass fronts of the stores there were riddled with big bullet holes and it looked as though they had been prised open either by the occupation forces or by local vandals and thieves exploiting the situation to loot the jewelry on display. One day, I made my way to the Old Souq and found it partly open, with the stores stocked. As I was strolling around the place, I noticed a Kentucky Fried Chicken sign. When I approached it, however, it did not look like a restaurant at all and I realized the place had been converted into a currency-exchange business without anyone bothering to remove the old sign. However, construction work was progressing swiftly everywhere in the city, thanks to the initiative taken by the government and the Kuwaitis themselves.

As I was walking around the city one evening, I ran into Saleem and his wife who were surprised to see me back in Kuwait and invited me to their house in Salmia. He was working as a sales associate at Boodai Company which imported construction machines for resale or rent in Kuwait. Saleem, his wife and his three offspring (the eldest, Meena, was in her teens, the two younger ones still children) had stayed back in Kuwait during the war years and gone through the agony of occupation and the chaos it had brought into their lives and those of others residing there. I could not help noticing the very visible scar on Meena's body. While cooking one day, she had apparently received an electric shock that had very nearly killed her. I remembered Saleem's tasteful collection of oriental rugs from my last visit to his home, but saw no signs of them this time. I gathered he must have sold them during the occupation to raise money to feed his family. He told me about his volunteer work during the occupation, when he had undertaken to carry food and water supplies to those in dire need. I could detect the telltale signs of exhaustion on the faces of every member of the family, but they were obviously relieved that now with the war over, they could pick up the pieces of their lives at school, at home and at work.

While Saleem had decided to live through the occupation, his brother-in-law, Fazlullah, had made a very different decision and had quite another experience to recount. When Anna and I had come to Kuwait for the first time in 1978, he had just graduated from Kuwait University and started teaching in a Kuwaiti government high school. A couple of years later, Saleem had followed and put up at Fazlullah's house in Romaitha, but subsequently brought his own family down to join him. During the occupation, Fazlullah had joined a group of Afghans and having discussed his plans with them, decided to leave an occupied Kuwait with his family and head out in their car to Iraq and from there through Turkey and Iran to Baluchistan. They had arrived in Peshawar, Pakistan, after an arduous two-month journey. It was a great risk to take for the father of six children, the youngest of whom, Maisa, was just a week old. When he eventually returned to Kuwait with his family, he would move into the second floor of the very house where he had lived earlier.

Recounting the hair-raising story of his two-month-long journey to Pakistan. Fazlullah described the hassles of going through various checkpoints and the strange demands made by the militia along the way through Iraq, Iran and part of Pakistan, until their arrival in Peshawar. On one occasion, he had gone to a hotel in Tehran to find out if he could put up there with his family. The manager had apparently asked him if he was a Sunni or a Muslim before giving him an answer. Fazlullah also described his one-week stay in the Sistan Baluchistan area, prior to crossing the border from Iran to Pakistan.

Later on, I would come to know about the experiences of other Afghans who had gone through the trauma of occupation or left Kuwait, only to return to their jobs in the country once the Iraqi troops had pulled out. For them, it was a second home and they had taken pains to adapt to the country. Almost all the Afghans I would meet there had learned to speak Arabic and communicated easily with both Kuwaiti and non-Kuwaiti Arabs.

They were less fortunate than other foreign nationals, however, when they tried returning to their country of origin during the occupation. With the Russian forces having left Afghanistan to the *mujahideen*, the country was in a state of total anarchy. About a quarter of the population had crossed the border into Pakistan and Iran and were living in refugee camps. Warlords had taken over, dividing the country into small pockets of influence and coercing the local population into supporting them. Checkpoints had been established to mark these areas, each the domain of a warlord with its own set of "laws." Travelers passing through had to pay fees at every checkpoint they crossed in order to arrive at their destination. Those traveling long distances were forced to cross several checkpoints and pay fees at each of them. It was obvious that law and order had taken a backseat in Afghanistan, while repression and torture held sway.

It was hardly surprising, under the circumstances, that the Afghans in Kuwait should be the only foreign nationals to feel uneasy at the prospect of returning to their own country. Many, like Saleem and his family, had, therefore, opted to stay on in Kuwait and endure the hardships the occupation brought upon them. Others, like Fazlullah and his family, had decided to go to Pakistan or Iran and stay with relatives in the refugee camps. Not that they could have done so indefinitely for fear of exhausting the period that covered their guest status. They would, therefore, have sought to return to Kuwait as soon as the situation in that country permitted it.

Curiously, while the embassies of other countries helped their compatriots in times of distress, the Afghan Embassy in Kuwait did quite the opposite. During my earlier stint in Kuwait, I remember all the employees of the embassy being communists, with some belonging to the Khalq faction and others to the Parcham faction. If the Political Attaché was from one, the Commercial Attaché would most certainly be from the other. Representing two hostile factions, they were, nonetheless, united in one quest: to clandestinely sell liquor from their official quota to local businesses and hotels at more than four times the subsidized price the embassy personnel were entitled to and to overcharge Afghans for renewing their passports on an annual basis. Holding, as I did, an Afghan passport during my earlier stay in Kuwait because of my American Green Card, I remember paying between thirty-five and 135 Kuwaiti dinars (a Kuwait dinar was the equivalent of over three US dollars) to renew it annually. There were even rumors that embassy officials were selling Afghan passports to local Palestinians who did not have passports of their own and could not, therefore, travel outside Kuwait. And it was alleged that during a two-year employment period, each embassy staffer could make enough money through such clandestine means to leave Kuwait and settle in another country of his choice. The embassy was, therefore, the last place where an Afghan would seek help.

The university housing complex in Shuwaikh, where my three-bedroom third-floor apartment was located, consisted of five twelve-story buildings and a few old one-story villas accommodating about 500 families belonging to faculty and staff. Some of the shattered windowpanes at the housing complex had been replaced, so the signs of war were less visible. The structure of neither the apartment buildings nor the nearby villas had sustained any damage. The area around my apartment building was a junkyard full of old and broken furniture that had been taken out of various apartments awaiting renovation and refurbishing. The faculty club had been damaged and work was in progress to repair the swimming pool and the building, which contained offices, recreation rooms and a restaurant. I would walk on the paved road inside the campus every day and pass by the power-distribution room. I could see that it was empty and full of torn wires. One day, I went in and found a guy from Eritrea working there. He introduced himself as James and explained that he was an employee of the American AT&T Company. On another occasion, I noticed two men inside. I went in and found James with his supervisor, who had come down from the State of Washington. They were trying to reconnect the wires to restore electricity to all the residential buildings in the area. Across the street from my apartment stood a small grocery store, a branch of the supermarket at the Shamia Cooperative, where the residents would buy their grocery and articles for the household.

The Language Center, where I was employed as Assistant Director for Curriculum, was located across the street from the football stadium on the Shuwaikh campus. Although most of the center's buildings were in ruins, a few rooms had been renovated to serve as offices for the director and other officials. The Assistant Director of Administration was an Egyptian. The director was a cousin of the Emir of Kuwait, who would occasionally drop in for a couple of hours. There was no way we could have overlooked his presence when he was there, because all the secretaries and those in charge of serving coffee would be running around, trying to cater to the director and his royal guest. On one occasion, I was invited to the director's house, along with a large group of guests. Located in Yarmuk across the Fourth Ring Road from the university campus in Khaldiah, the place turned out to be no less palatial than a castle, where the director lived with his large family. The centerpiece was a high dome, which could actually be opened in pleasant weather to let the fresh air in. The room beneath the dome, abundantly decorated with plants, looked like a rainforest café. It did not surprise me to learn that an Iraqi general had appropriated it for his own use during the occupation.

My two secretaries at the Language Center were both from India. Since they had been employed at the center from way before the occupation, they were familiar with the kind of work that had been done there. We spent a long time sifting through the dust and rubble, looking for information about the English Placement Test (EPT), which had been developed at the center and had been used for placing students in the English language units at various colleges. It was evident that someone had forced open the file cabinets with tools specially made for the purpose, because they were lying open, with their contents scattered all over the floor. I remember spreading something on the floor and squatting on it so that I could collect all the papers lying under a thick layer of dust. I managed to recover all the test items on the CDs and flash cards that lay on the floor. We also recovered other papers on the work that had been done at the Language Center and reports prepared on test administration throughout the years. We redeveloped the test-item bank and compiled information on test administration. By the beginning of the school year, we had a copy of the test to be administered for placing students in the Language Program according to their proficiency in English.

During the school year, I organized a program for training high-school graduates and government employees—all Kuwaiti citizens—who had been selected for academic scholarships in the USA. The training program was conducted late in the afternoon, after the official work hours. Using a selected sample of test items from TOEFL publications for placement purposes, we divided students into four groups and employees into two groups. The instructors for the program were selected from among those who were already teaching at the Language Center. The program covered the duration of the semester and every student's progress was periodically evaluated. At the end of the program, the students were expected to sit for the official TOEFL test and pass it to qualify for a scholarship. By the end of the school year, however, I had been removed from my post at Kuwait University and was unable to follow up and find out how many of the candidates had passed the TOEFL and obtained scholarships.

Which brings me to the issue of my one-year contract, renewable by mutual agreement between my employer, Kuwait University, and me. It was the kind offered to all non-Kuwaiti administrative staff members at the university and while no conditions had been stipulated as to how the two parties would go ahead and terminate that contract, should the need arise, it had never occurred to me to worry about it. I had no idea what lay in store for me.

Although I had been working at Kuwait University for a fairly long time, I had not yet mastered the art of saying the appropriate things in the presence of high-ranking officials who had the power to hire and fire non-Kuwaiti faculty and staff members. I probably made one of the biggest mistakes of my life when I dropped in on Dr. Shuaib, the university's new rector, at his office. During our conversation, he asked if I was planning to bring my family over to Kuwait. I replied that in the country's current scenario, it would probably not be the right thing to do, but I would consider the possibility in the future.

I dug my own grave when I emerged from the rector's office and stopped by to see the director of the rector's office; in other words, the rector's personal secretary, Izzat Saleh, an Egyptian who had worked there for several years. Anyone working or teaching at Kuwait University had to know Izzat, because he was the main instigator behind hiring and firing university personnel. I sat down to chat with him and he offered me bottled mango juice to drink. During our conversation, I casually asked him about the possibility of changing my status from "staff" to "faculty." Faculty members were entitled to higher salaries and more extensive benefits. Unfortunately, I did not realize that by uttering those seemingly innocuous words, I had dropped a bombshell. I had touched a sensitive nerve and from the expression on Izzat's face, it was clear to me that my days were numbered at the Language Center and that my contract would not be extended under any circumstances. Izzat had been holding the same official position from before my first time in Kuwait in 1978. Rectors would come and go, but he remained in place, advising every one of them on administrative issues, including the recruitment and dismissal of faculty and staff members. I remember talking to Jasem Al-Kandari, a Kuwaiti citizen who had become dean of the College of Education after leaving his position as director of the Center for Evaluation and Measurement. And even he confessed that he feared Izzat. It had not struck me, until that moment, that the all-powerful Egyptian could also ruin the careers of Kuwaiti faculty members, the only ones with tenure.

The gist of my conversation with Izzat must have been reported to the director of the Language Center, because I found her behavior decidedly frosty when I next met her. Earlier, she had treated me like a colleague and during our meetings, we would have cordial discussions on everything related to the center, including ways of improving its performance in the future. But on that day, I found her trying to cut short our conversation and make it clear that I was not welcome. No matter what I said, her response was one of utter indifference, as though I were a rank outsider. I heard from someone at the center that the director had expressed her intention to hire a real American in my place. The fact that I too, was an American citizen did not matter, because I did not look like a true-blue American. I should have paid heed to what Pauline, an ESL instructor and an American from Massachusetts who had acquired Kuwaiti citizenship after her marriage to a Kuwaiti, had told me one day in a parking lot in Shuwaikh. She had quipped that although I was an American citizen, I did not look like an American. I had joked in response that she, on the other hand, definitely looked like a Kuwaiti. I had known that physical appearance went a long way in Kuwait, but had obviously underestimated its importance

Meanwhile, I continued working at the center. However, with thoughts of Izzat's intentions at the back of my mind, I got in touch with friends and explored the possibility of finding another job. The only other place for post-secondary education in Kuwait was the Public Authority for Applied Education and Training (PAAET), which consisted of four colleges: Basic Education, Business, Medical Technology and the Institute of Technology and Communication. There was a vacancy at the Measurement and Evaluation Center (MEC), which I could fill. The one person I knew there was the director of PAAET, a Dr. Ahmad whom I approached, explaining my shaky position at the Language Center. Impressed with my résumé, he offered me the position of Assistant Professor and Measurement Specialist.

After my services were terminated at the Language Center, I decided to take a break and return to the US during the summer. With the new job in hand, I stayed on a little longer in order to sell the kiosk I owned at Rhode Island Mall, because it was becoming too much for Anna to handle, along with her job and other responsibilities. The women hired to run the kiosk were unequal to the task and it had turned out to be a losing proposition all the way. Most businesses at the mall usually made a profit during the holiday season in the fourth quarter of the year. I took over the management of the shop in September and stocked it with fresh merchandise. The holiday season was approaching and I listed it with a real-estate agent who would later become a friend. In December 1992, I was able to sell the shop, just in time to return to Kuwait in January, the following year, to take up my job at the Measurement and Evaluation Center at PAAET.

As a Measurement Specialist, I was entrusted with the responsibility of developing a program for the evaluation of faculty performance. I had done this kind of work at Kuwait University and had at my disposal copies of the material we had used at the Center for Evaluation and Measurement. Using them as a template, I developed a tool for evaluating the faculty performance at PAAET. The offices of the director and other staff members were located in the city, whereas the college campuses were scattered all over Kuwait. While PAAET was constructing an office complex for its use on the campus of the College of Basic Education for Men along the Third Ring Road in Adailiya, it had rented a floor of a commercial complex, where local businesses had their offices, for its director and other staff. When the new PAAET complex was completed after two years, I moved into my new office on the third floor of one of the buildings.

Unlike the university, PAAET did not have housing facilities for its non-Kuwaiti faculty and staff members. The faculty received a house allowance for renting residential accommodation, the amount being commensurate with the kind of accommodation required: bachelor's quarters or accommodation for a family. I moved into a one bed-room furnished apartment in Jabriya and settled in. My commute to work was along the Fourth Ring Road and that was the route I traversed every day.

After moving to my new office, I decided I knew enough Arabic to start teaching a course in Educational Research at the College of Basic Education. It was convenient that the administration had given me an office at the Adailiya campus, where the college was located, with other faculty members at the Curriculum Department. After the evaluation program was up and running, I started teaching a course in Educational Research at the College of Basic Education. At first, my Arabic was a bit rusty, but it improved with practice and I was able to teach my course and communicate with my students in fluent Arabic.

While the colleges at Kuwait University had been co-educational, the colleges at PAAET had separate campuses for men and women students. While the College of Basic Education for Men was located in Adailiya, the College of Basic Education for Women was in Shamiah. The faculty members who taught at both the campuses had offices in both. Unlike the university, PAAET had no shuttle bus for students to travel in and they drove to their classes.

I soon discovered that I was paying an exorbitant rent for my furnished apartment. With the same money, I could have rented a two-bedroom apartment in the same area. I found one and moved into it after furnishing it. The area on the other side of the Fourth Ring Road from Jabriya is called Hawalli. Most of the estimated 400,000 Palestinians, the largest community in the country after the Kuwaitis themselves, had lived there before the Iraqi occupation. It had been a congested locality, thick with shops and residences, and I would buy *kharouf* (roasted sheep with rice and nuts) from a restaurant called Zahrat al-Madayen (flower of the cities). But now Hawalli was a ghost town, as I discovered when I visited it one afternoon. Most of the houses and shops had been destroyed or abandoned.

Its fate was sealed when the Palestinian leadership supported Saddam Hussain in his military takeover of the Kuwaiti occupation. I am not sure of exactly when it happened, but shortly before or soon after the country's liberation, there was a noticeable Palestinian exodus from Kuwait. I thought of Ibrahim, a Palestinian who had worked at the Housing Department of Kuwait University before the occupation.

If anyone living in the university residence had a problem, all he would have to do was go to the housing office and look for Ibrahim, who was always there to help. When I went back in 1991, I too, had gone to the housing office looking for Ibrahim. He was not there and, knowing the situation, I did not inquire about him either. However, on an impulse, I did ask Muhammad, a Kuwaiti employee at the housing office, about Ibrahim's whereabouts and was advised never to mention his name again. According to Muhammad, Ibrahim had apparently worked as an informer for the Iraqi occupation forces, misusing his knowledge of those living in the residence to report on Americans and other Westerners present in the country. Having understood the situation, I made no further efforts to find out what had happened to Ibrahim or, for that matter, to other Palestinians I had also known Afeef, the janitor at the Center for Evaluation and Measurement, whom we would address as Abu Munzir; in other words, "father of Munzir," his eldest son, the first of a brood of ten, being so named. Abu Munzir had lived in Hawalli and invited Anna and me to the wedding of his third son, Nasser. After returning to Kuwait, I visited the Center for Evaluation and Measurement to see if Abu Munzir was still there. Evidently, he was not.

THIRTEEN

Departure from Kuwait and Back in the US

I had now been living in Kuwait for five years without my family. While I was only able to visit Anna and the children in summer, they had come down from the US to Kuwait just once during those five years and spent two weeks with me in the spring of 1994, when the city was still recovering from the Iraqi invasion and occupation and most of the destroyed buildings had been reconstructed. During those two weeks, I would take my family to visit some of our old friends and drive around the city, reviving our memories of the places we had seen together earlier. I was in a carefree mood, for the change in administration at the Public Authority for Applied Education and Training (PAAET) was still two years away and I had no idea that my seemingly secure job would be in jeopardy.

In February 1996, I was invited to visit the Ali Institute of Education in Lahore, Pakistan, for two weeks. I requested an additional week so I could spend time in Peshawar with my old friend, Jalat, who was then working at the United Nations. During my stay at the institute, I visited a couple of classes and made a series of presentations to the students that focused on the methods of planning and conducting a research project in education. I also made a presentation to schoolteachers on how to construct and administer classroom and placement tests and use the results. I was even ready to install the Statistical Package for Social Sciences (SPSS) on the computer so that the students and faculty could use it to analyze the results of their research instruments, but they did not have the software to permit such installation. I advised the administration to buy the software and promised to not only come back and install it on their computers, but also to train the students and faculty on how to design and implement a research instrument and analyze the results. I was even ready to revisit the institute for a week to instruct the students and the faculty on the use of the software.

The last time Jalat and I had seen each other was as far back as January 1977, before my departure for the US. Naturally, I was eager to see him again and stayed with him and his family for a week, hoping, at the same time, to see members of my own extended family and, particularly, my siblings, Wadood and Jahantab. That week was the last one in the holy month of Rozha, following which Eid al-Fitr would be celebrated to mark the end of the period of fasting. We sent a message through a truck driver to Jahantab's husband, Jameel, in Jalalabad, informing him that I was in Peshawar. My sister received the message and informed Wadood, who lived in Kabul. The following day, Wadood, his wife and four of their children arrived to see me. Jahantab too, joined me with two of her children. I was meeting my niece and nephews for the first time, because none of them had been born when I left for the USA in 1977. Had I thought it safe to cross the border into Afghanistan with my American passport, I would have visited as many relatives as I possibly could. But by this time, the Burhanuddin Rabbani government in Kabul was shaky and the Taliban were gaining in strength and making their presence felt. It was, nevertheless, a great consolation to be meeting my siblings after nineteen long years.

While my friend and my family had gone through far more trying situations than I had during their lives under the *mujahideen* and the Taliban, it is a measure of Afghan hospitality and adaptability that neither the host nor the guests ever complained about the living conditions or the lack of privacy, with sixteen of us sharing that three-roomed house, with a single bathroom between us. Jalat and his wife slept in the room with the attached bathroom. The rest of us would spread out a mattress anywhere there was space on the floor and sleep. If we needed to use the bathroom, we had go through the room our host shared with his wife. But despite the discomforts and the inconveniences, we enjoyed every minute of our time there. We spent a happy Eid together and when the time for my departure drew near, we were despondent.

As soon as I arrived back in Kuwait, I heard the news of the change in administration at PAAET. When I reported for work on the first day following my vacation, I met Dr. Waleed, who was also working at the Measurement and Evaluation Center. While I hadn't known him initially, I had been acquainted with his brother, Sameer, during my time at Kuwait University. A month after I first joined the center, I noticed that he had shut his office here and moved to his other office at the Department of Curriclulum in the College of Basic Education. It did not occur to me to wonder if my arrival at the center had prompted the director to ask Waleed to move out. Years passed and when I started teaching at the college, I would meet Waleed and even socialize with him, accepting his invitation to dine at his house with his family. We were both doing research and he needed my help to analyze his data. He had the software, Statistical Package for Social Sciences (SPSS), on his computer at home and appealed for my help on one occasion. When I went over to his house for the purpose, I found he had gone out and it was his wife who met me at the door and let me in. I was both surprised and touched. In Kuwait, only those visitors are allowed into a home in the absence of the master who are either relatives or deemed close friends. I had concluded mistakenly that Waleed not only looked upon me as a colleague, but considered me a friend too.

In hindsight, I feel my arrival at the center had aroused feelings of insecurity and rancor in Waleed and he was just biding his time before the opportunity to get back at me presented itself. That opportunity would come in 1996 when the PAAET administration was reshuffled and Dr. Ahmad, the person who had hired and supported me, lost his job. The College of Basic Education had a new dean and the center, a new director. By this time, Waleed had been appointed Head of the Curriculum

Department. It was unusual for a non-Kuwaiti to be inducted into that post, but his appointment might have had something to do with the recent marriage of one of his daughters to a Kuwaiti citizen. Something else may also have worked in his favor. He had managed to publish a book on Educational Research in Arabic, attributing its main authorship to Dr. Abdullah, the former Head of the Department. When the same Dr. Abdullah became vice-dean of the college, what could have been more natural than for him to use his influence with the new dean and have him appoint Waleed as the new head of the Curriculum Department?

No sooner had he assumed his new responsibilities than Waleed questioned the legality of my appointment in two different positions, brought the situation to the new dean's notice and convinced him that terminating my services would be the appropriate step to take. By losing the faculty position, I would become an administrative employee and my salary would be reduced to one-third of what I was being paid. Moreover, I would no longer be entitled to the housing allowance and the complimentary round-trip ticket home during the summer vacation. The new Director of the Center, Dr. Fauzia, was aware that I would not compromise and accept my modified position. It was time for me to leave PAAET and, consequently, Kuwait.

To me, it seemed like a hostile takeover by the new administration, because Dr. Ahmad, who had once talked to me as he would to a good friend, began ignoring me. The semester had been over in June and I could leave Kuwait, but decided to stay back and make an effort to extend my contract. I visited the office of the new PAAET director, Dr. Mudhaf, and was told to go and talk to Waleed. Unbeknownst to me, the letter terminating my contract had already been written and someone had to deliver it to me by a specific date. On an evening I am unlikely to forget, Waleed called me around six p.m., expressing his desire to visit me. Unsuspecting, I invited him over to my apartment and he promptly delivered the letter to me in person. I would later learn that going by the regulations for termination, it was the last day for delivering that letter. I suspected Waleed was behind it all, but was not sure if he was the only one. Well, he had had his revenge.

With all doors closed, there was no way I could stay in Kuwait. Leaving the country in the middle of summer 1996, I returned to the USA—this time, for good.

Once back in the USA, I was ready to move on and focus on my new life. By now, I had come to the conclusion that I was getting too old for undertaking temporary jobs. I had realized that as the years went by, it was increasingly difficult to find a job in one's area of specialization. I needed to do some serious rethinking if I were to support my family, get ahead in life and build a nest egg for Anna and myself when we retired. My children were about to graduate from high school and would need financial assistance so that they could obtain admission to colleges of their choice. Anna was working at Johnson and Wales University. I had been saving a part of my salary in Kuwait, which I had carried in the form of a bank check when I took the flight back to the US. I recall the Customs Officer at the airport asking me what I intended doing with the money and my reply that I was planning to put a dormer on my house in the US. The officer didn't have anything more to say and had handed the check back to me.

While employed at the Rhode Island Department of Education, I had sat for the National Teachers Examination (NTE) and received the license for teaching and administration at elementary schools. I now renewed my license and got a job as a substitute teacher at Pawtucket Public Schools. In 1997, I became a long-term substitute teacher. My daily allowance went up from seventy-five dollars to $165 and I was called to work almost every day, five days a week. Anna and I were earning enough to meet our daily expenses, but we did not have any savings that could have gone toward sending our children to college or securing our old age. Although I was working in Providence, I was open to offers of a better-paying job in education or in another field. My dismissal from my job in school administration in Rhode Island had made it virtually impossible for me to obtain a similar position there.

With my career prospects looking bleak, I responded to a blind ad in the *Sunday Boston Globe* for the job of a linguist. With my knowledge of four languages—Pashto, Dari, Arabic and English, I thought I might have an edge over other candidates for the post. I received a response to my application and was informed by the organization that had placed the ad that I would be among the most sought-after candidates they had fielded so far. I then received a phone call from the organization, informing me that I was required to appear for a test in the three foreign languages I knew and translate a one-page text from each of those languages into English. I received the three texts and was given an hour to translate each and fax the translation to the office. I began working on the first translation at nine a.m. and had completed them all and faxed them by noon.

A week later, I received a phone call from a person who informed me that director of the organization would be coming to Providence to test my aural skills. In a room especially reserved for the purpose, I began taking the test at nine a.m. When it was over and the director had been through my translations, he announced that while those from Pashto and Dari into English were excellent, the one from Arabic was less than promising. However, the gentleman was satisfied enough with my performance to offer me a contract of employment. I signed it promptly. Looking through my papers much later, I would find the date: 24 July 1997.

The new job was in Northern Virginia and I needed a clearance to begin working. The clearance was going to take a while, but I was in no hurry. I was teaching and earning some money to supplement Anna's income to meet our daily expenses. I also had the option of working in the new office on weekends, with an open invitation to go to the DC area, whenever I had the time, and work for the new office. I took advantage of this option and worked in the new office on most weekends and public holidays. I spent the whole of summer at the new office in 1998 and was informed that I could start working there full-time by the end of August.

While I did so, I still had to wait for my clearance to come through and mentioned it to my new boss one day. He heard me out and promised to get back to me in a week's time. True to his word, on the Thursday of the following week, he came to my office and informed me about my full-time employment at the new organization. Since I had been employed as a substitute teacher before I joined my new workplace, I had no obligation to notify the Providence Public Schools before becoming a full-fledged staff member of another organization. It was a matter of luck that I had received this offer just as Khushal was graduating from high school. Anna and I could now afford to send him to Salve Regina University at Newport, Rhode Island. It helped that our firstborn, a committed student, had received a partial scholarship to study at the university. As a Resident Assistant, he was also entitled to free housing and money for incidental expenses. All Anna and I had to do was cover the rest of his expenses until he graduated.

Meanwhile, I had rented an apartment a couple of miles from my new workplace and settled in. During that year, I would also buy a new townhouse that was then under construction and the family would come over for a visit soon afterward. When Khushal graduated from Salve Regina University in Criminal Justice, I invited him to come over to the DC area so that we could both look for a suitable job for him. This would help him pay back the remaining portion of the student loan of $35,000 he had taken earlier, for I was still contributing to its repayment through mandatory monthly instalments. Khushal is now gainfully employed and lives in Washington, DC.

When Jamal, my second son, graduated from Pilgrim High School, he was accepted at Roger Williams University in Bristol, Rhode Island. He had chosen architecture as his major and historical preservation as a subsidiary subject, but a year later, changed his major study area to social studies. Jamal was more fortunate than his older brother, because he was able to graduate without any loans to pay off. The credit, of course, goes to my wife. Since she was working at Johnson and Wales, which was affiliated to Rogers Williams, Anna was entitled to tuition assistance for one of her children. Jamal was the lucky one. Johnson and Wales paid his tuition for four years until he graduated. Anna and I covered the rest of his expenses, for room, board and athletic activities. Following his graduation, Jamal worked for the March of Dimes mission at the Central High School in Providence until the end of August 2007, then accepted a teaching position in Massachusetts in September the same year.

Our daughter, Shireen, graduated a year later than her classmates from the Metropolitan High School in Providence and started studying at the Community College of Rhode Island (CCRI), but her performance in most of the courses she had taken was unsatisfactory. We got her transferred to Northern Virginia Community College in Loudon County, Virginia, but she decided to take a break and started working at Starbucks, moving on later to work at the CVS pharmacy. In the beginning of 2005, she became pregnant and gave birth to a son who arrived nearly three months before his due date. After Brody's birth on August 17 2005, Shireen took a psychology course at NOVA, but completed it with a C grade, which convinced her that raising a child was a full-time job that covered twenty-four hours a day and seven days a week. Brody's father lived with us for eight months, but having him with us did not turn out to be a pleasant experience and we had to ask him to move out. He moved to Rhode Island to live with his mother. Shireen now lives with us and is trying to adjust to her new life. The court in Loudon County awarded her sole custody of Brody and we share the responsibility of raising him.

When Jamal graduated from college, Anna decided that it was time for the family to get together and live as a unit. She resigned from her teaching job at Johnson and Wales after fifteen years of service and we sold our family house in Rhode Island in the summer of 2004. It was a very difficult decision for Anna, because we had been living in that house for eighteen years. Our children had been very young when we moved into the neighborhood and they had grown up with friends they did not want to leave. We moved to Northern Virginia and began living in our townhouse. Then we sold the townhouse and invested the money in a new house in South Riding, Virginia. We have been living in that house since April 2005.

Anna's first job here was that of a reading specialist at Youth for Tomorrow. She was, at the same time, taking evening courses at George Mason University to get her doctorate. She now understands the importance of that degree, because not having one had held back her promotion at Johnson and Wales and prevented her from becoming a full-fledged professor. She has completed the course work and is working on her portfolio to get her doctorate. The rest of us are here in DC; only Jamal is still in Rhode Island and visits us once in a while. Although I tried convincing him that teaching jobs were more easily available in northern Virginia, our son feels comfortable living in Rhode Island. The area we live in now is growing very fast and new schools are being constructed to meet the growing needs of the residents. I read in the newspaper that Loudon County needed 800 new teachers and school administrators for the school year, 2007-08. However, the economic situation is deteriorating, the housing boom coming to an end and the County administration contemplating ways to scrimp and save in order to compensate for the deficit in its budget.

FOURTEEN

Family and Relatives

I n Afghanistan's patriarchal society, relatives from the father's side are considered members of the same extended family, whereas relatives from the mother's side lie outside this group. The extended family in my country usually consists of a married couple, their sons, the latter's wives and their children. The father remains the head of the family as long as he lives. The mother usually supervises the daughters' activities and takes care of the household. When a son gets married, he brings his bride over to his parents' house. When a daughter gets married, on the other hand, she becomes a member of her husband's family. When parents pass on, the sons inherit the family property. They usually live together under one roof, as long as there are no disputes between them and they have enough income to sustain themselves. However, with growing families and space at a premium, disputes are inevitable. In such an eventuality, the brothers usually divide the property between themselves, in conformity with Sharia, and build their own small family compounds in the same area, provided the entire property is large enough to accommodate all the households. A woman is entitled to half of her brother's share of the property, but usually lets him have it. Those sons in the family who can afford to eventually buy their own property usually sell their share of the ancestral property to one of their male siblings and move out. But generally, male siblings live together and consider themselves members of the extended family.

My father and his three older brothers, for example, lived in the same family home that belonged to their father, Abdul Ali, while it could accommodate them all. All four sons helped their father, a *Jula* (weaver), in his business. They would buy cotton from the farmers and use the *alaji*, a locally made hand-operated gin, to separate the seeds from the fiber. Using a hand-operated spinning machine called a *tsar-kha*, the women would then spin the fiber into thread, which would be woven by men on a hand-operated loom to produce a kind of rough fabric called *khamta*. Neither my grandfather nor his relatives in the trade had a retail outlet for selling the fabric and villagers would come to their house to buy it. My uncles were able to generate enough business to support their families. But after they passed, the demand for the fabric dwindled, because tastes had changed and people preferred factory-made textiles for their durability and superior finish. Local shopowners began bringing factory-manufactured fabrics from Kabul and Peshawar and selling them in the area. *Khamta* was now a thing of the past.

My grandfather depended less on my father, his youngest son, than he did on the others, because they worked full-time in the business. My father was less involved in the business, because he went to school and focused on his education. As soon as he was able to earn enough to live independently, he bought his own property and moved out of his parents' house. It was while working for the government that he married my mother. Although I considered myself a member of the extended family, I was actually born in my parents' house. My case, however, is somewhat different from that of most Afghans, because as my parents's firstborn, I only have memories of growing up in a nuclear family. My father's eldest brother, Mehmed Wali would pass away while still living in my grandfather's house. His only child, my cousin, Rawoulf, would come to live with us, when his mother, my Aunt Haleema, married again, choosing Faqeer Mehmed, my grandfather's third son, as her second spouse. Like my father, my cousin would also move out, once he had bought his own property, but would take his mother and his stepfather over to live with him. Faqeer Mehmed had three sons with Aunt Haleema: Abdul Qudus, Abdul Wahab and Abdul Qadeer. The daughter born to them died in childhood. My grandfather's second son, Sayed Wali, was married to Aunt Mulko. They too had three sons: Omara Khan, Wakeel Khan and Jalal Khan. My father's first cousin, Omar Khan, was a weaver. So was Ameen, Omar's nephew and son-in-law. When income from the weaving business dwindled and the trade itself became obsolete, Omar and Ameen grew desperate in their quest to find an alternative means of livelihood and began looking for other work.

Like a few other villagers from Khas Kunar, Omar started going to Peshawar to work as a daily laborer. In the spring season, when citrus fruits were harvested in abundance, there was high demand for labor in Peshawar and residents of Khas Kunar would rush there to earn some extra cash. Winter being a slow season for farmers in our village, they would travel over the Shalai Mountain, cross the border into Pakistan and, after a daylong trek, arrive in Gandau, the tribal area. From there, they boarded a vehicle for Peshawar. On arrival, they would stay on right through the spring harvest, until the citrus fruits had been picked from the trees. Once the season was over in Peshawar, the people from Khas Kunar would return home in time to harvest their spring/summer crop.

Ameen had been working around the house and helping Omar with his business. Grateful for his help, his uncle had married him off to his daughter. Although Ameen could not find any work either, I don't remember him ever going to Peshawar like his uncle to earn some money during the slow season. My father's other first cousin, Hazrat Wali, married a woman from the *Kulalan* (potter) community and moved to live in Da Kulalanu Banda (the local equivalent of the potters' village). Another cousin, Saleh, lived in Kunar village and was a *Padawan* or herder, who would take cattle owned by villagers out to graze every day. It was the job of residents in every village to take their cattle out early in the morning after the cows had been milked and gather in a designated place. The *Padawan* was present to ensure that all the cattle were in before leading them to the *jaba*, the grassy land along the river, or to the desert between the Shalai Moutain and the residential area.

The cattle would graze until late afternoon. The *Padawan* would bring them back to the gathering place at the village from where their owners would collect them and lead them home. Although there would be a *pada* (herd) of cattle from each village grazing in the *jaba*, the *Padawans* were able to keep their animals separate from other herds and bring them safely back home every evening without losing track of a single one. The *Padawans* were paid a share of the farmers' crops at harvest time. The village carpenters, blacksmiths, barbers, *Jalawans* and Imam too, were paid by the farmer for their services in the same way.

When I was growing up in Afghanistan, every family in Khas Kunar was directly or indirectly involved in agriculture. Those directly involved were the farmers who cultivated their own farmland or someone else's, looked after it and harvested the crop. Some of them did both at the same time, because the income from their own parcel of land was not enough to make ends meet. Those involved indirectly in agriculture helped the farmers either through the services they provided them or by buying their products. Among this group were the carpenters, blacksmiths, *Jalawans*, weavers, barbers and *Padawans*.

As local agriculture becomes increasingly mechanized, the way farming was done earlier will change slowly, but surely. For with mechanization making inroads into farming, it will save the farmer both time and effort if he hires someone else to prepare the soil, sow the seeds and harvest the crop. Of course, the daily routine of farming will continue to be followed, with the farmer spending his day on the field, while his wife carries his homemade midday meal out to him without fail. But the backbreaking labor that farming entailed earlier may become a thing of the past. Moreover, the fees a farmer had to pay other workmen like carpenters and blacksmiths to maintain his equipment will be reserved, instead, for the person who brings his machinery down to the farm to prepare the soil for cultivation and harvest the crop. There is a third fee that the farmer will no longer have to pay. I have heard that the bridge constructed on the Kunar River near the White Mosque has made the *Jalawans* redundant and the farmer need no longer pay for their services with a share of his harvest.

196

Considering the situation from the point of view of the carpenters, blacksmiths, *Jalawans* and others who had once provided essential services to the farmer and depended on him for their livelihood, the future appears bleak. The carpenters may yet survive by concentrating on making wooden spoons and legs and bars for cots and taking up carpentry work for the houses, schools and mosques coming up in the area. The blacksmiths, for their part, could turn their focus on maintaining agricultural machinery. The jobs of barbers, Imams and *Padawans* are still safe, because local farmers and other villagers will need their services.

To return to the subject of family and relatives, my mother had five siblings in all—two brothers and three sisters. Both her brothers lived with their parents. While the older one managed the property, the younger one went to school. They lived in peace, until the young brother graduated from high school, married and had his own family. Tensions rose between the siblings and finally, they were left with no alternative but to divide the property, the house and the land they had inherited from their father.

My stepmother Gul Bebu's father and uncles were carpenters, having inherited the profession from both their parents' families. They repaired yokes and plows for farmers, who would pay them in kind, giving them a share of the crop at harvest time They worked in their small courtyard during winter and under the mulberry trees in their gardens during summer. In their free time, they made wooden spoons and legs and bars for cots which were locally used as benches during the day and as beds at night. Since cots were in great demand, the carpenters did brisk business. Gul Bebu's maternal uncle was a contractor who would undertake individual projects involving carpentry work at sites where schools, mosques and private houses were coming up. Her brother helped their father on serving their clients, the farmers. During the slow season, however, he would join his maternal uncle, helping him to meet his contract deadlines.

The people living in Khas Kunar belong to different tribes. Over the years, they have intermarried and tribal affiliations are now less clearly defined than they used to be in the past. In fact, many Afghans from the region have established their loyalty, instead, to their families and occupation-related clans. My father's family, for example, belonged to the clan of weavers, while my stepmother's came from the carpenters' clan. Similarly, there lived in the village families of potters, *Jalawans*, judges and *Sayeds* (descendants of the Prophet Muhammad), among others. It was not imperative for a person born in one clan to remain affiliated to it for the rest of his life. One of my father's cousins, for example, would become a *Kulal* (potter). Another became a *Padawan*. The *Jula* clan would exist in name only, after the local demand for *khamta*, the fabric they wove, dwindled and the trade eventually became defunct.

Bandai, my mother's village, built by her great-grandfather, is different, because his descendants have been steadfast in maintaining their affiliation to the Mohmand tribe. Villagers from Bandai have intermarried with those from other areas without surrendering their tribal identity. As a child, I remember a strong community feeling prevailing in my mother's village. I was not merely considered a nephew by my maternal uncles, but also by their cousins and every other villager in Bandai. Whenever I visited the place, everyone would address me by the Pashto equivalent of "nephew." There would be much affectionate teasing, with my uncles referring to me as a *Krangalai*, "the person from Krangal." I no longer remember why they did so. As a child, I may well have alluded to a group of people from Krangal village in the mountain region of Pech as "the people from Krangal." Nowadays, the Krangal I read about in the newspapers is sadly different from what it used to be. It is described as the valley of death for overseas forces battling the al-Qaeda and the Taliban.

My father was the first member of his family to leave the weaver's trade. And this was facilitated by his own father, who thought he had enough help from his three older sons to be able to spare his youngest who was allowed to attend the local elementary school, where Grades One to Four were taught. My father recalled Amanullah Khan being the king of Afganistan during that period. Amanullah had, in fact, ascended the throne in 1919, when his father, Habibullah, was assassinated. Overthrown ten years later, he would go into exile, choosing to live in Italy for the rest of his life. My father was a year older than the last monarch of Afghanistan, Mehmed Zahir Shah. While my uncles stayed home, helped in my grandfather's business and got married, my father's determination to get ahead in life, after graduating from the elementary school, took him to local and regional mosques, wherever he was welcomed, in fact, for further studies. Having learned to read and write, he worked for the government for a year as a volunteer, without earning a salary. The director of his office gave him his meals and enough pocket money to take care of his other expenses. How my father's benefactor was making that much money to be able to feed him and meet his incidental expenses is, of course, the million-dollar question.

It was while working for the government in Pech as a treasurer, a salaried employee, that my father married my mother. As I have mentioned earlier, my birth would be followed by the birth of two siblings who died early. But Wadood arrived later, followed by Jahantab. By the time he started going to elementary school, we were living in Chaghaserai. While my sister, despite her intelligence, would be unable to go to school for reasons I have already explained, my brother would go to the local elementary school, graduate from there, and continue his education at the military high school in Kabul. He finally graduated from the Air Force Academy as a first lieutenant, with a major in Air Defense. Jahantab is now married to one of our relatives from Kunar and living with her husband and children in Jalalabad.

My half-brother, Torialai, and all my three half-sisters, Najiba, Latifa and Ghotai, were more fortunate. They were school-going age when the family settled in Imam Sahib and all of them had a chance to get an education and graduate from high school. My youngest half-sister is married to my cousin Rawouf's son and lives in Kabul. My other two half-sisters live in Imam Sahib and teach in the local school there. My half-brother has a shop and used to work at the Spinzar Company, where our father used to be an employee.

**

I was on my winter vacation at my father's house in Khwaja Ghar after completing the first year at the College of Education at Kabul University, when he, along with Gul Bebu, asked me if I would be interested in marrying her younger sister who was my age. My answer was, of course, an emphatic no. I softened the blow by explaining that I would be going abroad on an academic scholarship and did not like the idea of leaving my wife on her own for several years. If my father seemed skeptical about the sincerity of my response, he was justified.

My real reason for turning down the proposal was my aversion to the idea of becoming my father's brother-in-law and sharing the same set of in-laws. I secretly felt my parents should not have come forward with such a proposal at all. I suspected it had been my stepmother's idea in the first place and my father, being so much older than her and easily manipulated, hadn't had the nerve to shoot it down. For my stepmother and, perhaps, her mother, I was tempting bait, because by marrying me, Gul Bebu's sister would accomplish two things: become the wife of a college graduate and stay in the family. I was angry, hurt and dismayed that neither my father nor my stepmother had spared a thought for my own happiness or what would be in my own interest. They had probably assumed that if I were unhappy with my first wife, I could acquire a second one quite easily with the full approval of Afghanistan's polygamous society, where men are allowed to have more than one spouse, but restricted by their religion from marrying more than four women.

There would be more proposals in store for me and the fact that marriage between cousins is very common in Afghanistan and its neighboring countries merely added to my problems. I recall an occasion when I was visiting my mother's older brother and staying with the family overnight. It was the holy month of fasting and we all had to wake up very early in the morning to have the *peshnamai*, a special meal we would finish before dawn broke. As soon as the meal was over, my uncle declared he had been contemplating me as a prospective bridegroom for his daughter and wanted to know how I felt about the idea. I fell back on a noncommittal, politically correct and culturally acceptable response, explaining that it was not for me to decide, but for my father to come down from the north, where he was living at the time, and ask for his daughter's hand in marriage on my behalf.

Later, I would discuss the matter with my cousin, a military officer who would, had I consented to the match, have become my brother-in-law. The real reason I did not want to marry his sister was because she was my first cousin and illiterate, in the bargain. I recall once suggesting to my uncle that he send his daughter to school so that she could at least learn how to read and write. In fact, there was an elementary school for girls in Tanar village, within walking distance from their home. Being illiterate himself and like most men of his generation, my uncle was probably less interested in educating his daughter than his son. Male heirs had earning potential. They could take their place in the family business or obtain government jobs to enhance the family income. They would also live with their parents after marriage and be a support to them in their old age, for Afghanistan offered no social security or health benefits for its senior citizens. Daughters, on the contrary, got married and became members of another family, with no further responsibility toward the one to which they had belonged from the day they were born. Their new allegiance was to their husbands, who would support them for the rest of their lives. Daughters were, therefore, not worth investing in. Naturally, the birth of a baby boy was an occasion to rejoice over, the birth of a girl less significant in the scheme of things. I remember discussing the issue of education for girls with my aunt, the lady who had been keen to become my mother-in-law, and her reaction. She remarked that since she and her husband were feeding her daughters, she expected them to contribute by working for the family until they got married and moved out.

I was relieved to have escaped being part of such a regressive family. And I considered myself fortunate to have found a way of avoiding commitment and showing respect for my father without compromising my elder uncle's dignity. But the fact that I had been forewarned about the impending proposal by my uncle's younger brother, who was not on amicable terms with him, probably helped considerably. Had I married his niece, I would have become a member of his older brother's family and stayed with them during my subsequent visits. My elder uncle would have been my father-in-law, a situation his brother found quite unacceptable. I am not sure why these two men, separated by an appreciable age gap, never got along. In his bachelor days, the younger one had lived with his brother and his family. No sooner did he get married, however, than a dispute arose between the two brothers and the *qala* was divided equally between them. While my older uncle's family continued using the original front door to the residence, his brother had a separate entrance made for his residence.

Disputes between male siblings were not uncommon among the Afghan families I knew. For example, my cousins, Akbar Khan and Jaleel, the sons of my father's elder sister, could not see eye to eye either. With the sons of an Afghan family often sharing the same family compound and living in close proximity with each other, minor issues are bound to arise. And once male siblings marry and have children, their wives enter the fray, quarreling among themselves or instigating their husbands into fighting their battles on their behalf. The friction increases, with conflicts usually raging over living space and facilities, particularly if both are limited. The interesting aspect about such arrangements is that while families live separate lives under the same roof or in the same compound, they keep running into each other and their children usually play together. But when mishaps occur, as they sometimes do, leading to tragedy, the existing breach is likely to widen. That is precisely what happened in the case of my two maternal uncles.

My mother's two brothers had a garden adjoining the southern wall of their *qala*, where they had planted plum, apricot and pear trees. A small back door in the wall between the *qala* and the garden allowed direct access to the latter. Both families would use that door to go in and out of the *qala*. One day, my elder uncle's family dug a hole in the garden so that they could use the excavated mud for repairing a damaged section of one of the walls in the house. They left the hole, now filled with water, unattended for a while. My elder uncle's young grandson came out to play soon after, fell into the hole and drowned to death. His family immediately blamed the other family for the incident and the bitterness between them intensified.

Coming back from family disputes to the subject of my marriage, the third proposal came from my Aunt Mulko, who wanted me for a son-in-law. The widow of my father's second brother, she had breast-fed the motherless Jahantab and taken care of her. Aunt Mulko's own daughter was Jahantab's age and the two girls were close enough to look upon each other as sisters. In local culture, children fed from the same breast are considered siblings and Afghan tradition prohibits marriage between them. When the proposal came, I knew how to avoid committing myself. But it did not come directly.

I had come down to the village from Kabul for a week-long vacation and had gone to see my aunt. I was tired when I arrived at her place and lay down on a cot. Soon, I was fast asleep. When I woke up, lunch was ready. She had invited a family friend, Hasan, to join us for the meal. Afterward, Hasan asked me to join him for a walk. We strolled to the eastern edge of the garden and then turn north toward a secluded area, where we sat under a tree to chat. Hasan asked me then if I was interested in marrying my cousin, Aunt Mulko's daughter. My answer was a polite no, because I had never regarded the prospective bride as anything other than a sister. My aunt was disappointed, of course, but bore me no grudge.

In retrospect, I can only wonder at the kind of self-restraint I was able to exercise in turning down such proposals. Most young men my age would have jumped at the opportunity to get married. But as a college student, I was probably more concerned about getting my life sorted out so that when I did marry, I would be able to support my family. A typical young Afghan probably did not have the option in those days to follow in my footsteps, because he would live with his parents' and work for the family, foregoing the opportunity of getting an education. As a member of a large family, he probably felt secure at the prospect of a great many people being around to take care of his children. He could not, perhaps, anticipate the reality of a future where he was not so young anymore, his parents were advanced in years or dead and he had no option but to squabble over inherited property with his brothers.

I, on the other hand, had my own house in Kabul. I had graduated from the AUB and returned to Afghanistan to work in the Ministry of Education, I thought I was ready to get married. But finding a suitable bride turned out to be more difficult than I had imagined. I was interested in marrying the daughter of my cousin, Rasul, a schoolteacher in Khas Kunar, because the young lady was a graduate of the local elementary school and I assumed she could read and write. It was not the custom, especially in rural Afghanistan, to propose directly to a young woman or even raise the subject with her parents. The prospective groom was expected to send one of his close relatives to the girl's family to ask her parents for her hand in marriage. I thought my father would be the best person to negotiate, because he was the maternal uncle of the prospective bride's father. I was living in Kabul at the time and asked my father to come down from Imam Sahib, where he was living, and visit Rasul, who was spending his summer vacation at his younger brother's place in Kabul. My father happily complied. He went to visit his nephew and informed him of my interest in marrying his daughter, urging him to accept the proposal on her behalf, as I was a well-educated and hard-working person and would make a suitable spouse for the young woman.

It did not take me long to discover why my father had returned dejected from the meeting with Rasul. Apparently, my cousin had told him quite curtly that it mattered little to him if I was educated or not and he did not see himself getting his daughter married to me. I was quite baffled by his attitude and failed to make sense of his bitterness toward me. I thought back to the past, trying to recall anything untoward that might have happened to turn him against me. The only incident I could think of had taken place when I was a mere child. I had been carrying Rasul's first son, then a baby, in my arms, when I slipped, lost my balance and fell down, dropping the baby from my arms. Although he burst into tears, as any baby would have done under the circumstances, he stopped crying after a while and was fine. Much later, the boy fell ill and died. I could not help wondering if Rasul believed that internal injuries caused by the fall had eventually led to his son's death. The first suggestion that he might be bearing a grudge against me had come in my teens, when I was suffering from a bad case of acne. I remember asking my cousin about the possible cause of the rash on my face and his reply. According to him, it was cancer. Just as well that I had no idea at the time what cancer meant and what it could do to a person stricken by the disease!

When Rasul's family returned to live in Khas Kunar, I had asked Hukumai, my stepmother's mother, to drop in on them and speak to my cousin again on my behalf regarding the marriage proposal. I thought it magnanimous of her to agree, since she might have been secretly upset about my refusal to marry her daughter and could well have turned down my request out of spite. But her efforts were to no avail. Rasul turned down her request as well. In desperation, I did something a little rash and in defiance of local tradition. I went down to Khas Kunar from Kabul and put up at Rasul's house for a night. My cousin's father was still living and his younger brother, Rabbani, a military doctor, was visiting from Kabul. I repeated the proposal and the three men discussed the matter at night, but said nothing to me in the morning, when I was setting out for Kabul.

Rabbani doctor accompanied me to the riverside, from where I would cross over in a raft and wait on the other bank for the vehicle from Chaghaserai to take me to Jalalabad. Realizing that time was running out, I summoned the courage to ask him if his brother had an answer for me. He replied in the negative. That final answer helped me make up my mind. I decided it was high time I put my hopes of marrying my cousin's daughter behind me and started looking for someone else.

A colleague from my workplace suggested a woman he knew who was the headmistress of an elementary school in Kabul. He invited her to meet me at my office, where we saw each other and had a talk in private. In Kabul, where people were more progressive, I suppose you could meet a woman you were contemplating marrying without inviting censure. Once we had met each other, I tentatively agreed to meet the woman's family.

Accordingly, my colleague and I went to the woman's house over the weekend and met her elder brother over lunch. Money, or rather, my financial situation, was the main thrust of our conversation, as he turned it to the subject of my movable and immovable assets. In reply to his queries, I described the mud house I owned in Kabul and the plot of land my family owned in Khas Kunar. It was apparent to me that the prospective bride's brother was not impressed by the fact that I owned a mud house in the area which would later be named Khushal Mayna and become a part of Kabul City. I also had to be honest and inform him that I could only lease my father's land in Khas Kunar, because he was the owner. And I could lease it to someone and pay off the person later to reclaim the property. Our host then wanted to know how much I could afford to spend on the wedding party to preserve the honor of his family. After I gave him a rough estimate of the total value of my assets, he replied I would need twice that amount if the issue of my marriage with his sister were to make any headway. I realized it was an impossible situation. I had come all this way, unprepared for the difference between rural and urban traditions associated with matrimony. In the area of Afghanistan where I had been raised, the two parties discussed money matters only after the groom's family had agreed to his marriage to a young woman from another family.

The next day when I went in to work, I announced to my colleague that it would not be possible for me to marry the young woman he had recommended. My answer upset him a little, but when he deliberated further on the issue, he understood that my reasons for turning the girl down were valid.

A friend of mine came up with another proposal. His wife, whose family was originally from Kunar, but had moved to Kabul later, had been born and educated in the capital. She had a younger sister, also born and raised in the city, who was a high-school student and had two more years to go before graduation. My friend suggested that this young woman might make a good spouse for me, but cautioned that he did not have the clout to influence the family's decision in my favor.

The young woman's father worked in a government office where my house electricity bills were paid. I took the opportunity to pay my recent bill in person and meet the gentleman at the same time. During the conversation we had, it transpired that the gentleman and my father were acquainted with each other. I assumed that might work in my favor. I was hopeful when I sent my cousin Rawouf's wife to visit the family and find out if they were interested in giving their daughter's hand in marriage to me. But my hopes were dashed when she returned to inform me that the parents had not given their consent. I found out later that they had set their sights on a young man from a certain family whose senior member was a *Peer*, their religious advisor.

I had heard about the religious leader, Sahibzada, who lived in a large fort in the southern part of Tsawkai to the west of the main road between Jalalabad and Chaghaserai. I was going to elementary school in Khas Kunar at the time and we had been directed to make our way to Tsawkai and line up along the main road to welcome the king who was visiting the area. I had stood waiting with the other students for a long time, but the king did not turn up. It was then that I decided to go to Sahibzada's house and stay overnight with the family of Uncle Mehmed Gul, who was working on his farmland. Mehmed Gul used to work on our farmland in Khas Kunar and I called him "uncle," because I would play with his son who was a few years older than me. Mehmed Gul's wife, Aunt Gul Harama, was home when I turned up from the rally. She lived in a small compound attached to Sahibzada's house. I spent the night there and returned the next morning to line up again along the road with many others and wait for the king. His Majesty finally arrived from Jalalabad, allowed his car to slow down for a moment, so he could greet the spectators, and proceeded on his trip to Chaghaserai. After his departure, I was free to cross the river and go back home.

Coming back to the matter of my marriage, I guess his relations with my father meant little to my friend's father-in-law. He was far more interested in expressing his allegiance to his religious advisor.

It was now January 1977 and I was ready to leave for New York to study at Teacher's College, Columbia University. My search for a spouse in Afghanistan was over.

The matter, however, was revived again in the USA, when a group of Afghan colleagues at the Curriculum and Textbook Project arrived on a temporary visit to New York City. It transpired that I was the only bachelor among them. The young woman who had accompanied the group belonged to a very wealthy family in Kabul and I did not initially take my colleagues' broad hints about her being a good match for me too seriously. In the summer of 1977, we were all invited to a technological exhibition in Houston, Texas, and we left for the city in separate groups. I took the bus with two other friends and arrived in Houson after overnight halts in Atlanta and New Orleans. We were put up in a house belonging to a female classmate at Teachers College, who was originally from Houston. Her husband, who had been living alone in the place, was away and we were given the house key, so we could stay there for the duration of the exhibition. The rest of our group, including the single Afghan lady, had put up at a hotel. One day, my colleagues and I had all gathered in a room at the hotel. The lady was not among us and the others started seriously probing the issue of marriage and asked me if I were interested in her. I politely replied that I had to think about it.

Later, I contemplated the pros and cons of being married to her, giving due consideration to the kind of life I would be expected to lead in the future. The more I thought about it, the more I felt that going ahead with it would not be the right decision for me. There were so many differences that stood between us that it would have been foolish for me to ignore them. First, the difference in lifestyle. I came from a remote village in Afghanistan. Born in Kabul, she was city-bred. More significant still was the difference in our respective financial situations. Her family was filthy rich, whereas mine was dirt poor. Having money at your disposal that you yourself have earned makes you feel powerful and in control. If I married this young woman, I would end up living with her in a nice house in the center of Kabul that belonged to her family. Having gifted us the house, they would automatically have precedence over my own family, who would feel uncomfortable about coming over to visit us. I too, would feel awkward about entertaining my parents and other relatives in my home, which did not actually belong to me. If word about my situation got back to our village, there would be gossip about me and I would lose face and be forced to distance myself from my family and other relatives in the village. I remembered the cases of others who had been in a similar situation and ended up alienating near and dear ones and losing their place in their rural community. I suppose my allegiance to the folks in the village was too strong to be denied. Besides, having visualized our life as it would be in its entirety, I thought that as the husband of a wealthy urban Afghan woman, I would be forever at a disadvantage. It was better to be disappointed now than to be miserable in the future. I made my final decision and turned down this matrimonial opportunity as well.

Looking back on my life in the village, I realize that matrimonial matters did not seem so complicated at the time, although certain restrictions were in place. For instance, while it was not all that difficult for a man to meet a woman before marrying her, he was forbidden from addressing her directly. Such meetings were naturally easier to arrange in a man's native village or district, where he was locally known, than in a place where he was a stranger and might be regarded with suspicion. It was, of course, an advantage if the family of the woman he was interested in was related to him. He could drop in casually and observe her from close quarters without giving offense. Marriage between cousins was considered highly desirable, because both families regarded it as a way of strengthening existing ties and consolidating resources.

I was the exception to the rule. First, I did not approve of the idea of marrying my first cousin. Second, it was difficult for me to see a young woman outside the extended family, because I lived in Kabul, not in my village. Even when I went home to the village, I could never spare the time it took for close relatives to find a way for me to visit the family of a person unrelated to us. Wadood's mother-in-law did come up once with the name of a person whose daughter, she felt, might make a suitable wife for me. But she discovered later that the family intended to marry her off to a young military officer who was studying in the Soviet Union. Had I lived in the village, it would, no doubt, have been easier for me to find an Afghan wife of my choice.

Another good place to check out the local village women was a shrine behind our house in Khas Kunar. The groups which came to visit the shrine and supposedly offer prayers consisted mainly of women. Their primary objective, I suspect, was to find an excuse to go out and they used the occasion to dress up, organize a picnic and enjoy themselves. A young man could either observe them covertly or approach the group if he found a member of his family among them. When I was too young to be interested in the opposite sex, I would visit the shrine and collect the money the women had left on the tomb of a holy man we called Lachi Baba. It was only later that I would discover the shrine's potential as a hunting ground for a future wife.

Another good opportunity for wife-hunting presented itself late in the afternoon, when young women would emerge from their villages in groups, carrying empty clay pots on their heads which they filled from a canal or spring before returning home. The place they gathered in to fill the pots was known as the *guder*. There were sure to be young men lurking around the area and spying on them, for the women usually took their time, because it was one of the rare occasions they could leave the house and mingle with others of their age, gossiping about the kind of men they liked and hoped to marry. In fact, I remember a couple of folk songs celebrating this occasion. One addresses young men with the words: "Oh, young men, you will go crazy if you see what is happening late in the afternoon in Tsawkai." Tsawkai village is located on the western bank of the Kunar River, while Khas Kunar lies to the east. The folk song mentions a spring near Tsawkai, where all the young women from the village go to fetch water. It must have been sheer heaven for local men to spy on all those beautiful young women languidly making their way to the spring and chatting in a leisurely fashion with each other at the water source before heading home. And surely, it was one of those men who had declared: "Each bush in a *guder* is medicine, because my beloved must have washed her face in it."

The other local folk song, a very famous one that renowned Pashto singer, Qamar Gula, would sing, is about the village of Jalala, north of Asmar and to the west of the Kunar river, where the Gujar live and work for their Khan. The latter lives with his family in a large *qala*, whose gate opens out on to the main road. The poem goes, "The water in Jalala is sweet. The young women from the village fill their clay pots with it." The evocative quality of the lyrics must have stirred my imagination, for I had this yearning to see the village of Jalala.

My prayers were answered when I was sent there with a delegation from the Ministry of Education to inspect schools in the area. I noticed pots of geraniums adorning the wall flanking the road in front of the Khan's *qala*. I was determined to visit the Khan on my way back from Kamdesh, without sharing my plans with my colleagues. We made the journey in two vehicles, with the provincial Assistant Director of Education and my former classmate, Malang Ghundiwal, traveling in my group. A couple of American advisors, Don Schutte and Frank Fairchild, were accompanying us and we planned to pass through the area and visit the local schools in Barikowt and Kamdesh. Instead of spending one night there, as scheduled, we ending up staying for two, because our vehicle got bogged down in the water on the road between Kamdesh and Barikowt. We walked to Barikowt and spent the night with some elementary schoolteachers at their residence. We had left our driver with the vehicle and persuaded a jeep driver in the bazaar to go and pull our vehicle out and bring it to Barikowt.

The next day, we went to Kamdesh and stayed there overnight. On our way back to Chaghaserai, I persuaded my companions to stop at the Khan's *qala* and pay him a visit. I summoned up the courage to knock on the main door. When the Khan himself opened it, I introduced myself and the rest of the group, explaining that we had come to inspect schools in the area. Setting a true example of Afghan hospitality, the Khan welcomed us warmly and ushered us into his guest room near the main door. We spent over an hour chatting with him, during which tea and cookies were served, and during our conversation, the Khan mentioned his son who had graduated from the Police Academy and was then working as a police officer in Kabul.

Having met the Khan, a character in the folk song I have referred to, I have no doubt that Jalala village is still full of young women who fetch water from the local spring, while the men spy on them and fall in love. And that song must still be in demand.

The third—and last—opportunity for me to see young women in my quest for a wife was at the wedding of Omara Khan, the eldest of Aunt Mulko's sons, who was a few years my senior. I should add that my aunt was proud of her boys—the other two were Wakeel and Jalal— and insisted that the word "Khan" be appended to each of their names. Omara Khan was considered a complete name and no one would think of addressing him as Omara. But Wakeel and Jalal were common names and did not require a "Khan" attached to them. However, in deference to my aunt, we all complied with her wish. Invited to Omara Khan's wedding as a family member, I was, nonetheless, taken aback when I was appointed the new bride's *nikah plar* (designated father). I was to represent her at the wedding ceremony, negotiate on her behalf for a fair share of my cousin's property and hand it over to her as her *mahr*. It was the first time such an honor had been bestowed on me and, being a bachelor, I was uncertain about my ability to handle the responsibility. But I thought I managed well enough, bargaining with my cousin to get a fair share of *mahr* for the bride. This was my cousin's second marriage and I managed to persuade him to put one of his two houses in Kabul in his new bride's name and had this endorsed in the agreement drawn up for the *mahr*. While I enjoyed the status of being the *nikah plar*, it prevented me from going out and eyeing the women. Instead, I had to stay with the men all night, listening to the songs being sung and making plans for the wedding ceremony the following day and the wedding dinner, to which my cousin was expected to invite everyone in the village if he didn't want to undermine his reputation as a wealthy man.

I would return to the village later to attend the wedding ceremony of Aunt Mulko's youngest son, Jalal. I thought it very magnanimous of her to let bygones be bygones after I had refused to marry her daughter. She had put it behind her and was my loving aunt all over again. While the women's party at the wedding was on, Aunt Mulko suggested that I go into one of the rooms in the house and stay there for a while. The room had a large window that overlooked the courtyard and from my vantage position, I could gaze down at the activities there. I saw the women guests arrive and gather in the courtyard before engaging in much singing and dancing. I realized then that my aunt had given me the opportunity of observing the women from the privacy of that room, so I could decide if I liked any of them. All the women were in their finery and beautifully made up and it was a pleasure to gaze at them, but it did occur to me that I might not be the only man watching them.

Of course, sighting women and choosing one as a life partner was the least complicated part of the whole, elaborate process. If a man saw a woman whose appearance and general manner pleased him and whose background met with his approval, he would confide in his mother about his interest in her. The man would then step aside, while his family entered into negotiations with the young woman's family members. While the negotiations might seem to focus on preserving the honor of the respective families and ensuring the suitability of the concerned young man and woman as a couple, the deciding factor was always the amount of money the prospective groom's family was willing or able to pay the bride's clan. Theoretically, what was paid to the bride's family in cash and kind became her personal property. And, indeed, when she became a member of the groom's family after the wedding and went to live with them, she would take along the clothes, jewelry and household supplies she had received from them. However, the *mahr* (cash) she had received would be handed over to her father for him to decide how it should be spent, although in principle, it was meant to serve as the bride's social security in the event of a divorce. Since *mahr* is an Arabic term with religious connotations and failure to credit it to the bride's account could be construed as a breach of accepted religious beliefs, the local term, *warwar* (bride price), was used, instead, to circumvent the hurdle.

The main purpose of marriage was to establish blood ties between two families, the bride's and the groom's. Once the wedding was over, the bride was dispatched to the groom's home, where she was waited upon by the members of the new family. Seven days later, she was expected to visit her parents as a new bride and stay with them for a few days. This was known as the *owema* (the seventh day).

When the bride returned to her in-laws, she was considered a regular member of her new family and expected to assume responsibility for her share of household duties. The transition was smoother if a clear pecking order had been established in her new home. As the original mistress of that home, the mother-in-law naturally expected to be given precedence over the new bride. The latter's sister-in-law, that is, her husband's sister, also expected a measure of deference from the bride. However, if the newcomer asserted her rights too soon, worked to get the upper hand or manipulated her husband into speaking on her behalf, chaos would reign. Afghan men wisely refrained from involving themselves in their women's affairs and allowed them to sort things out for themselves. However, if the bride was truly unhappy in her new home, word would get around to her female relatives and a showdown between the families was inevitable. Her in-laws often retaliated by refusing to allow her to visit her parents, but usually the matter was resolved to the mutual satisfaction of both families. It was the only way out in a society where divorce is not an option, even today, because it is believed to bring dishonor to both families.

While it may seem, at first glance, that men played a dominant role in Afghan society and women were expected to be subservient to the male members of their family, it is not quite as simple as that. In the matter of worship, a certain level of equality was maintained, although men prayed publicly in mosques, while women did so in the privacy of their homes. For example, Islam decrees that both Muslim men and women must keep their bodies covered while saying their prayers five times a day at the stipulated hour. Men are expected to cover their heads and wear plain, long-sleeve shirts and *partoog* (loose, full-length trousers) in pale colors. Women wear long, loose patterned shirts and trousers, both in dark shades, that cover them from neck to ankle. Both sexes use an outer wrap that goes over the head and covers the body. As far as I know, women are not required by religion or tradition to veil their faces, because this would surely have come in the way of their work, for especially in rural areas, women are very active both indoors and outdoors. Their men leave home early to work in the fields while it is still cool. Women stay home and finish their housework before setting forth with the midday meal for their husbands and joining them in the field. While men are the ones who earn a living either by working on the family farmland or making business deals, once they return home, their income is handed over to the mistress of the household who assumes responsibility for its safekeeping and decides how it should be spent. I recall my father handing his entire salary over to my mother and later, to my stepmother, who would decide on how it should be spent. When he himself needed money, my father would ask for it from the woman of the house.

Afghan families are generally interdependent, with relatives pitching in to help in times of trouble. However, such closeness has its disadvantages too, for not all individuals are equally generous and prepared to curb self-interest for the greater good. I remember my father being the most helpful and caring member of his extended family, but his contribution to their welfare did not always meet with appreciation and his kindness was not always reciprocated. In fact, if he chose to leave his native village, Khas Kunar, and seek a better life in the north, it was primarily because of his sister-in-law Haleema's resentment toward him. For reasons I have yet to understand, my aunt, who was our next-door neighbor, did not spare any effort to get him into trouble whenever she could. On one occasion, finding one of her chickens lying dead on our farmland, she had promptly filed charges against my father with the local authorities. As a result, he had to spend a week in jail. On another occasion, when her youngest son, Qadeer, fell off a donkey's back, she accused me of having caused the mishap. Since I was a minor at the time, the local government could not have me arrested and jailed my father again for a week. Even when he had left Khas Kunar and would return for periodic visits to his family, Aunt Haleema, unlike our other relatives who welcomed my father warmly, would start badmouthing him and cast aspersions on him as an upstart who had only recently acquired his assets, as opposed to someone like her, who had inherited her wealth from her forefathers. I remember how her son, Rawouf, who was down from Kabul had stood up for my father, reprimanding his own mother for her harsh words.

Presenting a refreshing contrast to Aunt Haleema was my Aunt Mulko, who had been the most helpful of our relatives when my mother died, taking charge of us and breast-feeding my infant sister. Relatives on my father's side were poor, but supportive, though we would meet his cousins only occasionally.

My mother's relatives, on the hand, mostly kept to themselves and we would virtually lose touch with them after her death. My stepmother's family, though, was very supportive and Hukumai, her mother, took care of my brother and me, whenever the need arose. In fact, I thought she was a more loving mother to me than her daughter, Gul Bebu.

So while not all our relatives were equally supportive in times of need, there were enough of them to stand by us during hard times.

Note: Rawouf died in Khas Kunar on 5 October 2008. Rabbani, my cousin Rasul's younger brother, died in December 2008. Qadeer died in January 2009.

***

The issue of women's rights is as integral to Afghanistan as it is to any other country in the world. The problem lies in the Western perception of Afghan women. The *burqa*, a woman's garment, has been described by Westerners as a cage within which Afghan women are trapped. In fact, the use of the *burqa* is a recent phenomenon and, in no way, related to religion. The West would probably be surprised to learn that most women in the rural areas of my country still do not wear a *burqa* within their local communities. During a trip to Nooristan, for instance, I was told about an American couple who had gone to Kamdesh, lived among the villagers and learned their language. I do not know if John and his wife ever wrote a book about their experiences, but while my colleagues and I were having breakfast in the home of the local school's head-master, the latter brought out a photo album full of pictures featuring the village folks with the American couple. In answer to our questions about them, the headmaster replied that John and his wife had come to Kamdesh and lived among the locals for a couple of years. And judging by the photographs, it was apparent that the rural women weren't self-conscious about being unveiled in their presence. In fact, from what I would observe during my own visit, women in Kamdesh were very visible, going out to the fields with baskets on their backs to help their husbands. Living within a close community, where almost every resident was a relative, they could move about freely without veiling themselves. However, the fact that the appearance of a stranger could put them on their guard became evident when we made our way on foot from the main road to Kamdesh village by climbing a mountain and stopping several times to catch our breath. Halfway up, I recall looking down and spotting a couple, probably husband and wife, in the field. I was carrying a camera and asked the man if I could take a picture of the two of them. He refused right away and I went my way without another word. I understood the man had turned down my request, because I was a stranger to those parts. And had he known he would come across us in that secluded area, he would certainly not have permitted his wife to leave the house and join him on the field.

For urban women, dress restrictions eased when they were allowed to go to college and some of them permitted to take up employment in government offices. Before the 1960s, educational opportunities had been available to both sexes only in Kabul. The four boys' high schools and two girls' high schools in the city had turned out graduates in sufficient numbers to keep Kabul University, the only co-educational institute for college education in the country, functioning. In other parts of Afghanistan, only elementary schools for boys existed and few of the students who graduated from those schools were ever given the opportunity of study in Kabul's boarding schools. Boys from the provinces were, therefore, deprived of the chance to pursue higher education. Women, on the other hand, were denied such opportunities altogether, except in Kabul, in an unequal and often corrupt educational system that was weighted in favor of men and managed by equally corrupt government officials.

Once an absolute monarchy ceased to exist and the 1964 Constitution was set up, a few women in Kabul and other cities began going to school or work without wearing a *burqa*. Girls' schools had also been opened in the villages and despite initial resistance from a few locals, rural girls began going to school. The progress in the area of women's education continued through the 1970s. But if it ran into troubled waters and slowed as the decade drew to an end, it may well have been due to the growing resistance against the forced imposition of the women's liberation movement by the communist government or the one preceding it. This was, perhaps, part of the increasing religious opposition to the communists and by the time the eighties came around, the latter had been ousted from power.

With the *mujahideen* taking over, the situation for women became dangerous, especially in the rural areas, where they could no longer risk leaving their homes to go out and work. In the mid-1990s, the Taliban came to power and, under pressure from their Arab mentors and supporters, initiated measures ensuring that the progress Afghan women had made from the early sixties onward, both in the urban and rural areas, would grind to a halt. Had the movement for women's emancipation in the country not been impeded in so many different ways, there would have been a great number of educated women today in the cities and villages of Afghanistan working in different areas of the labor market.

Looking at the brighter side, if it can be described as such, given the increasingly harsh strictures imposed on Afghan women, the world was moved to devote greater attention to the need for women's liberation in the country. Books were published, articles were written and the media covered the subject extensively. While some of the reports succeeded in giving the subject comprehensive coverage, others missed the point, with the writers' personal feelings overwhelming the need for objectivity. I would urge members of the latter group, in particular, to familiarize themselves more thoroughly with the culture in which Afghan women were born and bred before broaching the issue of their status in society. Over the ages, their men have always taken great pride in being the breadwinners of the family and fulfilling their every need. For the last thirty-odd years, however, the very same men find themselves in a situation that prevents them from fulfilling their traditional responsibilities, trapped as they are between the shenanigans of corrupt government officials and the uncertainty of life in a land overrun by powerful foreign military forces on the lookout for insurgents. Their hope for a reprieve seems dim. I would suggest that Afghan men be allowed to win back their lost pride and they can only do so if they are allowed to work again and fulfill their family responsibilities, assuming the traditional role in which they have always seen themselves. Forcing them to submit to the latest newfangled ideas of women's emancipation in complete contravention of their cultural ethos may merely harden their resistance and come in the way of their women achieving even the minimum level of progess they are entitled to.

As for Afghan women, the government could surely devote some effort to their education and to the promotion of small industries that would engage them and help them to earn. It matters little if young Afghans do not study in co-educational schools, so long as the government invests funds in equal educational opportunities for both sexes. Being allowed to graduate at different school levels will not only increase the literacy level of women, but also help a number of them to take up professions in their area of specialization. And women in different professions can, in turn, contribute in valuable ways to the progress of the future generation of Afghan women. I would, therefore, urge those unfamiliar with our culture, yet driven by the impulse to express their views on the status of women in Afghanistan, to first orient themselves, keeping in mind the finer nuances of the Afghan family framework and the woman's place within it.

I have mentioned earlier that wearing the *burqa* was not a common practice among Afghan women in rural areas, especially within their own communities, and that its use was revived by the orthodox edicts of the *mujahideen* and the Taliban. I will maintain, however, that wearing it has, over the years, become a part of an Afghan woman's identity, both in her own eyes and in the eyes of the male members of her family. Nomad women and those living in the rural areas, surrounded by members of their own communities, often don't need to wear the garment. Women in Kabul and other large cities, however, choose to wear *burqas*, because they move among strangers on their way to school or work or even when out shopping. If they do discard the garment, it should be of their own volition and when they are ready for it. For an outsider to decide on their behalf would be both unfair and presumptuous, for oftener than not, his perceptions are based on his observation of a narrow segment of Afghan society—the urban one. If the outsider were to assume from that limited perspective that women in Afghanistan are all submissive creatures who have no say whatsoever in their homes, he would be sadly mistaken. For believe me, when those same women he sees outdoors in *burqas* return home to their families, they are the undisputed queens of their domain. Within the four walls of their home, they wield more authority than their husbands. The Arabs put it so well when they refer to their spouses as "ministers of the interior."

The status of women needs to be viewed within the context of the particular society they belong to. If that society is allowed to progress, the status of women living within it will also improve. The West needs to appreciate this important point and also remember that progress is not made in a day. It takes years of perseverance and hard work to move forward. Western women enjoy their position today, because much effort was expended over the centuries to get them this far. My academic advisor at the AUB had, in fact, shared with me the story of the first woman who had enrolled at the university as a student. The woman's family would apparently accompany her to the main gate, where the university president would be waiting to escort her to her classroom. After her classes were over, he would escort her back to the main gate, where her parents were waiting to take her home. The situation had obviously changed over the years and by the time I became a student at the AUB, it had evolved into a Western style co-educational university, where men and women shared classrooms, the library, the cafeteria and the campus in general. In fact, students of both sexes would organize open-house days once a year and use the occasion to visit each other.

My point is that any change that is positive needs to happen spontaneously, with the consent and approval of the people it is intended to benefit. I believe that by leaving Afghans to their traditional ways and respecting the choices they make, the West, and through its influence, the local government, would make greater strides in bringing about progress in their lives, than if they resorted to brute force to achieve the same end.

Consider the case of King Amanullah, a man revered by all his subjects as a national hero for resisting the British occupation of the country, defeating their forces and declaring Afghanistan's independence in 1919. However, even a hero is human and capable of making serious mistakes. During a six-month tour of Europe, Amanullah was enamored by the lifestyle he observed in those countries and was eager to introduce drastic changes in Afghan society during his lifetime. As a contemporary of Mustafa Kemal Ataturk of Turkey, he was probably inspired by the other leader's initiative in separating religion from the state, introducing Western customs and imposing a modern dress code on his citizens. In fact, during my visit to Ataturk's museum in Ankara in 1966, I would see, among the exhibits, a letter that Amanullah had sent to the Turkish leader whom he had addressed as "Dear Brother Mustafa Kemal." Without studying the ground realities, Amanullah had sought to emulate his idol and banked too heavily on the assumption that he would easily win the support of his people. In fact, when he returned from his European trip, his consort disembarked from the plane in a Western-style skirt. It could not have won the approval of his subjects who were conservative at heart and not ready for the dramatic changes their monarch was eager to usher in. In his impulsive and injudicious desire to modernize his country, Amanullah had moved too hastily and ended up alienating his subjects. In this context, I remember my history teacher at Kabul University claiming that at one point in his reign, Amanullah had moved to Qandahar, because he knew his life was in danger in Kabul. Not long after, he would decide to test the waters by flying over Kabul. The airplane was shot at from the ground and Amanullah barely managed to escape with his life. Shortly thereafter, he went into exile, spending his last years in Italy. After his death, his body would be brought back to Kabul.

Similarly, Daoud, the first president of Afghanistan, was considered a courageous leader who had won the love and respect of almost all his countrymen. But his popularity began waning rapidly, when he insisted that, in keeping with Western custom, the wives of government employees accompany them to public meetings, where men other than relatives were, inevitably, present. When my father was working at the Spinzar Company in Khwaja Ghar, news arrived from the company headquarters in Konduz that Daoud was visiting the area, accompanied by the company's president, Ghulam Sarwar Nasher, and all employees had been directed to take their wives to the meeting. While my father desperately needed his job and was afraid that disobeying the company president's orders might lead to his dismissal, he would not allow his wife, my stepmother, to accompany him to the meeting. He would subsequently discover that that the company had fined him a day's salary for his insubordination. I remember talking to an employee of the company about the situation. He remarked that if he had taken his spouse to a similar meeting, neither his boss nor his colleagues would have gained much from the discovery that his wife walked with a stoop and was almost toothless. In hindsight, I feel neither Amanullah nor Daoud read the situation correctly, lending the full weight of their authority behind their rash decisions, instead of acting responsibly. I cannot help wondering if the enthusiasm of these two rulers to forge ahead without thinking of the consequences had anything to do with the promise of a reward by some foreign power or the other for effecting changes in a country which was patently unprepared for it at that juncture. At least Daoud, I feel, should have moved with greater caution, given the fate of Amanullah who had been a far more popular leader, at least to begin with.

The way I see it, if allowed to evolve at their own pace, women in Afghanistan have every chance of graduating from the local schools and going on to pursue higher levels of education and eventually serving as role models for other rural women. This is, no doubt, a long-drawn process, but if initiated by the people themselves, it will gather its own momentum. This was evidently not a thought that had occurred to those leaders of a certain era who had tried to hasten change. Subsequent regimes, on the other hand, would swing to the other extreme, deliberately keeping the rural people ignorant of the changes taking place across the world. It was clear that they had failed to anticipate the scientific and technological developments whereby Afghans would discover in the not-too-distant future the level of deception to which their government had stooped to keep them in the dark all these years.

The author with his brother and his family, 1996.

The author with his sister and her children, 1996.

The author with his brother and his son and Jalat Hekmaty
and his son, 1996.

FIFTEEN

My Nuclear Family

I have been happily married since 1978 and am blessed to have a very supportive family. Our children have grown up and are settled. Anna and I are still working at our respective jobs and have been living in a middle-income neighborhood since 2005. Although my wife's first impression of South Riding was unfavorable—she likened the community to a cemetery—it has grown on her and she is now comfortable living here. To our son, Jamal, who still lives in Rhode Island, our community is a neighborhood of fancy houses with a fake town hall. I admit that it lacks the cachet of a neighborhood with old colonial houses, but it is a modern, multicultural community and looks like one, accommodating as it does people from diverse ethnic and linguistic groups. I am very comfortable here and have to say that Rhode Island doesn't have a counterpart. Whenever I return there on a visit, I hear the same distinctive language that most people native to that area use while communicating with each other. It is the kind of speech I neither had the chance nor the talent to master and it made me self-conscious about my own accent while living in Rhode Island, for I could not make myself understood to the locals and had to keep repeating what I was saying. After settling in the DC area, however, I am much more at ease conversing with anyone I meet. For a great many people living here have mother tongues other than English and speak English with a distinctive accent. I feel so much more at home among them.

Before I refer to my life with Anna, I need to add that given my history of rejected proposals and aborted attempts to find a wife, it was natural that I should be disillusioned and worried about my future. Was I doomed to eternal bachelorhood, I often wondered. Those anxieties must have been playing on my mind when I had a hernia operation in New York in May 1974. I remember the first question I had asked the doctor when I met him after the surgery: would I still be able to father children? The doctor had assured me that I would. But all those hurdles along the path to marriage and fatherhood were actually leading me to Anna. I now feel that I was fated to meet her.

Anna Scott was a fellow student at Teachers College, Columbia University. I clearly remember the moment when we first began talking to each other and I learned she was from Rhode Island. Until then, I had no idea that such a state existed. In fact, I had passed through it, a few years earlier, without even realizing it, while on my way to visit with a friend in Boston, Massachusetts. Anna's situation at the time was tougher than mine. While I availed of a full scholarship that took care of all my expenses, she was working in the college library to earn her graduate studies tuition, because her family was not in a position to help her. Of her close relatives, the only one she could truly depend on was her mother, Evelyn, a divorcée twice over, who lived in a two-bedroom house on Harbor Island, Narragansett, and was working as a secretary in the Department of Oceanography at the University of Rhode Island. Evelyn had married and divorced Anna's biological father, whose where-abouts were unknown. Her second husband, who had adopted Anna and given her his family name, was living in Connecticut.

Before I got to meet Evelyn, however, Anna had visited her mother's house, intending to stay with her for a week. But by midweek, she was back in New York. It seems her biological father had showed up at Evelyn's place and Anna found she just could not relate to him. The ambiance at the house had been rife with tension, prompting her to return to New York. I could not help but empathize with Anna. My own family members were, at least, together. Besides, coming as I did from an underprivileged background, I could relate to Anna, who herself belonged to a family of limited means. In fact, she had also worked her way through her undergraduate studies in Connecticut.

While we had much in common, what initially stood in the way of my considering her as a future partner were our religions—she was a Catholic Christian; I was a Sunni Muslim—and the inevitable cultural differences that would crop up between an American and an Afghan. While I was concerned about those differences, I was hopeful about resolving them if we both worked at it.

In Islam, Christians are considered people of the book and there is no religious law mentioned in it that prohibits a Muslim man from marrying a Christian woman. However, a non-Muslim woman marrying a Muslim man is required to convert to Islam. I reflected on the matter at length and decided that I could live with a person of the book. What endeared me greatly to Anna was her genuine desire to come to my assistance when I really needed her help. Being on a student scholarship (J-1 visa), I was not eligible to work in the USA. At the same time, I was adamant about not returning to Afghanistan, because I had no intention of living there under the communist regime. Anna quietly helped me to work toward a solution by typing the first draft of my dissertation, writing my résumé and subscribing to the *Chronicle of Higher Education* so I could look for jobs overseas. Since I could not work in the USA, she was willing to travel overseas with me if I got a job and had to leave the country. And sure enough, after the first draft of my dissertation was ready, I would receive offers of work from Iran, Saudi Arabia, Occupied Palestine and Kuwait. When we finally discussed the topic of marriage, I saw no reason to say no.

With my scholarship terminated as a result of the communist coup in Afghanistan, I was focused on getting a job and accepted the best offer I had received—from Kuwait University. Arriving in Kuwait, Anna and I settled in the two-bedroom apartment the university had allotted us and made friends with two Pakistani Pashtuns, Taj Mehmed and Mushtaq, who lived in the neighborhood. Taj was a flight engineer at Kuwait Airways. Mushtaq, who was working for Caterpillar, an American company, lent me money to make the down payment on the first car Anna and I would buy after a month in Kuwait. It was a simple deal between friends. I told him I needed money and Mushtaq promptly handed me 200 Kuwaiti dinars in cash, without even asking me to sign any papers. It was a transaction based on pure trust and when I had the money to pay him back, I would, in cash.

Later, Anna and I would discover that there was a sizeable Afghan community in Kuwait. The first Afghan I located was Fazlullah Reshteen who had recently graduated from Kuwait University and was teaching in a local public school. He was the son of well-known Pashto scholar Sedeequllah Reshteen, who had been president of the Pashto Academy in Kabul for a long time. I had read some of his books and listened to his speeches. Fazlullah's brother-in-law, Saleem, would arrive later and find a job at the Boodai Construction Company. He later brought his wife and daughter with him. Another daughter and a son would be born to the couple in Kuwait. Anna and I were lucky to have a fairly large group of friends and acquaintances, because we socialized not only with Afghans, but also with Americans and people of other nationalities. I had no problem finding a place of worship, because no matter where one lives in Kuwait, there is a mosque within walking distance. For Anna, however, there was a solitary church next to the Sheraton Hotel in Kuwait City where she could go for Sunday Mass. The other members of the congregation, she said, were mainly from India, Sri Lanka and the Philippines.

Anna and I organized the occasional party, entertaining our friends in our two-bedroom apartment in Khaitan. The situation changed somewhat after the children arrived. Our first child, Khushal, was born at the Al-Salam Hospital on 5 February 1980. Anna had applied for a sixty-day maternity leave and when she went back to work, we had Ramia, a Sri Lankan lady, come in to look after the baby. Ramia would arrive before we left for work in the morning and leave after either Anna or I had returned home around three p.m. Ramia's husband, Hiram, worked for an auto sales and maintenance company in the city. When Anna and I visited Sri Lanka with our sons, Khushal and Jamal, three years later, Hiram would pick us up from our hotel in Mount Lavenia and take us to visit his parents' place located in a short distance from the hotel.the same area. During supper with the senior couple, I recall Hiram's father telling us that he had worked for the local radio station and his nickname at the time was the Minute (or Mighty) Man.

While Anna was expecting our second child, we decided on employing a live-in maid and needed more spacious accommodation. The university appreciated our concern and moved us to a three-bedroom apartment on Haroun Al-Rasheed Street in Salmia near the Shaab Sea Club. While our residence in Khaitan had been far from the main shopping area, our apartment in Salmia was more conveniently located. It was also near the Gulf Coast along which Anna and I would go for walks in the late afternoon from November to the end of March, when the weather was still mild. For the rest of the year, it was simply too hot, both during the day and at night.

Aware that we were looking for a live-in maid, one of my colleagues strongly recommended an Indian lady who had worked for his brother-in-law and gave me her address in India. We wrote to her and she accepted our offer to come down to Kuwait and work as a live-in maid for us. It was while we were still living in this apartment that our second son, Jamal, was born in the same hospital as his older brother on 12 November 1981.

In 1983, the university built its own housing complex for faculty and staff in Shuwaikh and we were given a three-bedroom apartment on the first floor in one of the five blocks. This apartment was more spacious than the previous two we had lived in. There was even a separate room near the kitchen for the maid. We had been living in this apartment, when Anna gave birth to our daughter, Shireen, on 21 February 1984 at the Al-Sabah Maternity Hospital. But just two weeks before the delivery and four days after Khushal's birthday, a vehicle driven by a faculty member knocked down our son in the university campus where our apartment block was located. I remember picking the child up in my arms and realizing right away that his leg was broken. Fortunately for us, Wiyam Younis, one of the newly graduated doctors at the University Hospital in Jabriya, lived with her parents in the faculty residence and had just returned from work when the mishap occurred. Instead of entering the building, she would stop when she saw Anna and me and offer to take us to the University Teaching Hospital in Jabriya. One of the

English Language instructors offered to take us there in his car and we all got into the vehicle and set off. Arriving at the hospital's Emergency section, we did not stop at the gate, but drove straight to the children's ward. Khushal was admitted for treatment and had to stay at the hospital for two weeks. While Anna would spend the day with him at the hospital, I would stay nights. By the time Shireen was born, Khushal had been discharged from the hospital with a cast on his leg. I remember taking the boys over to the maternity hospital to see their mom and newborn sister and it was a very pleasant family reunion. Not everything had been running smoothly, however. Soon after her birth, the baby had come down with jaundice and had to be placed under special ultra-violet light. We had chosen this hospital, because being government-run, it offered free services and was better equipped to handle emergencies than the Al-Salam Hospital, which was a private enterprise and charged its patients fees. But Anna's accommodation—a crowded hallway lined with beds—that she was made to share with other recent mothers and their newborn babies, was substandard, to say the least.

Children pick up other languages after learning to communicate with family members in their native tongue. We began by enrolling Khushal in the Al-Bustan Nursery School, where the language of instruction was Arabic. The school was owned by Lulu Al-Qutami, a well-known Kuwaiti activist, and managed by a grandmotherly lady from Syria called Mama Aisha. After a couple of months, I noticed that my son was conversing with other children on the playground in Arabic, interspersed with a few English words. It seemed that neither he nor his playmates had any problems understanding each other. When Khushal finished nursery school, Anna sent him to the British-run Sunshine School, where the language of instruction was English. As time went by, our son gradually forgot the Arabic he had learned earlier.

We had a Pakistani neighbor in our apartment complex in Shuwaikh, whose children were more or less the same age as our own. The children from both families would play on the spacious platform in front of the four apartments on the first floor. It was interesting to note that during the time we lived in Kuwait, our children would speak English with a Pakistani/Indian accent. Whenever we visited Rhode Island during our summer vacations, however, they would switch to the New England accent. I remember musing that instead of devoting their energies to changing their English accents according to the environment they found themselves in at a given moment, they would have done well to learn another language, had they been given the chance to do so. I recall some local Afghan friends sending their children to a Pakistani school, where the language of instruction was Urdu. While all subjects were taught in that language, the school was also required to teach its students Arabic and English. I was amazed that children of eight or nine could not only speak Pashto, picked up from their parents, but also Urdu and English which they studied at school. Our children, however, didn't enjoy the same advantage. Since we spoke English at home, our children stayed monolingual, speaking no language other than English with a New England accent.

Anna and I now began thinking of returning to the USA, because the two of us had earned and saved enough money to not only invest it for a rainy day, but also to make the down payment on a house in a nice location for our children to grow up in. And eventually, we did return. Back in the US, we weighed our options and found what we thought was the right house. It was located in the Gaspee plateau of Warwick, where Anna had always dreamed of living. The neighborhood was a stable one and the local elementary school was just a walk away. The house had a small private backyard, which the children could use as a playground.The drive to my workplace at the Department of Education in Providence took about twenty minutes. Everything seemed just perfect and we thought it was a matter of time before we settled in and resumed a normal family life.

After buying the house, however, we discovered that it stood in an Irish nest. Our immediate neighbors on either side were Irish Americans, who seemed strangely uncomfortable about having a foreigner like me living in their midst. Some claimed I was black; others decided I was an Arab from the Middle East. It was not as if Anna and I did not make an effort to reach out to our next-door neighbors, but they preferred to keep their distance. Both families had children the same age as our own. I suspect that had their children been left to themselves, they would have ended up playing with ours, but their parents had probably warned them off us. We invited the son of one of our next-door neighbors to Jamal's birthday party and he came with his mother in tow. I am sure the child enjoyed the party, but would hesitate to say the same for his mother, because all the members of the family kept themselves aloof. It was an unfortunate situation, because the man taught social studies at the local high school where Jamal had enrolled after graduating from junior high school.

The other neighbor, a volunteer coach, was apparently made in the same mold. I remember an occasion when I had invited him over to have a look at the renovation we were carrying out on our new house to convert the back porch into a family room. He was gracious enough to come in, but after a quick look around, practically fled through the back door. He had two sons almost exactly the same age as our own. I do remember his older boy coming over to play with Khushal for a while. But eventually those children must have succumbed to parental pressure, for we did not ever see them playing with our boys again. Around five or six years after we had started living there, this particular neighbor sold his house and bought another one a couple of streets away from us. The teacher, on the other hand, continued to live there, even renovating his house to accommodate his growing family, but remained invisible.

We could not, however, let these minor irritations bother us. I was more focused on my children and enjoyed seeing them grow up. I could not imagine two brothers being as different as Khushal and Jamal. When my older son was growing up, he enjoyed participating in all three of America's well-known sports. He started with tee ball and went on to practice it with enthusiasm. At the age of eight or nine, he switched to soccer and played it for a couple of years. But it seemed that he preferred baseball and came back to play Little League baseball, until he had graduated from junior high school.

I had so much fun watching Khushal play that I begged Jamal to start playing when he was at the right age. One day, I implored him to accompany me to the store so that we could buy gloves and other equipment for playing tee ball. He retorted that he was not interested in playing any sport and I was simply wasting my time. I gave up and he never did involve himself in a sport.

When Shireen joined the tee ball team, I realized she was quite clueless. During the short time she played before giving up, I recall watching her participate in a game. I saw her gazing up at the ball moving her way, but when it came and landed near her feet, she was still looking up with her gloved hands raised to catch it. Shireen gave up playing baseball while she was still playing tee ball and never looked back. She would later take up dance lessons, but gave them up when she went to high school.

Meanwhile, Khushal continued playing baseball in the Little League. On the first day of the season, all the players and their parents or guardians would gather along Warwick Avenue, which was walking distance from the pit where they usually played. We would march to the pit for the inauguration ceremony and the exhibition game would begin thereafter. One day, Khushal's team was playing at the pit and he was meant to catch the ball. I was sitting outside on the steps among the spectators, when the ball came and landed next to me. I had tried to catch it, but didn't quite manage to. The coach shouted from the field that had it been Khushal, he would surely have caught that ball. I retorted that Khushal was a player; I was not. He was the insider; I, the outsider. On another occasion, I was watching a soccer game in which Khushal was playing. I was crestfallen when the opposing team scored two goals during the first half. But in the second half, Khushal evened the score with his two goals and the game ended in a draw.

I had played soccer for fun and knew the rules. However, I had no clue how baseball was played. I would practice with Khushal in our backyard when he was a boy and play tee ball with him. Later, I remember accompanying him to the neighborhood park or to the small field at the Wayman Elementary School. But once he had learned the game and started playing against other teams, I was out of the picture.

The American version of football had always been a mystery to me, because I could never figure out why anyone would enjoy watching a sport that led to human beings piling up on each other all the time. It was certainly not my idea of what a game should be. So when after enrolling in high school, Khushal decided to join the football team, I wasn't overly enthusiastic. I thought he had made the wrong decision, but went along with him, because he was so excited about playing and determined to excel at the sport. In fact, his team actually won the state championship for three years running and only lost the final game to East Providence High School in the fourth year. I remember the evening following the defeat, when Khushal had brought four of his friends over to our house. They had taken it for granted that they would remain the state champions forever and were naturally crestfallen. I recall how those boys had sat in the family room until late at night, eating the pizza they had ordered. When I woke up the next morning, two of my son's friends were asleep in the family room. Football was obviously a sport Khushal enjoyed and he has happy memories of his association with it, for he still keeps in touch with some of his former teammates. So it came as a bit of a surprise when he started attending college and gave up football, although he would continue to play different ball games.

Khushal was very sociable at college, where he did a double major in criminal justice and sociology. During his sophomore year, he was a Resident Assistant and did not have to pay for his room. He also received a stipend and was on a partial scholarship. To make up the deficit, we had to apply for an education loan. Although I continued to make the required minimum deposits toward its repayment while he was still in college, when Khushal graduated, he had a debt of about $35,000. I would carry on with those payments until he found a job.

Anna and I attended our son's graduation ceremony in 2002. He was on the honor list in both his majors. The award ceremony, during which the graduates would receive their degrees, was graced by the presence of invited guests, including the state representative at the US Congress, Patrick Kennedy. While all the other graduates shook hands with Mr. Kennedy, when Khushal went up on the podium, he hugged the senator. Taken aback, I would ask my son later why he had done so. It transpired that during his final year in college, Khushal had worked as an intern at the Urban League in Providence, to which Kennedy, a strong supporter, had been a frequent visitor. My son and the senator had, therefore, met and knew each other.

Khushal's graduation ceremony was an exciting and happy occasion, because he knew many of the faculty members and graduating students. There was much hugging and words of friendly advice for my son from his faculty members regarding his future. One young lady in a graduation gown and a cap would actually approach Anna to tell her that she was her future daughter-in-law. In fact, Erin and Khushal would live together in Washington, DC, for a couple of years before getting married on 14 August 2009. They the proud parents of Nico who was born on 25 April 2011.

My second son, Jamal, graduated from Pilgrim High School in Warwick in 2000 and enrolled at Roger Williams University in Bristol, Rhode Island. He intended to study architectural engineering, with the preservation of historical buildings as a subsidiary, but changed his major to sociology and education after the first year. He was luckier than his older brother, because Anna was teaching at Johnson and Wales University and was entitled to tuition reimbursement for one of her children if he or she were studying in one of its affiliated universities. Roger Williams happened to be among them. Anna and I paid for his dormitory during the first year and for the use of the recreational facilities until he graduated. Since his university was a forty-minute drive from our place, Jamal and I came to an agreement that he would live at home and commute to his classes. I would also give him the leased 1998 Honda Civic that I had bought at the end of the four-year period so he could drive it to the university. After a year of living at home, Jamal preferred to rent an apartment in East Providence, from where he could commute both to his university and to Bob's Store in Warwick, where he held a part-time job. He was still using the car, when he graduated from university in 2004.

It may seem strange to others that this sort of thing can actually happen, but Jamal almost missed his graduation ceremony. The previous evening, he had gone to a party in Providence with Khushal and his friends, returned home very late and fallen asleep in our study downstairs. I remember going downstairs early, the following morning, to wake him up so he would be in time for the ceremony. Jamal, however, had shaken me off and mumbled that he was sleeping. I had to be firm with him then, telling him that it was one day in his entire life that would never come again and it was a special one, since he would be getting his degree. I was certainly not going to let him sleep through it. Besides, I had come all the way from Washington, DC, to attend the graduation ceremony and enjoy it I would! I had dragged Jamal out of bed and asked him to go to his apartment, take a shower, wear a clean shirt and pants and be present at the ceremony. I am glad to say that he finally gave in.

Jamal's graduation ceremony was a low-key event, held under a huge tent on the university campus, where all the faculty members and relatives of graduating students had gathered. It was raining heavily and a corner of the tent near where I was sitting had collapsed, causing rainwater to pour in. Actually, Anna and I had been a little late in arriving and by the time we did, almost all the seats had been taken. While she had found a seat for herself, I could only manage a flattened cardboard box. With the rain pouring in, I moved to a vacant spot on the grass and began edging closer to the TV screen on which the images of the graduating students would be projected as they went up on the podium to receive their degrees. After a long wait, Jamal's name was announced and he appeared on the podium. I had my camera ready to capture that moment and managed to take two snapshots of him from the TV screen while he was receiving his degree.

By the time the degrees had been awarded and the speeches delivered by the faculty, high-ranking administrators and the valedictorian, the rain had stopped and the sun was out. We were advised to proceed to another area in the campus, where cookies and soft drinks were being served. After a brief stay, it was time for us to leave, for we had invited Anna's relatives from her mother's side to a restaurant for dinner. And there we all spent the evening, celebrating the occasion in our own way before heading home.

Shireen graduated from Metropolitan High School (MET) in Providence a year later than her batchmates. We then enrolled her in the Community College of Rhode Island (CCRI), where she spent two semesters. She took four courses and passed three of them, but lost interest in college and wanted to work. When we sold our house in Rhode Island in 2004 and moved to Northern Virginia, Shireen found work at Starbucks in a shopping center that was walking distance from our house. She was advised to take three courses at NOVA Community College and passed one before deciding to continue working full-time. Meanwhile, she had become pregnant and given birth to a son on 17 August 2005, two and a half months before the due date. As a premature baby, Brody had to stay in the hospital for two whole months before Shireen was allowed to take him home. She soon realized that taking care of a baby was a full-time job. During that period, his father, David, was living with us, but contributed in no significant way, merely creating tension within the family. He had come from Rhode Island, with the apparent intention of getting a job here and being with the baby. In fact, he did get a job and Shireen too, went back to her job, each working a different shift so that one of them would always be there with the baby at the hospital.

It was while we were vacationing in Jamestown, Rhode Island, at the beginning of June 2006 that Anna realized there was a dark side to David's character. During this time, he would apparently keep sending threatening messages to Shireen on her cell phone, saying that he could get at her and knew how to find her parents too. When Anna learned about the messages, she declared she felt unsafe in the house where we were staying and insisted on moving out to spend our last night in a hotel. We would leave Rhode Island the next morning without David.

A few days after we had arrived home, his mother called and begged Anna to let David stay with us. However, both my wife and daughter decided against it. Meanwhile, our grandson's health was improving and we found a babysitter for him so that Shireen could go back to work full-time to recover her lost benefits. Brody, a big boy, is going to the local elementary school. Shireen is working at a CVS pharmacy. The pharmacist has advised her to undertake further studies in that area. Having regained her interest in college in the meantime, Shireen had taken two courses at NVCC—one in psychology and the other in biology—and passed the national examination for pharmacy technicians, receiving a national certificate about which she is very excited.

When I compare my attitude to my parents with that of my children's toward us, I can confidently claim to have been more obedient, considerate and helpful. Of course, my children are still young and in quest of independence and may yet prove me wrong. For I am beginning to see some welcome signs of change in each of them. They are certainly more demonstrative in their affection for Anna and me. Perhaps their rebellious phase is coming to an end and they are beginning to recollect that though we, as a family, have been through tough times, we have always been there for each other in our hour of need. If they have been a little distant with me all this while, it could well be because I was either away in Kuwait when they needed me or too strict in my dealings with them during the most severe financial crises of our lives. Anna, however, has made up for the lack to some extent. A super mother, she has taken care of our children while working full-time at Johnson and Wales University.

Unconsciously or knowingly, Jamal expressed his feelings in the card I received from him on my birthday in 2008; it showed a young boy smoking a cigar, with a liquor bottle next to him. The caption said that all revolutionaries had eventually become great men. Shireen lives with us and we take turns caring for her son. I feel she does appreciate what Anna and I have been doing to help her out. Khushal got married in the summer of 2009; he will be the first one to settle down and, hopefully, raise a family. When he has children of his own to love and take care of, he will perhaps begin to understand what we have done for him.

It could be the kind of society we live in or the generation gap that makes it difficult for me to be on the same wavelength as my children, but caring about family members comes naturally to me. I remember being very grateful for all the help I had received from my father and was more than willing to reciprocate when I could. I had handed him part of the US/AID scholarship money I saved from my years at the AUB, so he could buy his dream house in Imam Sahib and live there after his retirement. As I had mentioned earlier, I also helped my brother, Wadood, who had found it difficult to sustain his large family of five sons and four daughters during the years of political turmoil in Afghanistan, by handing him my house, to be bequeathed after his death to members of his own family, and by having some of his sons trained to earn their own living.

This sense of duty toward parents and siblings is less deeply ingrained in my own children. I recall the time I had brought Khushal over to Northern Virginia. He had found a job and was living in the townhouse I owned. When he heard about our plans to sell our house in Rhode Island and the townhouse too, so we could invest the money in a family home in North Virginia, Khushal insisted that I sell him the townhouse at a lower price than its market value. But while living with us, our eldest son was at least helpful working around the house.

Jamal, on the contrary, couldn't care less. When part of the family was still in living in Rhode Island, I would go home to see them once in a while. Whenever I did, I would find the house in a mess. There were five pets—two dogs and three cats—and none of them were properly cared for. I noticed that instead of being taken outdoors, they would be allowed to go down to the basement, which they used as their bathroom. Almost every visit of mine was spent cleaning that filthy basement. The house was surrounded by full-grown trees and their cast-off leaves would pile up in the yard every fall. The job of raking the leaves and bagging them always fell to me and since they had been allowed to accumulate over time, it usually took me two whole days to complete the job. I recall an occasion when the leaves were heaped so high that I was almost buried in them. A neighbor passing by spotted me and while stopping to greet me, quipped that he did not envy me my predicament. Jamal was visiting us in August 2007 to be there for Brody's birthday and I remember asking him if he would mow the lawn for me. He was highly indignant that I had even asked him to do this lowly chore. Khushal lived with us until he got bored and moved out to Washington, DC, where he still lives. For the first couple of years, he rented an apartment. Then he bought his own condo in September 2009, where he lives with his wife Erin and their son Nico. . Jamal is still in Rhode Island and working for the public schools in Taunton, Massachusetts. He has bought a house and the closing is scheduled for 27 January 2010. Shireen, who has full custody of her son now and is planning to continue working in the pharmacy, is still living with us; she is not required to pay us rent. Moreover, we share the responsibility of raising Brody.

My journey through my years in my native country, Afghanistan, and later in Lebanon and Kuwait is over. I am now savoring life in my adopted country, the USA, where I have a job and a nice house. Our nuclear family is no longer nuclear; it is expanding, with Brody and Nico, our grandsons,. I have made both official and personal trips to Australia and to countries in Asia, Africa, Europe and the Americas. My experiences and pleasant memories will stay with me as long as I live. I love my wife and our children and have been in touch with my extended family in Afghanistan. With the passing years, Anna and I grow increasingly dependent on each other. Our relationship with our children is more of a long-distance one these days, but we hope we can sustain it and continue to ensure that our family remains a closely knit one.

Author's children on their first day back in the US from Kuwait, 1986.

Author's children celebrating first snow in the US,1996.

Author's children on Easter Sunday in front of the family house.

Mr. and Mrs. Safi with their children on Khushal's graduation from
Salve Regina University, 2002.

SIXTEEN

Religion, Beliefs and Practice

As a citizen of the USA, I have realized that in my adopted country, religion is a private matter. No one brings it to his or her workplace. My boss, for example, is aware that I am a Muslim, but that does not, in any way, affect my professional status. I have other colleagues who are either followers of Islam like I am or belong to other faiths. It has no bearing on their work or their relationship with their co-workers.

In Afghanistan, however, and in certain countries where I spent some years, religion is not a private matter at all. It is as public as can be and has a significant effect on a person's professional status in the workplace and social position in the community at large. Islam is the state religion in Afghanistan; every Muslim citizen is expected to practice it and every non-Muslim citizen to respect it. This is clearly stated in the Constitution and the court falls back on Sharia to determine whether a citizen accused of a crime is guilty or innocent. Different Islamic governments have used Sharia to their advantage to consolidate their position and ensure their political longevity. The same Sharia law had prevailed in the pre-Taliban era, but I don't remember ever hearing of a convicted thief's hands being cut off or of a person prosecuted for adultery being stoned to death. But once the Taliban came to power, Hindus and Sikhs were required, for the first time in the history of Afghanistan, to wear a yellow armband—a public declaration, as it were, of their non-Muslim status. With the advent of this Islamic group, dismembering, stoning or killing of suspected criminals became common, with the choice of punishment being determined by the alleged crime, according to Sharia, as interpreted by the Arab extremists who were both mentoring and financing the regime. In fact, under the Taliban, carrying out sentences in public was meant to serve as a lesson for all as well as an occasion for entertainment and the stadium became a venue for a different kind of sporting event: the torture of individuals deemed guilty of transgressions and, often, their gruesome execution for the same. If people turned out to witness these gory events, it was probably because they had nothing better to do, having been denied all forms of healthy entertainment by the regime.

In the name of al-Qaeda, the Arab extremists who had poured into the country, ostensibly to fight the Taliban's battles, abused Afghan hospitality, making themselves at home in a country where they did not belong. When the world ostracized the Taliban regime and isolated it politically and economically, driving it toward bankruptcy, these same Arab extremists provided its leadership with financial, military and political support. Such support rarely comes without strings attached and soon, the conditions imposed by the Arabs began to make their influence felt. The newly established girls' schools in the provinces and rural areas were closed down and the small minority of women who had been working in offices or teaching in the schools were dismissed and confined to their homes. When the Prophet Muhammad had declared that Muslims should seek knowledge, even if they had to travel to China for the purpose, I doubt if he forbade women from such a quest. But the Arab-influenced Taliban decreed otherwise. All public entertainment was declared anti-Islam, including movies, plays and musical soirées, as well as regular sports such as football, volleyball, basketball and field hockey. With that one diktat, Afghan youngsters who, like their peers everywhere in the world, enjoyed going out to socialize and participate in competitive games, found an important aspect of their lives cut off. In fact, in the late 1950s and early 1960s, I remember my high school in Kabul having two good teams—one for volleyball, the other for field hockey—that my classmates and I took great pride in. We would walk for hours to reach the campuses of other high schools and even Ghazi Stadium, where tournaments were held, to cheer for our team. I have been to that stadium several times to watch the parade of high-school athletes on the second day of the Independence holidays, attend football, field hockey and other matches and listen to the oratory of guest speakers or to children playing musical instruments and singing under the direction of Ustaz Ghulam Husain, a well-known musician and father of renowned singer, Ustaz Sarahang. The stadium and the area surrounding it were intended for public entertainment and enjoyment. My high schools, both junior and senior, and the stadium were located at opposite ends of the city, that did not deter me from spending most of the Independence holidays walking in Chaman-e Huzuri, listening to the singers at the clubs, set up for the occasion by various ministries and other government offices, or attending the games at Ghazi Stadium.

The clubs, all located between Chaman-e Huzuri to the west and Maranjan Hill to the east, were open during the seven days of the Independence holidays. Some required membership or admission fees; others, like the Pashtunistan Club, were open to all. This club was usually my main stop, because some well-known Pashto singers and entertainers performed there. Just walking around the area where the clubs were located and listening to the songs from outside their boundary walls was satisfying enough for me. If the weather was pleasant, it was a nice place to be.

When I had had my fill of entertainment, I would stroll around the area for the rest of the evening and then take the late-night city bus back to my school. To be denied the freedom to indulge in such pastimes was, therefore, a deprivation that must have hit the Afghan youth hard. But the restrictions imposed by the Taliban did not end there. To ingratiate themselves with their Arab mentors, the regime even removed all photographs and illustrations from children's textbooks and questioned the use of names that were common in Afghanistan, but prohibited in the Arab world.

When almost 3,000 innocent Americans were killed on 11 September 2001, every Afghan expected the Taliban to disown the fundamentalists of Arab origin. But that was not to be. On the contrary, the Taliban leadership continued to support the perpetrators of this atrocity. This was, indeed, ironic, because not a single Afghan had been involved in the despicable events of 9/11 and none of the terrorists eventually apprehended in the USA and in Europe and brought to justice was an Afghan. Even by their own standards, the Taliban had crossed all limits and the United States, along with the rest of the world, including the Islamic nations, would unite against them.

Before pressure was brought to bear on the regime, however, and the Taliban still held sway, its senior officials entertained themselves by acquiring several wives, that too, ones who were less than half their age. In Afghanistan, the family of a young, eligible woman usually demands a great deal of money when entertaining a marriage proposal for her from a much older man or one who is already married. By that reckoning, the Taliban leaders must have had a lot of money at their disposal. Although Islam allows a man to have more than one wife, the restrictions it imposes on multiple marriages are so stringent that most Muslim men usually content themselves with just one. Similarly, marrying a woman costs her future husband a lot of money in terms of the *mahr* he has to pay the bride's family and most Afghans are just not wealthy enough to go through more than one wedding without hurting themselves financially. I am told that in the early days of Islam, marrying more than one woman was permitted, because it was a way of providing for a great many women left widowed by the death of *mujahideen* in the war with infidels. But in times of peace, I don't see how a Muslim man can justify the same practice.

The first page of the 18 December 2007 issue of *Al-Hayat*, an Arabic newspaper, printed the UNICEF prize-winning photograph of the year. It captured the wedding ceremony in Afghanistan of an eleven-year-old bride and her groom, a man who was over forty. I remember printing out the picture and showing it to my friends and colleagues, who were shocked and disgusted. In all likelihood, the young girl's family had coerced her into accepting as her husband a man who was old enough to be her grandfather. I could not, however, help wondering at the man and his feelings as he sat next to his under-age bride in front of a large gathering of guests. The man's long beard, I noticed, had been dyed black. Its very length suggested he might be a mullah and that this was, perhaps, not his first marriage. It reminded me of a saying we have in Afghanistan: "Do what a mullah says, but don't do what he does."

Gazing at that photograph, I could only muse that while the Taliban leaders encouraged Afghan men to believe that Islam allowed them four wives, they never did bother to ensure whether those men could afford to maintain their four wives, nor if the latter were being treated, as their religion decreed, on an equal footing in every aspect of their lives within the privacy of their marital homes and being given the comforts they deserved. And the Taliban were certainly not concerned about the men's ability to provide for the great number of children they would father with these four wives, the number of offspring being increased by the absence of birth control measures in Afghan households. So the fact remains that while Islam permits a man a maximum of four wives, his financial burden increases with each additional one.

I recall that in Tanar village, where I had spent part of my child-hood, there were a few men who had two wives. One of those men was a teacher and the next-door neighbor of my stepmother's parents. I remember Jahantab remarking that the teacher's second marriage had so drained him financially that his wives had taken to cooking unpeeled potatoes to avoid wasting even a shred of the vegetable. She added that the unfortunate man was so distraught that he had now taken to spend-ing hours sitting at the window and staring out.

Among those of my relatives who sought to marry more than one woman was my cousin, Omara Khan, who had a stable government job, was earning a lot of money and believed he could afford to marry two women and support them without difficulty. He was mistaken, because during the political turmoil that engulfed Afghanistan, he lost his job and reached a point where supporting both wives and their children had become impossible. His first wife went off to Peshawar, where she lived with the six children she had had by him, while Omara Khan himself spent most of his time in Jalalabad with his second wife and the half a dozen offspring he had fathered with her. Later, his first wife would emigrate to Canada with her brood, leaving him in Afghanistan with his second wife and their other children.

From the dozen children my cousin would father, it is clear that with no system of family planning in place, parents in Afghanistan were unable to keep the number of offspring within the desired limit. If a man and his several wives remained fertile for years, they were likely to end up with more children than they could afford. My father would say that Islam defined a man's obligation to his offspring in terms of his ability to give them socially acceptable names, support them financially, provide them with a sound education and find each of them a suitable spouse. I would urge those men planning multiple marriages to first consider their duty toward the children they will father with those many wives. Would they be equally fair to all the children or would they tilt toward the ones their favorite spouse bears them? That would be a violation of the teachings of Islam. Consider the example of my maternal uncle, my mother's young brother, who would marry a second time and live with his new wife in Chaghaserai, while his first wife and their six children remained in Khas Kunar. He only visited the latter during a weekend, once a month or whenever he had the time, which proves that he wasn't treating his two spouses as equals. If he realized that he was flouting religious principles by doing so and persisted in that behavior, it was because he knew quite well that no one would hold him accountable.

The problem of having multiple wives is compounded when a man is unable to afford a separate establishment for each. With all of them living under the same roof and the women at home all day (since they are not allowed to hold a job), friction is inevitable. With the spouses fighting among themselves and clamoring for more attention and financial privileges from their husband, not only for themselves, but also for the offspring he fathers by each, peace is certainly not guaranteed. On the contrary, the situation leads to an atmosphere of mounting tension, apart from the division of income and property.

Consider the case of a wealthy farmer who earns a good income from his farmland. If he has several wives and children by them, the next generation is sure to divide his property between themselves. When their offspring divide the portion of the property they have inherited, each is likely to end up with yet a smaller portion of his or her grandfather's estate. The point I am trying to make here is the possibility of even a vast fortune dwindling if multiple spouses and their numerous offspring have to be maintained. Imagine, then, the predicament of the man who is not well off to begin with, but desirous of marrying more than one woman.

Consider the way my own extended family expanded. My paternal grandfather had four sons and two daughters. He owned no farmland, but he did have a house in the village and a small garden, where grapevines climbed the mulberry trees that grew there. In that garden, he had installed his weaving machine, his main source of income that helped him to sustain his family of eight. But as his sons married and fathered children, the number of family members increased. My grandfather had one grandson from his eldest son. The other three sons gave him three grandsons each. My own father had ten children from his two wives. During her short life, his first wife, my mother, would bear him five children, of which three would survive. My stepmother, his second wife, whom he married after my mother's death, would also bear him five children, four of whom are still living. Considering how numerous our family had become, we simply could not have lived on the property after my grandfather's death. There simply was no room for us. It was just as well that my father had bought his own property in anticipation of this moment.

When my father died in 1995, he left some property in Kunar, which Wadood is now managing. Our half-brother, Qader, is looking after my father's property in Imam Sahib. My extended family has decided to divide my father's property among his surviving wife, three sons and four daughters. My brother, Wadood, is keen that I sign over my share of the inherited property to him. He assumes that he will also get Jahantab's share. In other words, he aims to get half of our father's property. In fact, he actually sent me a four-page letter, explaining how this should be done, but I refused to go along with his plans. I made it clear that I wished to leave my part of the property to all my siblings, who would receive equal shares. Wadood is not happy about my decision, but I have every intention of standing by it. It is for my stepmother and my siblings to handle the inheritance between them. I am hoping they will resolve the issue amicably. If not, they are in for the long haul and the only people who will benefit from the squabble are the government officials who will exploit the situation by promising a resolution and demanding bribes at every juncture.

Like my father, my eldest cousin, Rawouf, had been smart enough to buy his own property. While we lived on our own, Rawouf would go off to the military school in Kabul. During his absence, his stepfather, who was also his uncle, lived on his property, managed it and lived off its products. The man also had his weaving machine, a second source of income. When he died, his three sons, Rawouf's half-brothers, who had grown up on the same property, continued to live on the income it generated for as long as their mother was alive. Once she passed, their future was uncertain. For Rawouf had got married and was raising his own family and needed the income from his property. His half-brothers owned no property of their own and had to find other ways to fend for themselves.

In fact, when Rawouf turned up to claim his property, his half-brothers found themselves in a desperate situation. The eldest one was blind and would try and learn to memorize the Quran from Mazum Pacha, our local Imam, also a blind man, who had succeeded in memorizing the Quran himself. When Rawouf's younger half-brother got married, the blind one lived with him for sometime, but not for long, because his health deteriorated rapidly and he died young. Rawouf's younger half-brothers—one married, the other single—had continued living in his house and taking care of his property. When Rawouf turned up, they found themselves with limited options, since neither had gone to school. The younger one left the house and started working as a gardener for the Department of Agriculture in Jalalabad. The other one learned sewing and became a tailor, making clothes in his spare time to support his family. He went to Kabul and rented a shop with a couple of tailors from Laghman, but was unable to make a success of it, because he did not know how to manage a business. Unable to attract clients, he returned to Khas Kunar, got married and started living on Rawouf's property and farming his land. Tailoring became a part-time job for him, supplementing the income from the land.

When our own grandfather died, we passed on his property to the family of our second uncle who had three sons and two daughters. Athough they did not have to pay rent in my grandfather's house where they lived, once the children grew up, the income from the property was not enough to sustain them. After their father's death, the weaving business ran out of steam and became obsolete and the children, therefore, saw no reason to pick it up. They bought a plot of land, instead, to supplement their income. All the three brothers had gone to school, the eldest one even graduating from college and proceeding to graduate school. The other two graduated from high school. The eldest brother obtained a stable, well-paying job, while the other two became teachers. Their combined salaries and the income from the property were enough to support the family.

Aunt Mulko and her family who lived in our grandfather's house, because they had nowhere else to go, took care of that part of the garden which belonged to my father, but treated his portion as her own property. Their combined share constituted half the garden. The other half belonged to Rawouf and his half-brothers, who had separated it from the rest of the garden and established their ownership over it. In order to establish my claim to my grandfather's property, I recall going to the garden one day and cutting down a tree. When my Aunt Mulko, who was living on the same property, asked me for an explanation, I told her that my family needed fuel for the winter to heat our house and cook our meals. In hindsight, I feel the idea had come from my stepmother, with whom I was living at the time in her parents' house. When she made an appearance in the same garden, however, a quarrel broke out between her and Aunt Mulko. My aunt probably assumed that having lived on the property for years, she had greater right to it than anyone else. When the two women eventually came to their senses, however, they agreed that Gul Bebu's father should chop down the fallen tree and the two of them would share the wood. This clearly proves that dividing family property is not a pleasant business, since it often leads to disputes between relatives, which may become violent enough to result in casualties.

I was not living in Khas Kunar when a similar dispute arose between Rawouf and Rasul's brother, Rabbani, over the demarcation line between our farmland and that of Rabbani's father, Shakar Khan. Gul Bebu, my stepmother, would later fill me in on the details. Apparently, Rawouf was representing my father who was then working in the north. The disagreement, it seemed, was over a ditch—from which both parties used water to irrigate their land—that lay between my father's property and Shakar Khan's. Rabbani contended that the ditch lay on his property and had to be moved to ours, because it did not conform to the demarcation line between our respective properties that continued

251

on the other side of the wall. With the modification he suggested, the monetary gain to either side would have been negligible and certainly not worth fighting over. However, the argument escalated and reached a point where Rawouf and Rabbani almost went at each other's throats. In fact, Rabbani's older brother, Rasul, even threatened to fetch a loaded gun from his house to settle matters. It was at that point that Gul Bebu's uncle, Fazal Rahman, stepped in on our behalf and resolved the issue. The irony of the situation was that while both Rawouf and Rabbani were college graduates and military officers, whose training should have taught them discipline, if nothing else, the man who eventually settled the dispute between them was illiterate. I still wonder how Fazal persuaded the hot-headed men to see reason. It could well be that the military officers considered it beneath their dignity to argue with an unlettered relative and ended the quarrel.

When Aunt Mulko's sons graduated from school and took up jobs, we, as their first cousins, decided to do something about dividing our grandfather's property among his four sons and organized a meeting in the village to formalize our agreement. Since the villagers were used to witnessing acrimonious quarrels and even fisticuffs between relatives over property, they were pleasantly surprised to learn that our family members had settled the matter amicably. We valued the house at 40,000 Afghanis and decided to sell it to Aunt Mulko's sons, since they had been living in it for years. They, the occupying family, would become the lawful owners by paying the other families with claims to the same property 10,000 Afghanis each. Rawouf's half-brothers, who did not have their own property, objected and demanded their share in the house. They were also entitled to their father's share in the garden which was was so small that dividing it into four parts would have yielded a minuscule area for each claimant. We would gain in no way from the division of my grandfather's property, because my father, who had settled with his family in the north, was not interested in claiming his share. My brother and I also stayed out of the deal.

When Aunt Mulko died, her sons found it impossible to live under one roof with their families. With her eldest, Omara Khan, living with his second wife and their children in Jalalabad, the second, Wakeel, bought over his father-in-law's property and moved out. The youngest son, Jalal, is the only one who still lives on the property with his family.

With Afghanistan's rural population on the rise and the plots of land owned by families limited, it is naturally difficult for growing families to live off the same parcel of land. Moreover, with increasing urbanization, a way of life is dying out, rendering many occupations redundant. Carpenters, blacksmiths, weavers and raft people, for instance, need to diversify and adapt themselves to other trades and professions for survival. My uncle, Mahmud Jan, the husband of my mother's sister, recognized the trend and went off to a textile factory to work as a clerk. My father was astute enough to leave his parental home when he could and make his own way in the world, ensuring that he could fend for himself and support his family independently. Looking back on my family's situation, I now realize how wisely he had acted. For had we stayed in Khas Kunar and depended for our survival on the property that had been bequeathed by our forefathers, we would have either led a miserable life or ended up harming or killing our relatives in the quest for our share. The crop from our father's property in Khas Kunar now comes to Wadood, who lives in Kabul with his wife, nine children and a few grandchildren. Jahantab lost her younger son, Abdul Zahid, to the *jihad*, a movement he would join under pressure from the regime. He never returned from Laghman where he was sent for God alone knows what purpose. Her older son, Ajmal, has returned from Pakistan and is married and living with the family. Our half-brother, Torialai, lives with his wife and seven children in our father's house in Imam Sahib and has a respectable income from our father's land and from his business in the town there. My three half-sisters, Najiba, Latifa and Ghotai, are married and teaching in their local schools. Najiba, a widow—her husband, Latif, an officer in the Afghan National Army, was killed by insurgents in the summer of 2010—lives in Imam Sahib. Latifa and her husband live in Kundoz City and Ghotai and her husband live in Kabul City. Every member of our family is settled, thanks to my father's foresight.

***

In an Afghanistan ruled or influenced by the Taliban, the best way to survive and avoid interference in your personal life is to fall in line or at least pretend to. The decision-maker about everything under the sun and particularly about religious matters is not necessarily the most intelligent or erudite of men. He could well have little formal education and even be illiterate. All that qualifies him for his position is a beard of the stipulated length and a gun. It is he who decides if you are a religious person or not, if you are a good Muslim or not—although he may have little idea of what that entails—or if you will ultimately go to heaven or hell after you die. Consider the manner in which cleanshaven Afghans were persecuted by the regime. If "advice" or intimidation didn't work, the so-called culprits were sentenced to a month's imprisonment and forcibly prevented from shaving. The administration would even decide on the length of the beard a man could keep. While most Afghan males have been forced to conform, deep inside, they resent such intrusion into what should be a strictly personal matter. Not for nothing do we have a saying in Afghanistan that is quite apt for the situation: "The beard is mine, but the mullah is in charge of it." No Afghan male likes a mullah to be in charge of his beard.

Religious education in Afghanistan begins early in one's life and every child, regardless of gender, is encouraged to be a good Muslim. In his early years, no child is bothered about praying five times a day, because God does not require him to do so. However, by the age of five, he is encouraged to start learning the Baghdadi Method. It starts with the child learning the Arabic alphabet. He is taught to pronounce each letter and study its shape. In the next phase of learning, he is directed to add a vowel to the sound of a letter, be it a consonant or a vowel. The vowels, A, O and EE, are combined with a consonant or another vowel. For example, adding each of the above vowels to the letter D will produce sounds that are equivalent to "da," "do" or "dee." The next step is to add a double vowel or *tanween* to each letter. The double vowels are pronounced thus: "on," "in" and "un." The letter D in the aforementioned example, when added to the double vowels, will produce "don," "din" and "dun." After a child has mastered the shape and sound of each letter and is able to combine it with vowels and double vowels, he is considered ready to memorize the prayers and the short verses in the last chapter of the Quran. As the boy or girl reaches adolescence, the focus is turned on using what has been learned while saying the daily prayers. And it is only when they are in their late teens that young Muslims are required to pray five times a day.

Young Afghan children learn the Baghdadi Method and the prayers they must say at home from their parents or other relatives or go to the local mosque early in the morning and wait for the Imam or one of his students to teach them after the latter have emerged from their morning prayers. Whether they are enthusiastic about the subject or have been roused from bed early in the morning by their parents to go to a relative's house or to the local mosque, the children diligently sit lined up against the wall, holding their Baghdadi Method books. Once they reach school-going age, boys continue going to the mosque, but girls are expected to stay home and carry on with the prayers, turning to their parents or relatives for guidance. And since many rural areas do not have schools for girls, this is where a girl child's formal education ends.

As a boy, I was entitled to praying at the local mosque and attending the local elementary school. But in my pre-school years, I would go to the local mosque that was a ten-minute walk from our home. Shakar Khan, Aunt Nabo's husband, who lived in the same *qala* as we did, was a mullah. His niece, Zulhejja, the daughter of Mullah Kamil Khan, a mullah himself, was married to his son, Rasul, and would teach me the Baghdadi Method. Of course, in keeping with Afghan tradition, I could not address any of them by name. Shakar Khan was always Baba; Rasul was Mullah Lala; his brother, Rabbani, an army doctor, was Doctor Lala and Zulhejja, my Mullah Bebu. I remember waking up early every morning to go to her house for religious instruction before returning home for breakfast. When I started attending school, I would leave for school right after breakfast.

While learning the alphabet, I probably fell short of Mullah Bebu's expectations, leading her to believe I was a slow learner. But when I reached the stage where I was adding a vowel to each letter, I speeded up the process considerably. For example, she taught me one day how to add the "A" sound to a consonant or vowel in the Arabic alphabet, but when I returned home, I managed to figure out all the combination sounds by adding the sound of "A" to each of the twenty-eight letters in the alphabet and gave her a pleasant surprise the following morning. I was able to move on right away to the next step; that is, adding the sound of "EE" to each of the letters in the alphabet. Following the Baghdadi Method, I would memorize the prayers and some of the short verses in the last chapter of the Quran. They all sounded so impressive, especially when recited by the local Imam, but I did not know what they meant. Since religious studies was part of our curriculum, I usually memorized the same material both at home and at school.

By the time I was required to recite my prayers, I was ready. I learned other things in school, which I could not freely discuss with my relatives and the other villagers. For example, I learned in my geography class that the world was round and rotated around the sun with other planets. That was not, perhaps, how the local mullahs and others who revered them interpreted the Quranic verse (the twenty-second verse of Surah Baqara, as translated by Abdullah Yusuf Ali) in which God says, "He made the earth your couch and the heavens your canopy; and sent down rain from the heavens." Of course, it was easy to think of the earth as flat; everyone believed it had four corners. I thought it would be prudent to leave the ideas I had picked up in geography class where they belonged. Bringing them home could only mean trouble, for any concept that did not conform to publicly held belief was considered contrary to religious teaching.

It did not take much to be branded an infidel by those who could not accept ideas which were scientifically sound, but incomprehensible to their limited minds. I feel increasing the literacy level and broadening their intellectual horizons would have gone a long way toward solving this problem. Unfortunately, many, especially the bearded ones, think they know everything there is to know about religion and related matters. We have a popular saying in Afghanistan that a person who knows nothing thinks he knows everything in the world. However, once he is receptive to the idea that there is much to learn beyond his own sphere of knowledge, he will realize that it cannot be explored in a single lifetime. Instead of misguiding those who look to them for religious instruction, the mullahs would do well to improve their own knowledge of Islam so that the younger generation will benefit from their guidance.

To return to the subject of my own religious instruction, during my early teens, my family encouraged me to go to the mosque and recite my prayers. At school too, some time would be set aside for our early afternoon prayers. The fifth and the last prayer of the day was performed late in the evening, before going to bed. While reciting all five prayers in a mosque was preferable, it was not an obligation; one could just as well say some of the prayers at home or anywhere else deemed appropriate.

The Imam at the local mosque as well as my father and other relatives at home insisted that I recite the prayers five times a day, preferably at the mosque, to ensure my place in heaven. While the other option, hell, was considered only a temporary place of residence for a Muslim who had sinned, going by my idea of how it was meant to be, I tried my level best to avoid the possibility of spending even a fraction of a second there. It is described in Surah Baqara, Ayah Number 24 (Abdullah Yusuf Ali's translation), as follows: "Then fear the fire whose fuel is men and stones which is prepared for those who reject faith."

No wonder I was diligent about saying my prayers five times a day, although with the chores I was entrusted with as my parents' eldest son, it was, by no means, an easy task to make time for them. At the end of the day, I would, however, make it a point to compensate for forgetting a prayer session. I respected Mazum Pacha, our local Imam, and tried hard to live up to his ideals by proving to him that that I was a good boy and capable of being regular with my prayers. I also felt the need to convince my father and other relatives that I was as diligent a Muslim as they were. But in my bid to impress everyone, I lost sight of the objective of my prayers. It began to seem as if it wasn't God Who sent humans to heaven or hell. The people, the very creatures He had created, had assumed the responsibility on His behalf. It even occurred to me that they might expect a fee to send someone to heaven. The situation was such that if a bearded man had decreed that I would be barred from heaven for missing out on a prayer session or failing to fulfill my other religious obligations, I would either be unable to question his authority or be prohibited from doing so. As a result, I would be denied the chance of defending myself against his allegations and his judgment. The combination of school work, homework and religious duties was, indeed, a heavy burden for me. And my early years were spent believing in a very limited concept of religion that guaranteed my place in heaven on the strength of mere ritual: reciting my prayers five times a day and fasting one month in a year. Helping my family andother people in the community seemed to have no place in the scheme of things.

Of the five pillars of Islam, the first has to do with reciting in Arabic the Kalima Tayyeba (the holy word): "There is no deity other than Allah and Muhammad is his messenger." Anyone who recites it and believes in its message is considered a Muslim. There are no other formalities to fulfill, apart from observing the other pillars of Islam in order to remain a Muslim. Once a person becomes a Muslim, he/she is required to pray five times a day, fast from dawn to dusk during the month of Rozha, pay *zakat* to the poor and perform the Haj, a religious pilgrimage to Mecca, once in his/her lifetime, if it is within the person's means. While the prayers are to be recited five times a day and fasting is confined to a specified month in the year, a Muslim is allowed to recite the Kalima Tayyeba as many times as desired. The payment of *zakat* may vary according to one's financial situation, representing as it does a percentage of a Muslim's annual income. The Haj pilgrimage too, is not mandatory for Muslims who are unable to afford the expense.

At no time is a Muslim exempted from his prayers. If he is traveling, an abbreviated version of the prayers is available for his convenience. If he cannot find water to cleanse himself before his prayers, he is allowed to use the dust from a clean cloth to perform the *taimum* ritual before he begins. If age or infirmity cripples a Muslim, he need not prostrate himself like his brethren, but is permitted to sit down in a comfortable position and recite the prayers alone or in the company of others. A bedridden person too, must pray, even if he or she does so simply through gestures. Menstruating women are exempted from the ritual prayers and fasting. If a Muslim, irrespective of gender, misses out on the prayer session at a designated time, he or she must make up for it later. A Muslim is not required to fast on days he or she is traveling or ill during the month of Rozha. However, this too, must be compensated for later in the year, taking into account the number of days he or she had missed out on.

The most difficult pillar of Islam for me was the one involving the five mandatory prayer sessions every day. On certain days, I was so tied up with some other work that I would miss out on one of the sessions. I must also confess that occasionally, I simply forgot to pray at a designated time. Yet I was desperately afraid of missing a prayer for fear that I might end up in hell. A time soon arrived when I just could not compensate for the number of prayers I had missed in the day. I had to lower my expectations of myself and accept the fact that I was just not going to be able to manage all five sessions every day. I still did my best and asked God to forgive me for my lapses, though I would feel guilty whenever I went to the mosque.

Fasting, however, was not as crucial a problem, because I did not have enough to eat anyway. My breakfast was a piece of homemade cornbread and a cup of tea, sweetened with a spoonful of sugar. Lunch at school was a slice of cornbread I had carried from home. Sometimes, if I was lucky, there would be wheat bread at home. My supper consisted of bread and vegetables that were fresh in summer and dried during winter. During the month of Rozha, I would eat two meals: one before dawn, the other, after sunset. Whenever I went to the mosque, I would carry a plate of vegetables and a loaf of bread. Everyone else who came to the mosque would also bring a plate of food from his house and we would all sit down and eat together. This meal, locally known as Rozha Matai (breakfast), started right after sunset, following the Azan, the call for prayer, and would last for a couple of minutes. We would then chant our prayers and go home. The major meal of the day was always eaten at home with the family.

Since I did not have an income at the time, the matter of paying *zakat* or going on a Haj did not apply to me.

My visits to the mosque for Friday prayers set me thinking about life after death. There were apparently a great many pleasures in heaven—drinking wine, keeping male servants and having multiple wives, all of whom I had sexual relations with—that would have amounted to a sin, had I enjoyed them in this world. The afterlife was considered permanent; the life we were living now, temporary, although the latter allowed us to earn merit for the former. How we conducted ourselves in this world would determine the kind of life we would have in the next.

These are reflections I indulge in even today. Heaven, for instance, is described in the Quran as a place where streams of water flow in the shade of trees. For a desert dweller, this image is an immensely appealing one. However, for a person living in a part of the world where trees are plentiful and streams abound, there would be little difference between life on earth and life in heaven. Also, since life after death is eternal, everyone who dies, regardless of his age at the time of his death, becomes a thirty-one-year-old in the afterlife and remains that age for-ever. I guess few would not enjoy eternal youth.

What strikes me particularly is the emphasis the mullahs lay on life after death for men, as if women did not come into the picture at all. Should Muslim women not question that assertion and try to find an afterlife for themselves too? According to my memories of what I was taught in my childhood years, a man's wife apparently becomes his senior wife in the afterlife. If her husband is legally married to several women in this life, would the senior wife have to compete for his affections with the others in the next world? What happens to a woman who does not have a happy married life in this world? Will she be forced to live with the same husband in the afterlife? What about a divorced woman who never remarried? What about a woman, such as my Aunt Haleema, who remarried after being widowed? Does she have to keep both of her husbands happy in the afterlife? If this is the case, heaven may not guarantee a happy life.

I am certainly worried about my own case, because Anna is the only wife I have and she is a Catholic. Will she be able to join me in the afterlife or will I be alone if God decides to send me to heaven? Or if we both die, will we be assigned to the Muslim heaven or the Christian one? Or will we be separated. The Muslim heaven may be barred to Anna, because she did not convert after her marriage. By the same argument, the Christians may not let me into their heaven, because I remained a Muslim even after marrying her. There is also the possibility of us being denied access to both heavens, because we did not faithfully follow the teachings of our respective religions. As a Muslim, I believe in one God. As a Catholic Christian, Anna too, believes in one God. However, each of us defines God differently. To me, God is above all human relations. To Anna, God is our Heavenly Father Who sent His son, Jesus Christ, to die for the sins our ancestors had committed. If the two Gods are different, each may use different criteria of judgment before determining which humans should proceed to heaven and which to hell. Apart from Islam and Christianity, there are countless other religions in the world, whose adherents believe in yet another set of gods. These gods not only have the task of determining which humans among their devotees should go to heaven or hell, but must also come to a decision about those who believe in another god.

Coming back to my case and Anna's, perhaps God will decide to send us to purgatory. I have been told that life in purgatory is a temporary phase. I assume the place is for those cases that are so complicated that God needs more time to think about them before arriving at a decision. Unfortunately, in our case, the appropriate permanent residence might just be hell, since we may both have been perceived to violate the principles of our respective religions. On the other hand, God could decide to reincarnate us and send us back to earth for a second temporary life to redeem ourselves. However, if He takes that long to deliberate on every controversial case on earth, the latter itself may cease to exist before we are reincarnated. In that case, God may send Anna and me to another planet to complete our temporary life before He assigns us to our rightful place in our permanent life. Since our case is far from unique, what troubles me is the thought of the monumental task He has ahead of him. And by the way, Abdullah, the Prophet Muhammad's father, and some of his other close relatives were not Muslims. So will they be sent to heaven or hell?

When I suggest that the afterlife may not be an improvement on the life we have in this world, I may be accused of blasphemy by some of our religious leaders. Yet there is a saying in Afghanistan that no one has returned from the afterlife, the implication being that no one knows about life after death. Those who preach the gospel of God could well be more concerned about improving their own lifestyles in this world than about what awaits them after death. Or they could be busy trying to establish a dream life after death that is way better than the life they have now. Exploiting our lack of knowledge about the matter, certain people claim they are closer to God than others, leading laypersons to believe that by respecting and obeying these self-styled representatives of God, they will be assured a place in heaven.

Let me tell you the story of Inzeri Mullah Sahib, who used to live in Inzerai, a mountain village north-east of Khas Kunar. Gul Bebu's father, Abdul Rahman, would often undertake a daylong journey on foot to carry a goat or a sheep as a gift for him. Almost everyone in Khas Kunar considered the mullah a saint and would visit him to ask for his blessings. Each *mureed* or follower would stay overnight at his monastery and be rewarded with a loaf of dry bread which he could take back home with him. The *mureed* would bring the bread home and distribute pieces of it among his family members and other relatives. By eating the bread, they believed they were sharing the blessing the mullah had bestowed on his mureed, thereby ensuring that God would forgive them their sins and facilitate their journey to heaven. I am now sure that the mullah and those living in his monastery were more concerned about improving their own lives than helping the *mureeds* or their families and relatives to go to heaven. Had Abdul Rahman slaughtered the animals he took as gifts for the mullah and fed the meat to his family and relatives, he would have done them a world of good and been better placed, as a result, in his quest to proceed to heaven when the time came.

The *hazrats* and peers of Kabul are famous for striking bargains with their *mureeds*: if the latter can show proper reverence for them—often, in the form of generous donations—they will be rewarded with a wonderful life after death. These much-respected men have already won over the fathers and even grandfathers of their *mureeds* by luring them with the promise of God's mercy and expand their sphere of influence by approaching their sons and grandsons too. By strengthening their support among the people in this manner, the *hazrats* and peers have consolidated their religious and political positions within the government. For example, Sibghatullah Mujaddadi aka Hazrat Sahib and Sayed Ahmad Gailani aka Peer Sahib were prominent leaders during the *jihad* in Afghanistan and played a significant role in its perpetuation by first supporting the Taliban, then conspiring against them by becoming part of the international initiative to rid the country of them and bring Hamid Karzai to power. Without support from their followers, neither would have been able to exert such influence in the political arena and if the government bows to their dictates today, it is because its survival would be at stake without their backing. Given Afghanistan's situation, it is clear that the *hazrats* and peers are more preoccupied in improving their lives in this world than in worrying about what lies in store for them in heaven—that is, if they go to heaven.

Peer Sayed Ahmad Gailani, in particular, enjoys living in his palatial mansion in England, condescending to visit his castle in Afghanistan for a while to show his face to his *mureeds* and ensure their continued support. During his absence from Afghanistan, a family member is, in all likelihood, appointed to collect donations on his behalf, intended, ostensibly for the poor among their *mureeds*. Being naïve, the devotees are unaware of the real intentions of these so-called holy men and get taken for a ride. It is hoped that with education available to a wider cross-section of the population and the knowledge that comes with it, these *mureeds* will be able to see their peers and *hazrats* for what they are—ordinary human beings like them who use false promises to hold them in thrall. The *mureeds* can then focus on improving their own lives instead of persuading their peers to negotiate with God on their behalf. God is there for all of us and everyone should be able to seek His blessings directly without having to call in a "broker" to present their case, as it were.

The gospel being preached by the Christian clergy to their congregations is, in no way, superior to the teachings of the Muslim mullahs. The preachers of both religions speak of God's infinite love, yet incite their faithfull to hate the followers of other religions. Those Christians who claim that Muslims are destined for hell, because they do not respect the Christian god, are surely mistaken. For Muslims worship neither Jesus nor Muhammad. They worship the god who created both men. What appealed to me in this context was a statement made by Kiven James in the final episode of "The King of Queens," where he told a Jewish Rabbi that the latter's god was the father of his own god. In fact, all three faiths worship the Father or Supreme Being. If Islam differs from the other faiths, it is in the belief that God cannot have a son, since fathering a child is a human attribute. The god Muslims worship is beyond that. God in the Quran is described in Surah Ikhlas (translated by Abdullah Yusuf Ali), as follows: "Say: 'He is God, the one and only; God, the eternal, absolute; He begetteth not, nor is He begotten; And there is none like unto Him." It is difficult to imagine that three religions, which started with the worship of the same God, diverged so radically as to have their followers become sworn enemies. It is a shame that in spite of living in the twenty-first century, many of us continue to insist that the god we worship is superior to the one adherents of other faiths believe in.

While Christians and Jews are free to hate Muslims without being perceived to violate the principles of their respective faiths, Muslims are bound by Islam to regard those very same Jews and Christians as people of the book. As a result, Muslims have the same respect for Jesus, Moses, Abraham and other prophets as they have for Muhammad. A Muslim risks jeopardizing his religious beliefs if he defames the roughly 124,000 prophets revered by the practitioners of other faiths. No newspaper in an Islamic country is likely to print a cartoon ridiculing any of the aforesaid prophets. It is important to note that this is the outcome of respect for the prophets revered by other religions, rather than of official restrictions on self-expression. Since making derogatory statements about the Prophet Muhammed and the faith he propagated is not construed to be against the principles of Christianity and Judaism, criticism of Islam has become virulent after 11 September 2001. A Christian leader, Jerry Falwell, even declared Muhammad to be a terrorist. I find the statement absurd in the extreme and ironical in light of the fact that Muhammad lived over 1400 years ago, whereas individuals like Falwell have equated the Prophet with terrorism only after 11 September 2001. A Muslim, on the other hand, would hesitate to make a similar statement about Jesus, because he would consider it a sin that might send him to hell. A Muslim preacher would never encourage such statements about Jesus Christ either, because Muslims regard him as a beloved prophet who received from God the holy book of Injeel (the New Testament). He is one of the four prophets deemed closest to God, the others being Moses, Ibrahim and Muhammad. Moreover, Muslims have accepted other prophets revered by both Jews and Christians. The fifth pillar of Islam, the Haj, is, in fact, about Ibrahim, one of those prophets, described as Khalilullah (friend of God) and revered by all three faiths. He is the first to have built the Kaaba and is said to have stood on a stone while doing so. Every Muslim pilgrim circumambulating the Kaaba during the Haj or the Umra must pay his respects to this sacred stone and honor the sacrifice Ibrahim made by sacrificing a sheep on the first day of Loy Akhtar (Eid Al-Adha), celebrated by Muslims all over the world at the end of the Haj ceremony. Therefore, for a Muslim to show disrespect to any of the prophets beloved of the followers of all three faiths would be to violate the principles of Islam. I can only assume that those who make pejorative statements like Falwell need to learn more about Islam and Muslims. The world would certainly become a better place to live in if the followers of each of the three Unitarian religions focused on the principles of their respective faiths and worshipped one god instead of allowing their politicized versions to dictate their thoughts, words and actions.

I was fortunate to learn about all the prophets—almost all 124,000 of them—chosen by God to teach people in their respective communities to abstain from sin and follow the right path to salvation. I was also taught to say, "Alaihissalam," (peace by upon him) after the name of each prophet, from Adam to Muhammad, was mentioned. One should think about the amount of networking in the twenty-first century if one has any respect for all the prophets dear to the followers of the three religions. In addition to the teachings of Islam, I learned a lot about Christianity and Judaism by attending the prayer services in mosques, especially the afternoon prayers every Friday. Being well acquainted with the teachings of the prophets whom Islam respected as much as the other two faiths did, the Imam of every mosque would take pains to explain to his congregation how the aforesaid prophets had always tried to guide their people along the right path. I can only wonder if Christians and Jews are similarly familiarized with the teachings of Muhammad when they attend services in church or in a synagogue. If they were, they would, perhaps, respect Islam more than they do now. They would not need to question the extent of their preacher's knowledge of Islam. Nor would they need to go to the main source of such knowledge—the Quran—to learn about Islam on their own.

My respect for all the three religions began early in life and was reinforced as I grew up. My religious education at home was supplemented by the religious studies courses I had taken in elementary and secondary school. Despite the fact that the language of the Quran is Arabic, which most Afghans do not understand, hearing someone recite its verses in a sonorous voice is enough for them to sense and savor their beauty. But beyond the mere melody of the verses and of the voice reciting them, the beautiful message underlying the words also needs to be conveyed. I was among the fortunate ones who would begin enjoying this experience quite early in life. I was in the sixth grade, when I joined my father, along with a few other government officials, who had decided to take translation lessons from Maulawi Abdul Khaliq, the new Imam of our local mosque in Chaghaserai. A graduate from a university dedicated entirely to religious studies in Deoband, India, he was a respected religious scholar and taught the course to the government officials without charging any fees.

Right after our morning prayers, we would all gather under a mulberry tree in the courtyard of the mosque and read and translate a few verses from the Quran, starting from the very beginning. The Imam would translate every verse literally and then interpret the underlying message for us. I am told that the Prophet Muhammad himself had learned the Quran in the same way, verse by verse, though they were apparently not revealed to him in sequential order. He would memorize the verse or verses he had heard from Gabriel and repeat them for the Ashab (pronounced "as-hab") Al-Suffa (friends of the patio) who, in turn, memorized the verses and probably recorded them in writing. From what I have been led to believe, the Bible—both the Old Testament and the New—on the other hand, was revealed in written form. While reading the Old Testament, I did feel it was written the way a history book would be. The Quran was put together in the form of a book only during the time of one of the Prophet Muhammad's caliphs.

Initially, the Prophet was hesitant about his ability to do justice to his responsibilities as the chosen messenger of God, for he was illiterate and unable to either read or write. I was told that the first verse of the Quran revealed to him was among the short verses in the second half of the last chapter. It begins with, "Proclaim (or read)! In the name of thy Lord and Cherisher, Who created—created man, out of a (mere) clot of congealed blood. Proclaim! And thy Lord is most Bountiful. He Who taught (the use of) the pen, taught man that which he knew not…" Thus inspired by the verse, the Prophet felt able to take on the mission of spreading God's word. I believe the last verse of the Quran was revealed to Muhammad on Mount Arafat. He addressed his followers and conveyed God's message to them, which was as follows: "This day have I perfected your religion for you, completed my favor upon you, and have chosen for you Islam as your religion." This is Abdullah Yusuf Ali's English translation of the third Ayah in Surah Al-Mayed. Those who had listened to the message grew despondent at the thought of Muhammad's advancing years and approaching death, for the Prophet had been chosen as God's messenger when he was already forty years old. He would die at the age of sixty-three, having served as the Prophet for twenty-three years.

By the time I had graduated from elementary school and accompanied my younger brother back to Khas Kunar because of my father's early retirement, I had already completed learning the first six chapters of the Quran. The extent of knowledge I had gained from this course became evident, when I went to Lebanon and watched the movie, *The Bible*, at a theatre on Al-Hamra Street in Beirut. It began with Adam, who was created from clay and assumed human form before rising to his feet. Then I saw Eve, his wife, eating a forbidden apple, which she also offered to him. By eating the fruit, both committed a sin and were banished from the Garden of Eden and sent to live on earth. Then came the story of Adam and Eve's sons on earth. One of them would kill his brother and then find out what he should do with the dead body after carrying it with him for a few days. This was followed by the story of Noah and the Ark, which carried his family and pairs of animals from every species on earth to save them from the Flood. There followed the story of Ibrahim (or Abraham) who obeyed God's command to sacrifice his son, but slaughtered a ram, instead. The last story is that of Moses who appeals to God about the fate of his people, the children of Israel. I have learned to say, "Kaleemullah" (the one who speaks to God) after mentioning the name, "Mosa." It is by reading the Quran, attending the prayer services in local mosques and being a participant in the translation course taught by Maulawi Abdul Khaliq that I have learned about all these prophets of other faiths.

Watching the movie, *The Bible*, I discovered that the prophets featured in it were respected and accepted in the other two religions and traced the historical era to which each belonged. The similarity in the stories about these prophets to be found in the sacred scriptures of each faith was evident. If there were a few differences, these were minor and probably came about because of the oral tradition of passing on stories from generation to generation, with variations inevitably creeping in from one narrator to the next. For example, in the movie, Eve ate an apple. In the Quran, the name of the fruit is not mentioned, but the rest of the story is identical. Ibrahim (or Abraham) was commanded by God to sacrifice his son Ishaq (or Isaac), the son of his first wife, Sarah. The Quran states, however, that he was ordered to sacrifice his other son, Ismail, whom he fathered with his younger wife, Hagar. Ibrahim killed neither of his sons. That God sent the sheep Ibrahim slaughtered, instead, is accepted by all three faiths.

A preacher has a choice between highlighting the differences in each faith or emphasizing the common elements they all share. How he chooses to interpret a particular scripture determines his followers' attitude to other faiths. Sermons are powerful instruments of communication and emotionally charged to engage the congregation's attention and ensure its involvement. If a preacher uses his power of communication to emphasize the differences in the three religions, he is paving the way to distrust and disrespect for any faith other than one's own. By highlighting the similarities, on the other hand, he can foster a feeling of unity, harmony and peace. It all depends on how a message is conveyed and the intentions of the preacher who is entrusted with its communication. He can either narrow down our focus or widen the extent of our knowledge, broaden our horizons and open our minds.

The program which really helped me to do so by acquainting me with the world's major civilizations consisted of four compulsory courses at the AUB, grouped together under the title, Cultural Studies. We started with the most ancient known civilization of Mesopotamia and the book we were required to read contained an epic poem called the *Epic of Gilgamesh*. The similarity between the stories of Gilgamesh and Noah's Ark is striking, though the events narrated could only have been possible in an era when people lived at the mercy of nature. Consequently, their folklore is full of tales about floods, storms, hurricanes and other natural disasters. Moving on to Greek civilization, the books we students read were Homer's *Iliad* and *The Republic* by Plato. During my tour of Europe in 1966, I would visit the Parthenon in Athens. As I walked up the hill and through the ruins on my way to the summit, I could imagine the oracles around the area involved in a discourse with each other. Our next area of focus in class would be Roman civilization and the birth of Christianity. The books we read in this context were the *Purgatory* of Dante and both the Old and New Testaments. Reading the Old Testament took me back to the teachings of Maulawi Abdul Khaliq and his translation of the first six chapter of the Quran. I discovered that almost all the stories of the prophets in the Old Testament were also featured in the Quran, some, albeit, with minor variations. On a subsequent visit to the Vatican and the Sistine Chapel during my trip to Europe, I would learn all that I was hoping to about Christianity.

Islam came next in our program and the book we were required to read was the philosophy of Ibn-e Rushd. Since I was already familiar with the contents of the Quran and had acquired preliminary knowledge of the teachings of Islam, I did not have to read a great many books on the subject. We then proceeded to contemporary civilizations or ideologies such as communism and existentialism. Marx's *Das Kapital* and Jean-Paul Sartre's theory of existentialism and socialism were required reading. In retrospect, all that I learned in those four courses unwinds in my mind like a long film about human evolution and the contribution of people from all over the world to the advancement of ideologies, science and technology. The Arabs imbibed much of what Greek civilization had to offer and passed it on to the Western world. And the Silk Road must have played its own role in enriching civilization in both Europe and Asia through such cross-cultural transfers.

While reading the history of my own country, I would discover that my ancestors were Buddhists, with schools all over the area that is now recognized as Afghanistan. The statues of their Lord Buddha in Bamiyan, the Buddhist school in Hadda, Jalalabad, and the ruins in Aya Khanem in the north of the country are all symbols of a very advanced civilization. With the subsequent conquest of Afghanistan by Alexander the Great, however, a strong Greco-Buddhist influence would be introduced. When Genghis Khan invaded the country, he brought with him a culture of violence and mayhem. The Arabs followed, conquering much of the country and converting its inhabitants to Islam, but for the Nooristan area, where the people continued to practice their indigenous faith. It was Abdul Rahman Khan who would ultimately convert the Nooristanis to Islam and change the name of the area from Kafiristan (the land of infidels) to Nooristan (the land of light).

SEVENTEEN

Discussion and Recommendations

While my life has been through its own share of upheavals, both in Afghanistan and abroad, my compatriots have experienced the kind of turmoil that citizens of few countries in the world have had to suffer. If my life took a turn for the better, it was probably because I was able to leave the country at the right time and pursue my dreams elsewhere. Many of my fellow Afghans were less fortunate and I can only feel a deep sense of regret over what they have had to endure. Forced to flee the familiar environment in which they had lived, most were either persecuted or killed during the mass exodus because of their religion, language and ethnicity. Those who survived lived under the constant threat of danger and starvation. A great number ended up in squalid, overcrowded refugee camps in neighboring countries like Pakistan and Iran, suffering from injustice, absence of adequate security and lack of health and educational facilities. The governments of both Pakistan and Iran made every effort to send the hapless Afghan refugees back across the border, not only accusing them of involvement in the illegal trade of narcotics and weapons, but also alleging that they were robbing their own citizens of employment opportunities and having a destabilizing effect on their society.

Afghanistan, unfortunately, had no place for these refugees either, because in the meantime, local warlords had parceled the country into sections and claimed these for themselves, with different factions fighting each other for supremacy. Thanks to three decades of anarchy and civil war in the country, the Afghan people could no longer expect to satisfy even basic human needs such as food, shelter, education and health care. Denied a normal existence, the generation born during the war grew up assuming that battles and gunfire were a way of life. Once the Soviet forces had pulled out of the country, the US government considered its mission accomplished and withdrew its aid and support from the Afghan government. It did not take long for the power vacuum to be filled. Extremist Arab mercenaries who had joined the *jihad* against the Soviet forces, with the full backing of the Western powers, now felt free to establish a terrorist stronghold in Afghanistan. Exploiting Afghan hospitality, they consolidated their position under the Taliban and exported their version of terrorism to the US on 11 September 2001. It was with this event that the American government would wake up to the reality of the monster in their midst and launch its mission against al-Qaeda and its supporters all over the world.

Back in Afghanistan, ordinary citizens were so traumatized by the rule of the so-called *mujahideen*, that they even began reminiscing about the years under the monarchy with a sense of nostalgia. With the king holding the reins of power, they had been poor all right, but had lived in peace. From the time the *mujahideen* had taken over the country, however, supposedly to fight the *jihad* or holy war, the people had not been allowed a moment of peace. For contrary to the tenets of Islam, this war against infidels was also being waged against other Muslims for abstaining from the violence these so-called holy warriors had unleashed upon the land or simply for getting in the way of their selfish goals. These *mujahideen*, as they called themselves, were motivated by pure greed—for money and dominance. Given the ordeal they were made to go through, ordinary Afghans had reason to feel they had been better off under the monarchy.

The absolute monarchy under the last king of Afghanistan, Zahir Shah, became a constitutional monarchy in 1964, paving the way for citizens other than those who were members of the royal family, to participate in government. The coup d'état that would take place within the royal family in 1973, while the king was abroad, ended the monarchy and brought in its place a version of a royal republic. The first president, Mehmed Daoud, cousin and brother-in-law of Zahir Shah, allowed the Communist Party to run the country's administration, because he had come to power with its support. The two factions of the Communist/Socialist Party united, but could not hold together as a single entity and split again, triggering not only the assassinations of their respective leaders and high-ranking officials, but also the murder of anyone outside the party who was considered an opponent of its ideology. Under pressure from the growing influence of Muslim *mujahideen*, the party collapsed, forcing the Soviet Union to withdraw its forces from Afghanistan in 1989. With their retreat, the Soviet empire suffered a fatal political setback that would lead to its eventual collapse and disintegration and the subsequent birth of several independent countries in Eastern Europe and central Asia.

The Taliban, who came to power in 1994, captured Kabul in 1996, executed the country's last communist ruler, Najeebullah, and did not waste time in setting up a fundamentalist regime, which they named the Islamic Emirate of Afghanistan. In doing so, they made every effort to drag Afghanistan more than 1400 years back into the past, to the very beginnings of Islam. The Arabs under the leadership of al-Qaeda who had arrived earlier, ostensibly to participate in the *jihad*, now found an opportunity to assist the Taliban government in conducting its military campaign against all opposition in the country. While the regime had mullahs and maulawis among their leaders, none was a scholar of Islam or had any experience in running a government. The vacuum thus created was just what the Arabs had been looking for: the ideal pretext to impose their religious and political ideologies on the Taliban. When the latter found themselves politically and economically isolated by international sanctions, the Arab extremists became their sole support in terms of financial aid and military expertise. With the events of 11 September

2001, the Taliban realized they would have to choose between distancing themselves from the Arabs and their support or abandoning Afghanistan altogether. They chose the latter option and paved the *way for the invasion of Afghanistan by foreign forces and the occupation of the capital city, Kabul, by the Northern Alliance.*

With the empowerment of the Northern Alliance, tensions escalated between the Pashtuns and various minorities, increasing the possibility of the country's division into the north and the south. Having managed to rid themselves of the mostly Pashtun Taliban, the north, where most of the non-Pashtun ethnic groups lived, rejoiced in its newly acquired sense of power. In fact, the Americans, the latest foreign military power to enter Afghanistan and occupy it, were unique in having done so with the support of the country's ethnic minorities. The British forces, on the other hand, had tried to invade the country, years earlier, through its Pashtun-occupied areas and fought the Afghans in three successive battles, but were driven back and forced to recognize Afghanistan as an independent country in 1919. The royal family had been ousted by a Tajik, after Amanullah was overthrown in 1929. King Zahir Shah's father, Nader Shah, and his two uncles, Hashem Khan and Shah Wali Khan, had entered Afghanistan through the Pashtun territory of Pakistan, conquered the capital city of Kabul and restored the monarchy. The Loya Jerga system created by the Pashtuns in Afghanistan had played a major role in resolving national disputes. And the Pashtuns themselves had been the dominant group in staving off invasions and preventing the country's occupation by foreign forces. The Americans and their NATO allies found an alternative way, relying on the minority groups to invade and occupy Afghanistan. It was with the support of their local allies that they launched their military offensive against the Taliban and the Pashtuns. *Unfortunately, the circumstances that had led to the occupation empowered the other ethnic minorities and encouraged them to settle scores with the Pashtuns.* Pursued mainly in the southern and eastern parts of Afghanistan by foreign and local government forces, the Pashtuns initially lost ground, but managed to regroup and continue their struggle. The Pashtun minority living in the north now felt threatened, as pressure was brought to bear against them by the other ethnic groups which accused them of supporting the Taliban. Their sense of insecurity deepened when a weak Afghan government hesitated to take a firm stand on the matter *and the foreign powers showed no interest whatsoever in supporting them. As a result, some members of the Pashtun minority in the north were either killed or forced to leave the area.* The foreign forces in Afghanistan initially claimed to be waging war against al-Qaeda, but they were also fighting the Taliban because of their allegiance to al-Qaeda. Being mostly Pashtuns, the Taliban would operate in the Pashtun areas of Afghanistan, with the local Pashtuns providing them sanctuaries to hide from the foreign forces. *Nocturnal raids were conducted on the family compounds of suspected Taliban sympathizers in the Pashtun areas.* Consequently, these areas were under perennial threat and most of the inhabitants fled, leaving their homes and settling elsewhere in the country. The lives of many innocent people living in the area were disrupted and some were killed because of a case of mistaken identity. The family members of those who had been exterminated in this manner retaliated by doing something which had, so far, been unheard of among the Afghans; they became suicide bombers. *Pursued by the military and security forces and ignored by the local government,* the Pashtuns had no support from any quarter. They are still suffering today and constitute the largest internally displaced community in Kabul and elsewhere in the country. Most of the Pashtuns now wear turbans and grow beards, making them indistinguishable from the Taliban or their foreign allies.

Due to the threat under which they lived in areas of the country to which they did not traditionally belong, members of the Pashtun minority in the north had been forced to protect themselves against the injustice and discrimination they faced from other ethnic and linguistic groups. The foreign forces were also apprehensive that the unstable conditions in the south and east of the country would gradually spread to the north. To prevent such an eventuality, the American government decided to establish a democracy in Afghanistan. The USA itself has a democratically elected government, whose seniormost officials, including federal government employees, representatives of the Congress and even the president, are voted to power by the citizens of the country. The Americans, in fact, come out in large numbers to cast their vote and take great pride in electing their leader and his representatives. In a democratic system such as theirs, the best candidate stands a good chance of winning. The officials and representatives thus chosen are subject to the laws of the country and accountable to the American public whose support has ensured their election to leadership positions. As an American citizen, I listen attentively to the speeches delivered by state and federal candidates, observe the debates they attend and follow the policy line they adopt before casting my vote. No pressure is brought to bear on me in the matter of my choice of candidate; nor am I obliged to divulge the name of the person in whose favor I cast my vote. The total number of votes cast for a candidate determines who will win with a majority. This is true democracy and it should serve as an example elsewhere in the world. In Afghanistan, however, despite the judicial system being in place, laws are often not enforced, leading certain individuals with clout to assume that they are accountable to no one. Their conviction is reinforced by the inability of most of the country's poor to afford legal action against their tyranny; all such downtrodden citizens can do is fall back on the use of arms which, for them, is a last resort when all else fails. The political longevity of those who come to power in Afghanistan, even if they do so through elections, depends on the power base they are representing. If they have a strong base, they usually stay in power longer than those who do not. The first elected president of Afghanistan, Sibghatullah Mujaddadi, for example, belonged to the latter group. He was a mere puppet, with the Northern Alliance in control of Kabul and its members making all the decisions on his behalf. When his term came to an end, he left, or rather, was forced to leave the office of the president. On the other hand, Burhanudeen Rabbani, a member of the Northern Alliance who succeeded him, was in a far more stable position because of his stronger base. When his term came to an end, he did not hand over the reins of government to someone else, as expected, but held on, confident that the influence he wielded was widespread enough to silence all semblance of protest. When the Taliban came to power, however, they upset the status quo by conquering Kabul and removing the Northern Alliance from the capital. Had it not been for them, Rabbani or another candidate from the Northern Alliance would have stayed in power for life. It turned out, however, that the Taliban were least interested in Kabul as a power base, for their leader, Mullah Muhammad Omar, ruled the country from Qandahar, which he treated, to all intents and purposes, as the new seat of government.

Given the turn of events, a coalition of mostly democratic countries then invaded and occupied Afghanistan, with the approval of the United Nations, their main goal being to rid the country of the Taliban insurgents and pave the way for a functional government to come to power. However, their well-meaning intention to ensure Afghanistan's security and stability by relying on a traditional form of power sharing—holding elections in the way it had always been done—would ultimately backfire, because in focusing on their own objectives, they ended up undermining the interests of the locals. The Loya Jerga system, created by the founder of modern Afghanistan, Ahmad Shah Baba (1747-1773), had always been used to settle both local and national disputes in the Afghan way. In June 2002, during George W. Bush's eight-year term as president—one of the least popular in the political history of the USA—a twenty-first-century version would be used for the presidential election in Afghanistan, bringing Hamid Karzai to power. It was unfortunate that the US administration which backed the Afghan president should be headed by none other than a man who had damaged the reputation of his Republican Party locally and reinforced the old image of the "ugly American" worldwide. The fallout was equally ugly. The Afghans, who had once regarded Americans as allies they could rely on, now began looking upon them as their most despised enemies, no different from either the Russians who had invaded their country with ulterior motives or the British who had preceded them with similar intentions.

A democratic system which does not cater to the interests of a country's citizens, favoring certain groups to the detriment of others in a bid to serve the interests of the occupying forces, eventually morphs into a form of government that is no better than a dictatorship. Britain had attempted to create a similar situation in an era when the sun was still shining on its Empire and the Indian sub-continent was still a part of that Empire bordering Afghanistan. Its military offensives against the country were a vain effort to retrieve its lost territories and keep the Empire intact. The Russians followed in their footsteps in the 1980s, intending to enforce the Soviet Union's so-called democratic system and run the government via a puppet regime. There were even speculations that their primary target was the warm waters of the Indian Ocean. Both foreign powers tried to subjugate the Afghans by deploying a divide-and-rule strategy and eventually, both were forced to retreat with their tail between their legs.

Having lost its empire and its glory, Britain is now territorially confined to a mere island, which it shares with Ireland. The disintegration of the Soviet Union has led to the loss of its status as a superpower.

Given the lessons Afghanistan's history has taught its previous invaders, the present coalition of occupying forces would do well to refrain from emulating the ways of the superpowers of the past. Their main goal should be the upliftment of ordinary Afghans. If they fail in that endeavor and merely continue disrupting their lives, chances are that the local governments set up by the occupying forces will come under pressure from their own electorate. The foreseeable outcome would be the withdrawal of the foreign forces from the country or its less palatable alternative: its continued occupation of a now hostile Afghanistan.

The present coalition of occupying forces may have ways of justifying their presence in the country, but ordinary Afghans are not likely to be easily won over by their argument. In order to achieve their perceived objectives, such forces typically consolidate their position by supporting the stronger political group in the country. However, the problem arises when the group supporting the foreign forces in Afghanistan is not necessarily the one with the stronger power base. For instance, the Northern Alliance, which supports the occupying forces, is composed of Tajiks, Uzbeks and Hazaras, who reside mainly in the north and constitute a minority. While they are united against the Pashtun majority, their own regional interests often come in the way and lead to clashes with each other. The present occupying forces are unlikely to progress in their mission if they fail to enhance the little success they have achieved in the Pashtun areas by improving the lives of the locals and bringing stability to that part of the country. Karzai's government, unfortunately, finds itself in a bind. The Taliban denounce him as a puppet, while the opposition groups object to anything his government sets out to do. For his re-election to the presidency, Karzai had to bend over backward to please his opponents in the Northern Alliance; the votes of the people residing in the north were crucial to his political future, for living as they did in a relatively secure area, they could venture out, visit the voting centers and cast their votes, unlike the residents of less stable areas for whom the option was not available.

The Afghans may have voted Karzai to power, but they can do little to keep him in the presidential palace. *What ensures that he—or a so-called elected leader like him—remains there is the support of the countries which have forces in Afghanistan.* Karen DeYoung and Graig Whittlock opened their article, "Kandahar offensive not on schedule," on the first page of the 11 June 2010 issue of the *Washington Post* with the following words: "When the Obama administration decided last fall to accept Hamid Karzai as the legitimate president of Afghanistan for the next five years, there were no illusions that working with him and his government would be easy." The point here is that the Afghans may have voted Karzai to power, but he is headed for certain failure if he does not succeed in aligning the interests of the foreign occupying powers with those of the local population. For the only way of ridding the country of the menace of insurgency and restoring stability is to improve the lives of ordinary Afghans.

The Afghans are not really demanding the impossible. In fact, having gone through a miserable quarter of a century under the communists, the mujahideen, *the Northern Alliance and the Taliban, they had almost given up on their country. But they began experiencing the first stirrings of optimism when, for the first time in years, the foreign occupation enabled them to send their 500-odd representatives to Kabul to participate in the first Loya Jerga. It seemed remarkable to them that despite being under foreign occupation, they were being given an opportunity to elect their own leader. They were ready to vote for ex-King Zahir Shah, a symbol of unity for forty years until the coup d'état engineered in 1973 by his cousin and brother-in-law, Daoud, coup d'état in had forced him into permanent exile.* But their hopes were fated to be shattered. In fact, had it not been for the Northern Alliance that compelled the former monarch to withdraw his name from the list of candidates on the very first day of the Loya Jerga in a bid to pave the way for some of its members to elect one of their own candidates, most of the Jerga would have voted the ex-king to power. This was the same monarch who had once enjoyed the title, Trustee of God. His name had been mentioned during Friday prayers in mosques all over the country and all who joined in those prayers would appeal to God to give him a long life. *The situation was different now. The first Loya Jerga was delayed for a day in order to facilitate the election of Karzai with an announcement by the ex-king that he was not interested in the leadership position. He was forced to accept the title of Father of the Nation, a so-called honor that divested him and his family of all political power. It was, indeed, a sad end for the man whose father had ruled the country since 1929 after overthrowing Bacha-e Saqau.*

The election of Karzai was, however, a judicious choice, because as a Pashtun, he represents the country's ethnic majority. The media had reported that his father, Abdul Ahad Karzai, had been killed by the Taliban in Quetta, Pakistan. *Rumors were that the first choice for the presidency in Afghanistan was, in fact, not Karzai, but Commander Abdul Haq.* However, that plan fell through when he was killed by the Taliban in Nangarhar province.

The first Loya Jerga had elected Karzai as the president of Afghanistan under pressure; when they reconvened, however, they re-elected him to the same post. Unless the Afghans amend the Constitution, however, to facilitate Karzai's chances of remaining president for the third five-year term, he is likely to be ousted from his position. But the point cannot be overemphasized that restoration of law and order in the country is imperative if the foreign occupying forces wish to reconcile their ultimate objectives with those of the Afghan national government and eventually leave Afghanistan in good faith. The Afghans, for their part, would regard the relationship they had shared with the foreign powers as the beginning of a lifelong friendship.

But much work remains to be done before that end can be achieved. *There is no certainty, after all, that the new democracy in Afghanistan will survive.* The only way it can do so is by preparing the ground for a real democracy to be set up, whereby the most deserving candidate for the presidency will be voted to power and each subsequent president will endeavor to improve the lives of all Afghans, instead of trying to retain his position by catering to the ethnic, religious or linguistic group whose support has brought him to power. *At present, time is on the side of the countries occupying Afghanistan. The latter has earned the support of the United Nations and that of a large number of countries in the world.* If the participating nations witness some progress that benefits the lives of ordinary Afghans and there is hope of normalcy being restored, they may well decide to continue their support of the country. If, however, Afghanistan under the occupation remains unstable, these countries may become disillusioned and question their support *for a never-ending and, ultimately, meaningless war.* Most of the democracies in the West would be well within their rights to conclude that the war in Afghanistan was not their war, after all. Their leaders have to keep public interest uppermost in their minds if they intend to win elections in their own countries. Without the support of their people, they would not be in power. And if the people decide against supporting a war, whose outcome does not impact their lives, being fought in faraway Afghanistan, the leader must, in the interests of his own survival, respect their wishes. It has already happened, with the citizens of Spain refusing to support their government's decision of deploying troops in Iraq. The leaders of participating countries in the ISAF forces may follow the same trend and *get out of Afghanistan, once and for all.*

Most Afghans are tired of the war that has shattered their country and if they fight on, it is because they still hope to restore a semblance of normalcy to their lives. *If their elected government, with the support of participating nations, is unable to restore law and order in the country, there is grave danger of the Taliban or a similarly repressive group wresting control and returning to power. A development of this nature may be too much for both the occupying forces and the local government to handle.* The Americans and other allied forces have a formidable challenge ahead of them: gaining the support of the general population and, at the same time, winning the war against the Taliban and al-Qaeda. So far, chasing the Taliban fighters and their leaders has resulted in large-scale casualties among the civilian population. *The international news media has been periodically reporting the loss of civilian lives in Afghanistan. The occupying forces and the Taliban have indulged in a mutual blame game, holding each other responsible for these unfortunate incidents. The loss of some innocent lives has even been described as collateral damage. Most of the civilian casualties have been in the Pashtun areas, where maintaining security has been as great a challenge for the local government as for the occupying forces.* The Americans have been operating in hostile terrain since 2001, when the defeat of the Taliban prompted the latter to join forces with their Arab and Pakistani allies and win the local population over to their cause. The Taliban mainly operate in areas where there is a Pashtun majority, with the local men wearing beards and turbans in their bid to emulate the insurgents. Some do so, because, like other Afghans, they consider it their religious obligation. For others, it is simply a means of survival, for alienating the Taliban might lead to death. *However, this does pose a problem for both the administration and occupying forces. If they fail to differentiate between the local population and the insurgents, be they Taliban or al-Qaeda, they may end up endangering the lives of civilians and forcing them into a situation that can be best described as being trapped between a tiger and a cliff, as an old Pashto saying puts it. Caught in a bind that would involve a choice between fighting, fleeing or perishing, many would leave their lands and native villages, adding to the swelling population of internally displaced people.*

A situation of this kind would also encourage members of other ethnic groups to join the local and foreign forces and, in the guise of weeding out insurgents from the Pashtun-dominated areas of both Afghanistan and Pakistan, avenge their personal grievances against the Pashtuns. The local governments in both countries are torn between soliciting support from their countrymen on the one hand, and appeasing the concerned foreign governments, on the other, in a bid to stay in power. The votes of the local electorate are as important to their survival as the financial assistance from the foreign governments. The problem arises when one kind of support can only be ensured at the cost of the other. The conditions imposed by the other countries on the local government may go against the interests of the electorate and deplete the vote bank considerably. The foreign governments may also identify certain Afghans and Pakistanis as insurgents and expect the the local government to target them. So far, most of the targets have been located in the Pashtun areas of both Afghanistan and its neighbor. Ably assisted by their foreign allies, the respective local governments may be equipped today to conduct operations in the unstable areas of their countries, but if the funds that pay for such military operations dry up in the future, there will be hell to pay. The insurgents will not only be back with a vengeance, but the local administration in both Afghanistan and Pakistan may find it difficult to hold on to the reins of power.

Military action is, therefore, not the ultimate solution. What the ISAF forces and local leaders, supported by their respective governments, should aim for is a reconciliation of the rival ethnic, religious and linguistic groups that had divided the country into their personal fiefdoms and waged war against each other. It is, possibly, of the most effective ways of empowering the local governments and ending the foreign occupation of Afghanistan.

Bringing about that reconciliation is no mean task. For the animosity between the Taliban, mostly from the Pashtun community, and other minorities is a serious matter and has been reported extensively in the international news media. Their rivalry goes back a long way. The Tajiks, Hazaras and other minorities do not deign to describe themselves as Afghans, because they associate the very term with a person who is ignorant. In fact, the word, "Afghan," is closely related to the local term, *ghul*, which means "ignorant." Going by that assumption, Pashto, the language Afghans speak, can only be a backward language and not of any importance. I shudder to think what might happen if a Tajik like Burhanudeen Rabbani becomes the president of Afghanistan and attempts, as Rabbani did, when he was in power, to ban Pashto publications and broadcasts.

And as Afghan history has proved, time and again, Rabbani is not the only member of an ethnic minority to misuse power. *Consider, for example, the course of action the non-Pashtuns chose once they had gained access to weapons and won the support of the international community;* they targeted the Taliban, in particular, and the Pashtuns, in general. The Uzbeks, under the leadership of Rasheed Dostam, for example, packed thousands of Taliban fighters in sealed containers and transported them to Sheberghan, where they were buried alive. The Northern Alliance put a group of Pashtun leaders aboard a helicopter bound for Konduz, but the 'copter crashed before reaching its destination, killing all its passengers, including members of the Nasseri Tribe from Konduz. This was tantamount to willfully killing prisoners of war when they should have been put on trial and prosecuted under local or international law. *Turning a blind eye to the atrocities, the local government of Hamid Karzai and his supporters have been ineffectual in bringing Dostam and other warlords of the Northern Alliance to justice, partly because they are too powerful and, partly, because he needs their support to ensure his re-election. It is in his interest to maintain the status quo.* But the Afghan president has gone further than that. He actually brought Dostam down to Afghanistan from Turkey on a temporary visa to conduct a pro-Karzai campaign among his followers in the north. In order to win the elections a second time, the president has even appealed to former warlords and war criminals to support him.

Lack of significant progress in the security situation in the Pashtun areas and the privileged status of the other minorities has merely increased the animosity between the two groups and hampered the progress of the ISAF and local government forces in defeating the insurgency. The dispute over grazing pasture between the Kochies, mostly Pashtuns, and the Hazaras in central Afghanistan, for example, has intensified. *Because of local and foreign support for other minorities, the Pashtuns have realized they are being marginalized.* The lack of stability in the Pashtun territories has even impacted international aid to Afghanistan. All the NGOs with a presence in the country try to invest their funds in the north, because it is relatively secure. This inevitably creates resentment among the Pashtuns who are also looking for stability in their lives.

They too, harbor hopes of restarting their lives and probably feel ignored by the local government as well as the international community. Morever, through their decade-long combing operations in the Pashtun areas in quest of insurgents, the Afghan and foreign armed forces have *alienated the local Pashtuns. The situation is, in fact, so unstable and fraught with risk that many have abandoned their ancestral property and moved to already crowded urban neighborhoods.*

Lending a twist to the already complex situation *is the tendency of the Americans and other ISAF forces to rely on native Afghans as their interpreters while conducting their combing operations. Reports about the use of unqualified and prejudiced interpreters that has resulted in the death of innocent civilians have surfaced in the news media. The interpreters either do not speak the language of the local people or are ignorant of local customs and unaware of how to deal with the residents of these areas without giving offense. And if they belong to non-Pashtun ethnic groups, they may have vested interests in targeting innocent Pashtuns and causing their deaths. The problem may be resolved by employing qualified interpreters who are not only familiar with the local language, but well acquainted with local traditions, thereby minimizing the risk of misleading the military forces they are trying to assist.* The interpreters and others on whom the ISAF forces depend should not let their tribal, ethnic, religious, and linguistic prejudices get in the way when guiding these troops toward a designated target. *An intensive training program in language and cultural orientation should be set up for these interpreters to improve their communication skills with the local residents.*

Every international-aid agency operating in Afghanistan should realize that Kabul is a city and concentrating major construction and development projects there may do little to improve the country's overall political and economic situation. A balanced development in various sectors such as education, agriculture and industry, among others, is the only way to bring stability to the country and its people. Employment opportunities should be generated for the rural youth so that they can earn a living in their familiar environment without being forced to migrate to the cities, where most of them merely add to the number of the unemployed and increase the population of urban beggars. The government needs to have a long-range plan to meet the basic needs of the rural population.

I had been following the news of the official visits in May 2009 to Washington, DC, by Afghan President Hamid Karzai and Asif Ali Zardari, president of Pakistan. I heard of their joint meeting with President Barack Obama, as well as other meetings with members of the US Congress. If these two gentlemen were expecting unconditional handouts, they must have returned home disappointed. They should have known that there is no free lunch in America and they would have to earn everything they asked for. Upon arriving home, they must have been preoccupied with thoughts of their political survival, dealing with the insurgents and keeping the aid money flowing in so that they and their supporters could maintain the lavish lifestyle they had created for themselves and grown accustomed to.

The political situation in Afghanistan and other developing nations has forced their citizens to flee their native lands and move to a place where they can find a better life for themselves. I would like to concentrate on the local problems which divide the Afghan population and use my own experience to advise those who emigrate to the United States in the hope of living a normal, fulfilling life there. Afghans have always been divided by four factors: religion, gender, ethnicity and language. The first is a powerful weapon, especially when exploited by government officials, local warlords and armed mullahs to ensure unquestioning obedience from the country's citizens. Unless they are divested of the right to expound on religion and twist it to their ends, all three groups will, in a bid to stay in power, continue to intimidate the general public rather than enlighten it. Legislation should be passed to protect the rights and ensure the safety of religious minorities so they can continue to live in their local communities, instead of having to move to other areas and seek refuge with other members of their faith. The religious minorities, comprising Hindus and Sikhs, find it increasingly difficult to live in the rural communities and have been moving to the cities in order to live in close proximity to other members of their faith. The antagonism between the Shias and Sunnis has intensified and new sects have appeared which are so extreme in their beliefs that they may well have moved beyond the boundaries of Islam. Among them are the Ahmadis, the Bahaees and the Druze. Muslims should learn that the way to peace and harmony does not lie in invading the places of worship frequented by the followers of these religions and sects and attacking them, but in reaching out to them and trying to work toward an understanding of their beliefs and practices. Assault and disrespect can only perpetuate more of the same through retaliation and counter-retaliation and the sad story never ends. Muslims today should remind themselves of the early days of Islam, when their forefathers lived in harmony with other religious minorities. They would do well to emulate the example of their wise ancestors.

To continue with the religious issue, the Sunni sect has a decentralized religious system, where lay believers may not know whom to contact for advice if they need answers to their questions. On the contrary, the Shias have a center or person authorized to advise laymen and answer questions they may have regarding their faith. In the absence of a designated adviser, Sunnis are often left to the mercy of the different individuals they approach for answers to their questions. The possible contradictions in the explanations they receive are likely to confuse them further and leave them vulnerable to manipulation by the bearded weapon-wielding men I have mentioned earlier, who are patently unqualified to dispense religious advice. They would be equally vulnerable to exploitation by a powerful government or local warlords who use religion for consolidating their position of authority. Consider the case of the last king, Zahir Shah, who was an absolute monarch during most of his reign. The title, *Tolwak* (Almighty), that the Pashto Academy created for him was an outright insult to the people of Afghanistan. This title, meaning, "the one with all the authority," encouraged the king's subjects to regard him as a demigod who could do no wrong. Therefore, whatever the nature of his deeds, he was above the law and his subjects had to accept his absolute authority. I feel it is unacceptable for subjects to look upon a king, who turns their religious obligation to his advantage, as the ultimate authority. They should know that elected caliphates, not absolute monarchs, are entitled to follow the Prophet Muhammad's tradition after his death. No politically elected authority, be they corrupt mullahs or government officials, should be guiding laypersons on religious matters.

In fact, the lack of a legally established religious authority in Afghanistan seems to have cleared the path for self-appointed religious advisers to manipulate the common people. Government officials have intimidated citizens by reminding them of the king's authority and the consequences of failing to bow to it. The mullahs continue to terrify people by threatening them with visions of hell, should they fail to recite their prayers and fast during the month of Rozha. As a boy, I had imagined that religion was all about praying and fasting and God relied on those two factors alone to judge if a Muslim should go to heaven or be consigned to hell. I remember watching a group of magicians who would open their books following their performance and show the audience lurid pictures of what kind of punishment was in store for them in the afterlife if they committed certain sins like having sex with the spouse of another person, stealing and accepting bribes from clients, among others. Those pictures were meant to frighten the audience into accepting their words as the unequivocal truth and donating generously for their show. While the language used by the magicians was simple and straightforward enough for the common people to understand, the language used by the mullahs was always too complicated to figure out. The mullahs usually recited a verse from the holy Quran or read a *hadith* (a saying of the Prophet Muhammad) in Arabic and then translated it into the local language in words too difficult for most of the audience in a mosque to decipher the underlying message.

Had I remained in the village where I was raised, without exposure to the wider world that lay beyond it, I would have grown up with a very narrow concept of Islam. I would have assumed that ensuring a place in heaven was just a matter of praying five times a day, fasting during the month of Rozha, finding out if I had enough property to pay *zakat* and/ or performing the Haj. Everything I did in accordance with the four pillars of Islam would have been confined to myself alone, without taking into account my relationship with other people. *Zakat* is the only pillar in which a Muslim reaches out to his brethren. If most Afghans live with this narrow concept of the religion, it is possibly because the mullahs have encouraged them to do so by convincing them that this world is a temporary place and a testing ground for the eternal life after death. But the reality is that we live in a society and have obligations to its other members. This has to do with the social aspect of Islam, which is clearly stated in several verses of the Quran about our obligation to our god, our parents and family, our other relatives, neighbors and traveling companions and even to a person sitting next to us. This also covers our treatment of non-Muslims who live in our neighborhood, be they people of the book or not. The Quran clearly states that Muslims have their religion as do non-Muslims. And indeed, as I have mentioned earlier, the Hindus and Sikhs in my neighborhood were treated with due respect by all the villagers. The followers of other religions are also our co-workers, friends and neighbors and should consider them as such and participate in their rituals of worship without being obliged to accept their beliefs as our own. If we have respect for other religions and understand that each has a core of positivism, we will contribute to the creation of a better world.

Among the factors that have divided our society, education, unfairly implemented in the government schools, has proved to be an important one. Education has never been available to all Afghan citizens without discrimination; it is a privilege reserved for the exclusive few who are already in a position of advantage vis-à-vis others. Most of them live in the cities and consider education as their God-given right. However, the great majority of Afghans live in villages, where educational opportunities are limited in the extreme. I would like to paraphrase a poem by Ajmal Khatak, a well-known Pashto poet, who says that big people are created big and born in heaven. They are destined to be in heaven. However, we must try to earn heaven for those who been born and distined to go to hell. . One can only wonder at this injustice. For like the residents of Kabul and other cities, rural people too, provide the government with revenue. Villagers pay taxes on the produce from their farmlands or from the profit they make on their businesses. Why, then, is access to educational facilities and programs not their fundamental right? In fact, if rural people were educated in the provinces and provided with suitable employment opportunities there, they could exercise the option of continuing to live in their native provinces instead of migrating to the cities and adding to the already high rate of unemployment there.

The other factor dividing the Afghan people is language. The Afghan government must resolve to address the language issue democratically by providing elementary education to the children of various minorities in their own language. Designating Pashto as the national or official language should be followed by a well-designed plan to promote it. Pashto as the national language should not be confined to Pashtuns alone. Programs and facilities should be provided across Afghanistan for the people to learn it. The Pashto language has come under pressure from Urdu in the east and Farsi in the west and north. The Pashtuns living in Pakistan, for instance, have been influenced by Urdu and owing to the influence from Iran, the distinction between Dari and Farsi has been gradually fading away. The importance of learning Pashto would be clearly felt in a situation where a government official employed in an area where the local residents do not speak his language is unable to open a channel of communication with those he is meant to serve and not only ends up feeling isolated, but fails to fulfill his responsibilities effectively. Speakers of other languages in Afghanistan should be discouraged from resisting the learning of Pashto. I hope the situation I noticed in Jalraize in the 1970s has been resolved throughout the country and the Hazaras and others belonging to minority groups are using their objective judgment to consider the language of instruction that would be appropriate for their local schools. During the years I spent in Afghanistan, I never heard Pashtuns opposing the use of Dari as a medium of instruction in their local schools. Probably half the people living in Kabul were Pashtuns when I was living there. Yet most of their children began their formal school education in Dari. I did not speak Dari when I graduated from the elementary school in Kunar and came to Kabul to pursue my secondary education. But I did learn the language before graduating from secondary school.

The next area of concern that Afghans from all walks of life need to address is the treatment of their women. It is time for them to understand that women are neither their fathers' property before marriage nor their husbands' after they tie the knot. Those men who choose to give their daughters in marriage to the person willing to pay them the highest sum as *mahr* are clearly anti-Islamic and guilty of violating the prospective bride's basic human rights. Instead of filling their own coffers with the bride price paid by the prospective groom's family, parents should respect their daughters' choice of husband, consider their happiness and remember that *mahr* is, by law, their daughters' property. Afghans, in general, and Pashtuns, in particular, should prioritize the education of their women. The international movement for the emancipation of women demands for every woman in her community the same rights that its men enjoy. Once educated, women will be able to contribute to their community in areas where they are more suitable or competent than men. To begin with, women, because of their disposition, temperament and special skills, are especially equipped to be better nurses, midwives and elementary school teachers. Afghans would, I believe, be happy to have their children delivered by a well-trained woman doctor or competent nurse and educated by qualified women teachers in their local schools. Similarly, with the progress of women's education, it will be easier for Afghans to find a woman doctor to take care of sick female family members like mothers, wives and daughters. If they resist sending their daughters or young female relatives to school, that possibility is unlikely to ever present itself. Moreover, educated Afghan women can serve as role models for other women in the community and gradually, education for women will no longer be considered an exceptional step, but a natural process of overall development.

Educational programs for Afghan children and youth should be conducted according to a well-organized educational plan that fosters pride in their own culture and tradition while encouraging them to learn about developments in the rest of the world, including in the field of science and technology, so that they can apply the knowledge to improve their own lives and the lives of those around them. Jamaludeen Al-Afghani, an exponent of this philosophy, would become a well-known scholar in Egypt and in the rest of the Arab world after leaving Afghanistan, where he had not seen a promising future for himself. During one of his speeches in the 1960s, the president of Egypt, Gamal Abdel Nasser, would describe himself as the second Jamal. It is hoped that resistance to scientific and technological progress will subside as the literacy level of the general population rises. A well-conceived educational program can also help promote a sense of national identity among non-Pashtun ethnic groups who have, so far, shied away from being labeled Afghans, because it equates them with Pashtuns. And, indeed, in private circles, Afghans are equated with Pashtuns and the Afghan language is deemed to be Pashto, although most Pashtuns working in government and private firms are bilingual. Hopefully, a well thought out good educational system will help ethnic minorities to integrate with the others in Afghan society, learn Pashto and be proud of their country.

During the twenty-five years of political turmoil that devastated the country under different regimes—communist, *mujahideen* and Taliban—about a quarter of its population was forced to flee across its borders and become refugees in Pakistan and Iran, where they lived in squalid conditions in the world's largest refugee camps. Other developing countries that have been through similar political unrest have seen many of their nationals forced, like the Afghans, to leave their homelands and look to the West for freedom from religious, ethnic and political persecution. Some of them, mostly affluent and educated citizens, would end up in the USA. A majority have become American citizens, with their children being born in a country which considers itself to be the world's greatest democracy.

For my part, I lived in Lebanon in the 1960s and soon after I had left it, the civil war began in 1975 and lasted for seventeen long years. I would go to Kuwait in 1978 and live there in peace until 1986. After I had left with my family for the US, the country would be invaded by Saddam Hussein's Iraqi forces in 1990 and occupied in a single day, leaving the royal family with just enough time to fly to Saudi Arabia. Had they stayed back in the country, most of them would have been killed. In fact, Sheikh Fahd, a younger brother of the Amir, Sheikh Jaber Al-Sabah, who had stayed back in Kuwait, died defending his country. The Iraqis would eventually be forced out of Kuwait so that its citizens could return, reclaim their country and rebuild it. A year after I left Afghanistan in 1977, the communist coup d'état would take place and bring untold misery to the people—the only constant in the turbulence that accompanied every subsequent change of regime. Anna had even quipped on one occasion that I would do well to stay put in one place, because every time I moved to another destination for the sake of work, some momentous political event or other would rock the country I had left behind.

I was born in a society where male children were considered their parents' only social security in old age. Afghans took great pride in their sons, because the latter were expected to learn the trade of their fathers, marry women chosen by their parents and continue to live in the parental home and support them when they were old and infirm. Even those who went to school and learned trades other than those of their fathers were expected to return home and live with their parents or take the latter along to live with them in their new homes, for the elders were unlikely to be able to fend for themselves. Young Afghans have been following this family tradition for generations. I am not sure if my father received any retirement benefits after his employment at the Spinzar Company was over. The only people who were left to take care of him in his old age were my stepmother, Gul Bebu, and Torialai, my half-brother. The latter would marry the daughter of my parents' next-door neighbor and set up his own family. Our parents were considered a part of his extended family and my father died while living within it. Torialai, would also assume ownership of our father's property and live on it. My three half-sisters, Najiba, Latifa and Ghotai, would marry and join their new families.

Raised in this milieu of interdependence and filial obligation toward elders, Afghans and other nationals from developing nations find themselves in a cultural and social environment that is quite alien to their understanding when they settle in the US. In their adopted country, parents have a broader support base; they can depend on all their offspring, regardless of gender. As naturalized citizens or legal residents, parents are, of course, entitled to certain old-age benefits like social security and health insurance and probably need more love and moral support from their children than actual financial assistance. However, children from other cultures growing up in the US adapt to the demands of a society that is quite different from the one in which their parents were raised. Inevitably, most of these parents are unlikely to grasp the significance or implications of the life and career opportunities available to their children, because they are beyond the former's sphere of knowledge and experience. Unable to understand what their children are studying in college or doing at work, parents may not be in a position to offer them informed advice about the educational or employment opportunities available to them. In circumstances like the ones I have described, parents should do what is best for their children: allow them to grow the way they want to grow. By allowing them freedom of choice in the matter of careers and life partners, parents are likely to earn their children's appreciation and respect and stay close to them.

In Afghanistan, the family circle is a comprehensive one and a young man—like the one I used to be quite a few years ago—has to move far away, both physically and emotionally, if he wishes to forge an independent life for himself. But at least, he has the option to go ahead. The same choice is, unfortunately, not available to a young Afghan woman, especially from the rural areas, until the time she gets married. She is expected, instead, to help her mother with the household chores until she is of marriageable age and ready to become a member of her husband's family. The family circle in the US is, on the other hand, comparatively circumscribed and a young woman has as much right as a young man to leave the parental home and set up on her own. As for me, I did flout local tradition when I left my village in my early teens to go to Kabul for furthering my education, but the welfare of my family was always uppermost on my mind. In fact, the only people I socialized with in Kabul with were my relatives and friends from Khas Kunar. Even when I went to Lebanon to study at the AUB, I would be thinking of my family and looking for ways to save money from my scholarship so I could either send it to them or reserve it for their use when I returned home to Afghanistan. I doubt if my children are as concerned about my financial situation as I used to be about that of my parents. I am also uncertain as to whether I can bring myself to ask their help if I ever need it. With my social security and other old-age benefits, in addition to the money I have saved for my post-retirement years in hand, they may well assume I have no reason to seek their help.

Given Afghanistan's cultural climate, where boys enjoy greater freedom than girls, certain aspects of life are frowned upon and considered to bring shame on the family. On attaining maturity, young Afghan boys have the liberty to leave home and travel without an escort. Women, however, can only step out of their homes with a close male relative who is a *mahram*; that is, someone ineligible to marry the person he has been entrusted to accompany, like a brother, a father, a grandfather or paternal and maternal uncles. Consider, in this context, the case of my brother, Wadood, who was eager to send one of his sons to live with me in the USA and pursue further studies here. I had no objection to his plans and tried to obtain student visas for two of his sons at different times. Since Afghanistan did not have a US Embassy, Wadood and his sons had to travel to Pakistan to apply for a visa from a US consular office in that country, but their applications were turned down. When my niece graduated from a high school in Kabul, I was ready to bring her to the USA for further studies and surmised that my efforts would be facilitated by worldwide condemnation of the Taliban government that was denying Afghan women their right to be educated. But Wadood voiced serious objections to the idea. Although I did not ask him for a reason, I understood that while I was a *mahram* for his daughter, my adult sons—her cousins—were not and my brother was against the girl living in the same house with cousins who were young men by then.

My own nuclear family would be sorely tested in this matter, when my wife informed me in the spring of 2005 that our unmarried daughter, Shireen, was pregnant. She called David, her boyfriend and the father of the unborn child, over to our house from Rhode Island where Anna and I had convened a family meeting to sort out the problem. While mulling over the issue in my mind, I thought of the way an extended family in Afghanistan would have resolved it. Putting myself in the shoes of an Afghan, I considered the three alternatives open to me: solve the problem once and for all, instead of allowing it fester indefinitely; endure the shame that everyone in my extended family and I would have to live with for the foreseeable future; or hush up the matter and continue with our lives, without informing the rest of the Afghan community. In Afghan culture, a permanent solution to the problem would involve killing both the prospective parents as a message to the community at large that I believed in preserving our honor at all costs and would not tolerate the birth of an illegitimate child in the family. In other words, I would risk inviting the lifelong enmity of the family to which the unborn child's father had belonged and trigger off a vendetta, whereby revenge killings would be carried out and provoke, in turn, further revenge killings, with the blood feud spilling into the next generation and the next. Of course, we could be prosecuted for murder by the authorities, but the vendetta would be kept alive. The second option would be to ignore the problem and become the laughing stock of the town for many years to come. The third would be to to get the couple married, so they could respectably raise the child that had been conceived out of wedlock and hope no other member of the community would be any the wiser. If the community found out the truth, the child's parents, the child himself and his mother's family would have to bear the burden of shame, with the child's maternal grandparents praying that they would not be permanently ostracized by their own relatives.

Living as I did in the USA, my own situation was somewhat different. My entire support system was my nuclear family—Anna and my children. My extended family and distant relatives lived thousands of miles away and had little connection with my life here. The only other Afghan friends I had lived right here in the US and there was certainly a possibility of them discovering our situation when they visited us. Pondering over the matter, I decided sensibly that it would not be entirely unreasonable for us to count on their understanding and empathy and, possibly, even their support. I did not feel that if I accepted the final option, I would be exposing my nuclear family to censure or shame. However, I was still the only one holding out as Anna, Shireen and David suggested the third option, which they felt was best for everyone involved. I finally gave in.

Our grandson, Brody, was due in November 2005, but arrived prematurely on 17 August. We allowed his father to live with us for eight months without charging him any rent. Shireen helped him find a job at a local CVS store. Both the young people modified their work schedule so that at least one of them could be with Brody at the hospital round the clock. However, David's presence in the house caused a great deal of tension and, finally, we had to ask him to leave. Shireen went back to her job full-time and managed to recover her lost benefits. We sent Brody to a child-care center in the neighborhood, where he enjoyed himself. He attended a Montessori school initially before going to an elementary school in the area. Shireen has learned a lot from the experience and has become a responsible mother to Brody. Mommy, Grandpa and Grandma are sharing the responsibility for raising the boy, who has spiced up life for everyone in the family.

When Shireen was in her teens, she would often complain that I treated her differently from the way I treated her brothers. I guess she was referring to certain restrictions imposed on her that did not apply to her male siblings. I remember sitting her down one day to discuss the issue. I admitted I was treating her differently, but I had my reasons. I explained that girls were far more vulnerable than boys when they reached adolescence, because while both sexes could give in to sexual desire, only girls were capable of becoming pregnant as a result and being saddled not only with a bad reputation, but with the huge responsibility of bringing up the child. I told her that while there were deadbeat dads in plenty, no one had ever heard of deadbeat moms, because mothers could not absolve themselves of the responsibility of raising their children, whether their fathers were around or not. Also, while a woman could sue her child's father for child support, the legal process to achieve that end was a long, elaborate one, with no guarantee of a judgment being passed in her favor. In fact, David was ordered by the court in Virginia to pay child support, but has either not found a job or refrained from acknowledging that he has one to spare himself the financial responsibility of providing for Brody. In the absence of child support from David, Shireen has to bear the burden of raising Brody on her own. I now shudder to imagine what would have happened to my daughter, if she did not have our home and her parents to fall back on. Shireen, who is a pharmacy technician and earns just enough to pay for her son's school expenses, now understands that while we, as her parents, were able to do everything for her when she was a child, she must largely fend for herself as an adult and manage a lot of things in her life without enlisting our help. Shireen and Brody live with us and Anna and I share the responsibility of raising him, because taking care of a child is a full-time job and a single parent is not always equal to the task. Shireen has also realized how much pressure she has put on the family by becoming a mother so early in life.

Children grow up and yearn to be independent of their parents, but those naturalized American citizens who come from conservative societies and expect their children to abide by the old family traditions that prevailed in their countries of origin may find themselves up against the law in their adopted country. Considering the unlimited opportunities these children can avail of in the USA and the freedom they enjoy in pursuing whatever course in life they aim for, it may not be feasible for their parents and guardians, however well-intentioned they are, to persuade them to follow the old ways. If the senior members of the family are insistent about asserting themselves and resistant to the choices their offspring have made, using force and intimidation to impose their will, the generation gap can only widen between them leading to acrimony, mutual disrespect and even the disintegration of the family unit. A far more sensible course of action would be for parents and guardians to discuss their differences with their offspring and arrive at an understanding. It may well be that some members of the younger generation eventually decide of their own accord to return to the traditional ways of their parents, but the lines of communication between parent and child must always remain open.

My own experience of leaving Afghanistan to settle in the US, by no means, unique. My fellow Afghans and people of other nationalities have similar stories to narrate of breaking away from their local traditions to seek a better life for themselves overseas. While living in our adopted country, most of us still follow the old ways we were accustomed to. We are gradually realizing, however, that our new life is rich with constant challenges that we must meet if we are to get ahead. And in order to do so, we must learn to adapt, remodeling our traditional ways of life as we go along. If I had belonged to a well-known family in Afghanistan, I would have used its status and influence to get ahead in life. In my adopted country, however, the only way I can progress is to work hard and contribute in significant ways to the society of which I am a new member.

Most of the countries from which people have made their way to the US have a designated religion that is recognized back home as the "official" one. The state religion is usually the one practiced by the majority of citizens in a country or by its leader. While living as an Afghan in Lebanon and Kuwait, I had observed that a citizen or resident's religious affiliation had a significant impact on his life at work and in the social space. I would discover the inherent distrust with which followers of the dominant religion viewed others. This attitude was, to some extent, fostered by the governments themselves, which failed to treat the followers of all faiths as equals.

In the US, on the contrary, there is no official religion as such and the adherents of different faiths enjoy the freedom of worshipping in their own way and according to their own beliefs. The work environment here is also quite a refreshing departure from that of the countries where I had once lived. I must confess that in Afghanistan too, as in Lebanon and Kuwait, those who belonged to faiths other than the one sanctioned by the state religion were not treated on par with the others.

While living in Lebanon, I made some interesting discoveries. I learned that only a Maronite Christian could become the country's president, while none other than a Sunni Muslim could occupy the prime minister's seat. The position of Speaker of the Parliament, on the other hand, was reserved exclusively for a Shia Muslim. The situation in Afghanistan while I was growing up was a subtle variation of the same system. The king had been a Sunni Muslim from the Hanafi tradition, while the prime minister and other senior government officials either belonged to the royal family or were closely affiliated to it.

In Kuwait, the same story had a different twist. I learned that the manual workers brought over from other countries were treated like subhumans. Women who had gone to Kuwait to work as household maids were desperate to return home, because they were overworked and abused by the families that had employed them. Members of the cleaning crew at Kuwait University and at the Public Authority for Applied Education and Training worked twelve hours a day. Some of them confided that most of the salaries they earned by performing certain services for their employer was being skimmed off by him. Some of them had come from Bangladesh and confessed that they were keen to return home, but could not do so, because they either lacked the funds to pay their travel expenses or were afraid to violate the rules imposed on them by their employer. They owed their plight primarily to their position as members of the expatriate minorities.

Here in the USA, however, I have colleagues from different ethnic, religious and linguistic backgrounds and all of us are as proud of our origins as we are of being citizens of our adopted country.

These very differences, however, continue to divide the citizens of my native Afghanistan. A quarter of a century of anarchy and fighting, mainly along linguistic, religious and ethnic lines, has merely widened the chasm between its citizens. Every ethnic and linguistic group in Afghanistan has a tendency to exaggerate its numbers in a bid to have a larger slice of the pie than it rightfully deserves. And if every group is as avaricious and grasping as its rival, the country's natural and financial resources are likely to fall short and lead to further dissension, with the prospect of inter-group cooperation and agreement on a shared national identity moving further and further away from the realms of possibility.

Unless legislation is introduced to ensure non-discriminatory treatment for all Afghans, irrespective of their affiliations, influential individuals from different groups may consider themselves above the law. It is, indeed, a distressing reality that a weak government *in Afghanistan* may be incapable of implementing the law effectively and bring powerful warlords, like Dostam, to justice. What the country needs is a stable, democratic government that can take the interests of all its citizens into consideration and find a way of unifying different groups. Afghanistan will remain united and prosper as a nation if the Pashtuns and other groups can all identify themselves as Afghans and be proud of their shared nationality and shared language.. If all Afghan citizens can foster mutual understanding and master the art of sharing, the pie they long for may be large enough to satisfy every one of them.

11033274R00170

Made in the USA
San Bernardino, CA
04 May 2014